# Contents

D0406185

your name.

your name.

## Previously...

Japan. The country eagerly anticipated the arrival of Comet Tiamat, which would be visible for the first time in a thousand years. Mitsuha, a high school girl living in a rural town deep in the mountains, found herself feeling down most of the time. The causes: her father's mayoral campaign and the ancient customs of her family's shrine. Because the town was small and cramped and because she was old enough to be painfully conscious of the eyes of those around her, her longing for the big city grew and grew.

One day, she dreamed she'd become a boy. An unfamiliar room, friends she didn't know, and the streets of Tokyo opened before her. Having wanted a life in the city more than anything in the world, Mitsuha enjoyed it to the fullest.

Meanwhile, Taki, a high school boy who lived in Tokyo, was also having strange dreams. He'd become a high school girl in a town he'd never been to before, deep in the mountains.

The mysterious dreams happened again and again. The two high schoolers were also clearly missing memories and time.

Although Taki and Mitsuha were bewildered that they were repeatedly swapping between each other's bodies and lives, little by little, they accepted the reality. They coped with the situation as best they could, sometimes squabbling through notes they left for each other, sometimes enjoying the other's life. However, just when they'd grown comfortable around each other, the switching abruptly stopped. Taki realized, during the time they were switching, that he and Mitsuha had been linked in a special way. He made up his mind to go see Mitsuha.

"We've never met, but I'm about to come looking for you."

When Taki reached his destination, he was confronted with an unexpected truth...

m a k o t o   s h i n k a i

r a n m a r u   k o t o n e

03

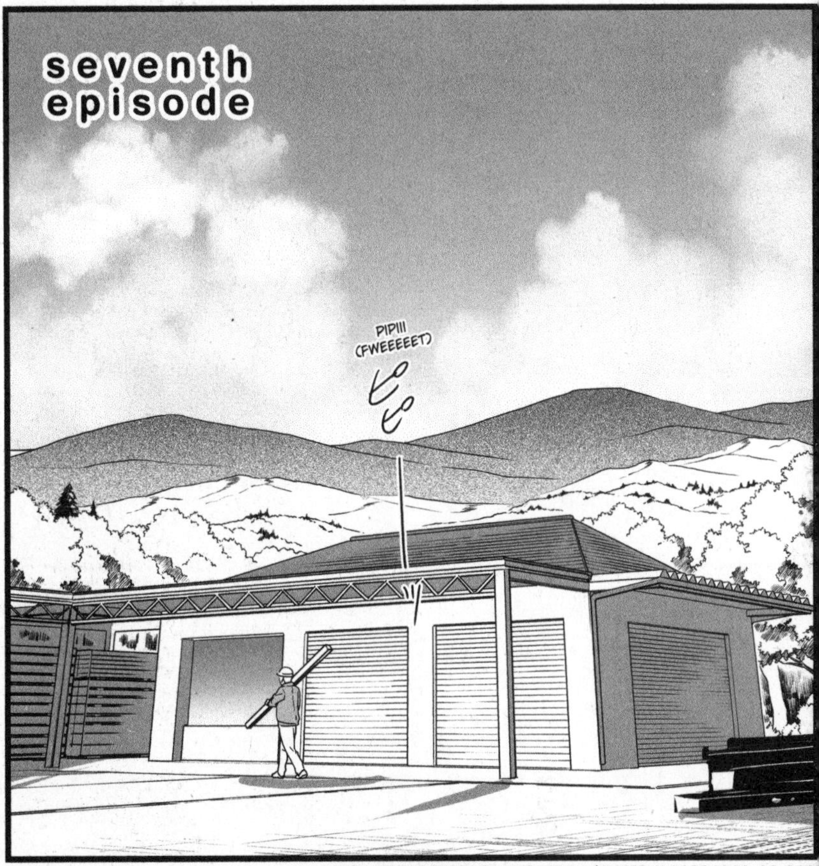
seventh episode
PIPIII (FWEEEEET)
ピピッ

SIGN: TESHIGAWARA CONSTRUCTION / MATERIALS LOT 0000-00-0000

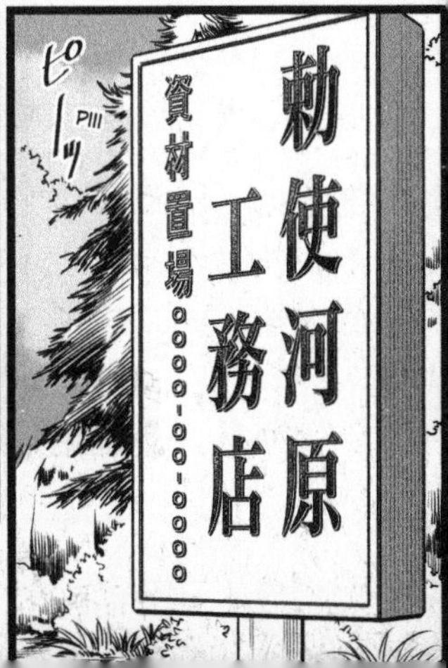
ピーッ
PIII
勅使河原工務店
資材置場0000-00-0000

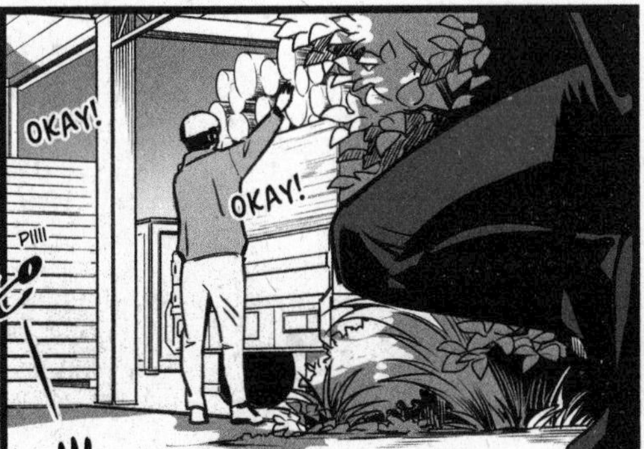
OKAY!
OKAY!
PIIII
ピーッ

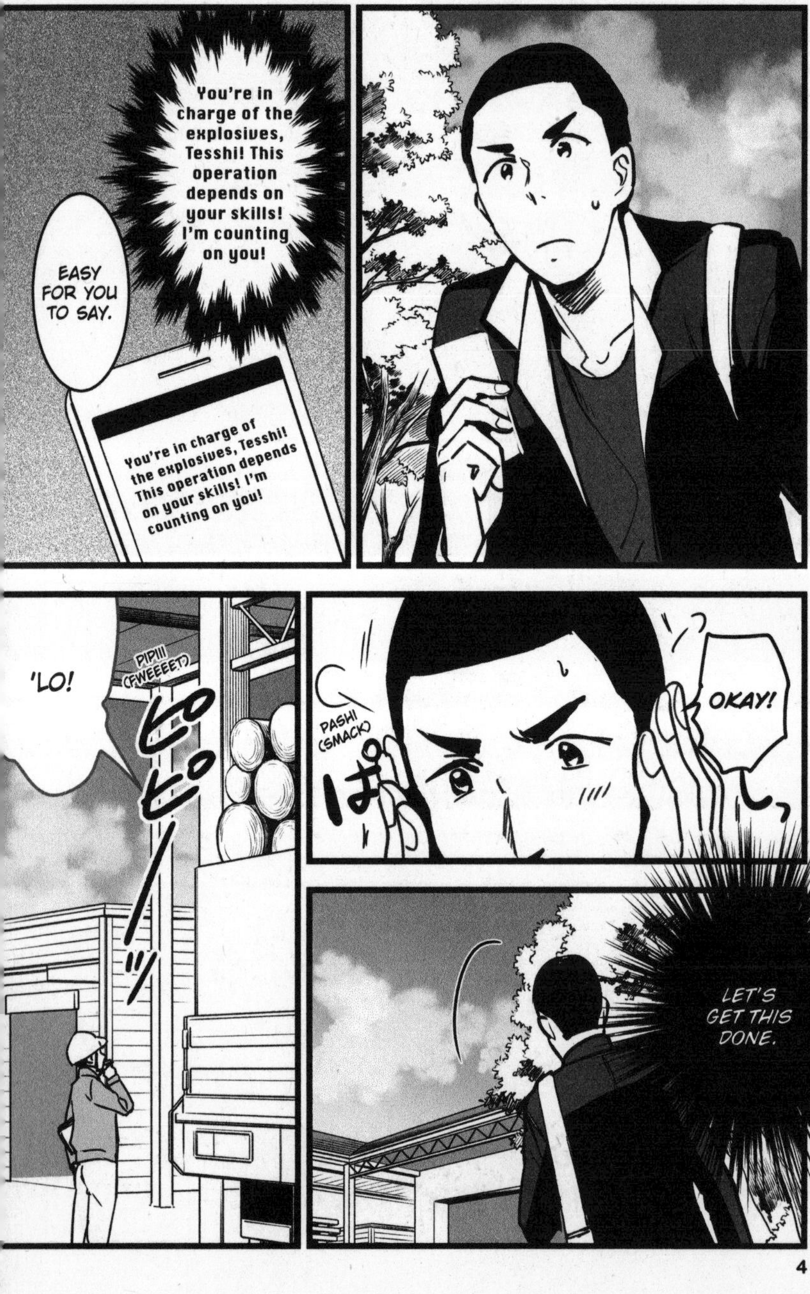
You're in charge of the explosives, Tesshi! This operation depends on your skills! I'm counting on you!
EASY FOR YOU TO SAY.
You're in charge of the explosives, Tesshi! This operation depends on your skills! I'm counting on you!
OKAY!
PASHI (SMACK)
ぱ
LET'S GET THIS DONE.
PIPIII (FWEEEET)
ピピピーッ
'LO!

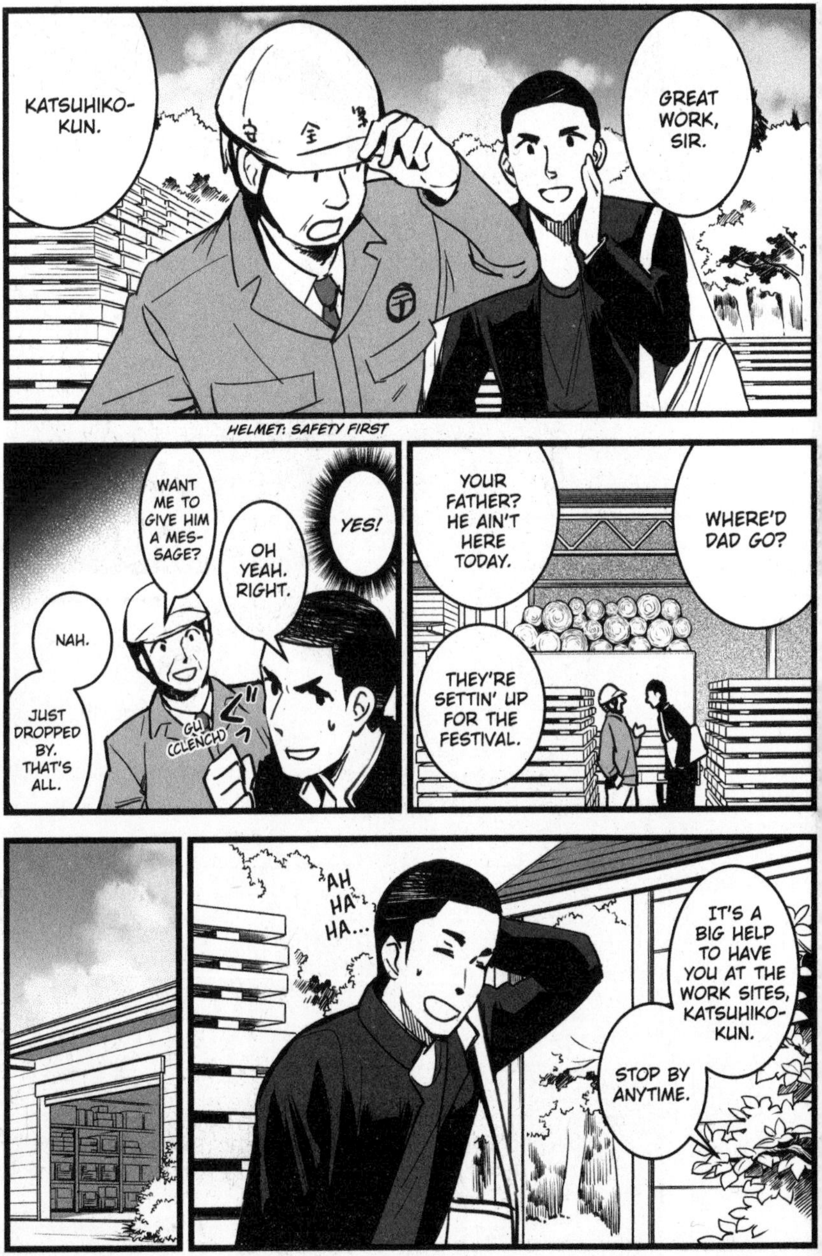
GREAT WORK, SIR.
KATSUHIKO-KUN.
HELMET: SAFETY FIRST
WHERE'D DAD GO?
YOUR FATHER? HE AIN'T HERE TODAY.
THEY'RE SETTIN' UP FOR THE FESTIVAL.
YES!
OH YEAH. RIGHT.
WANT ME TO GIVE HIM A MES-SAGE?
GU (CLENCH)
NAH.
JUST DROPPED BY. THAT'S ALL.
IT'S A BIG HELP TO HAVE YOU AT THE WORK SITES, KATSUHIKO-KUN.
STOP BY ANYTIME.
AH HA HA...

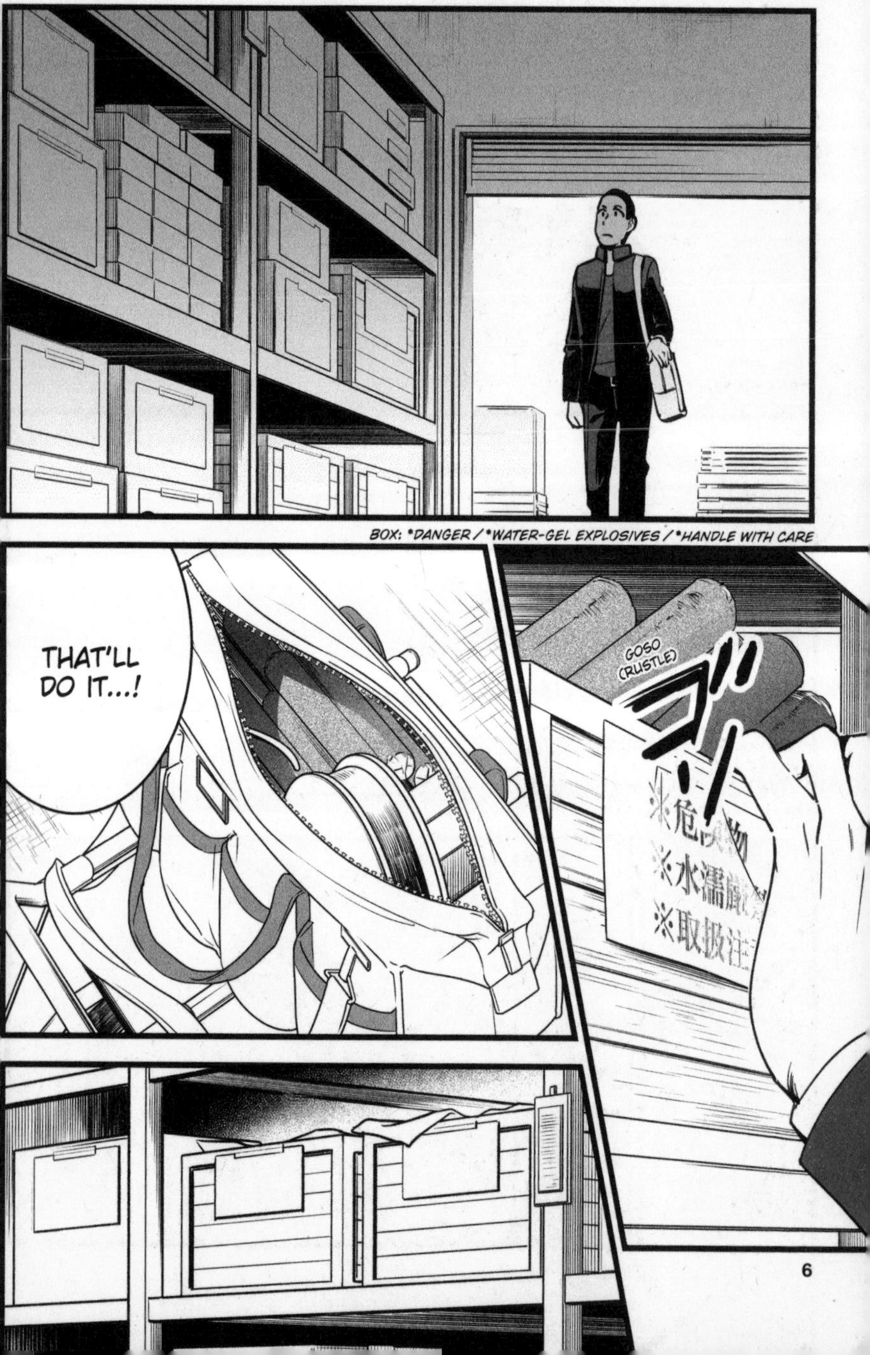
BOX: *DANGER / *WATER-GEL EXPLOSIVES / *HANDLE WITH CARE
GOSO (RUSTLE)
THAT'LL DO IT...!

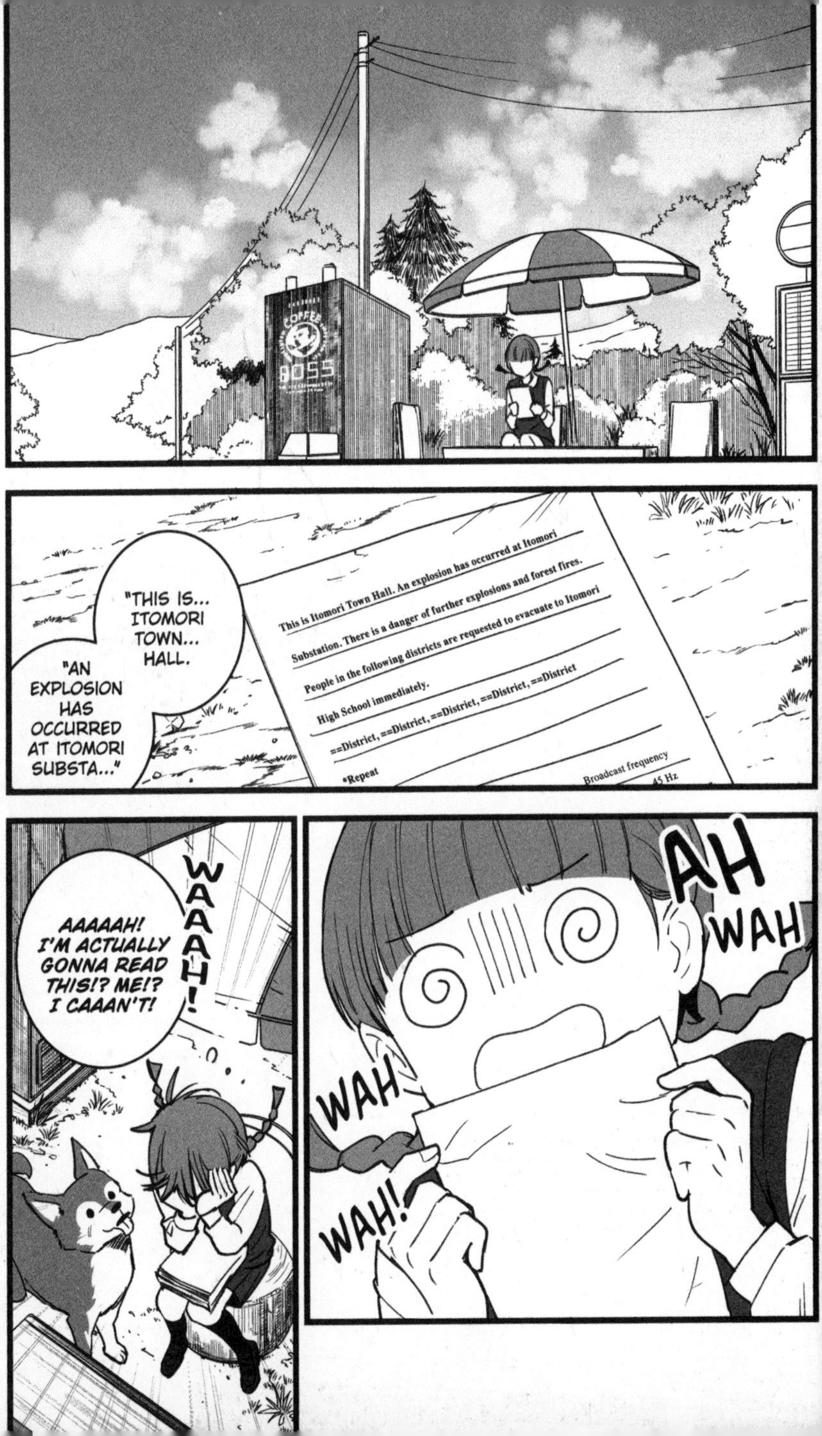
COFFEE
BOSS
This is Itomori Town Hall. An explosion has occurred at Itomori
Substation. There is a danger of further explosions and forest fires.
People in the following districts are requested to evacuate to Itomori
High School immediately.
==District, ==District, ==District, ==District, ==District
*Repeat
Broadcast frequency
45 Hz
"THIS IS... ITOMORI TOWN... HALL.
"AN EXPLOSION HAS OCCURRED AT ITOMORI SUBSTA..."
AH
WAH
WAH
WAH!
WAAAAH!
AAAAAH! I'M ACTUALLY GONNA READ THIS!? ME!? I CAAAN'T!

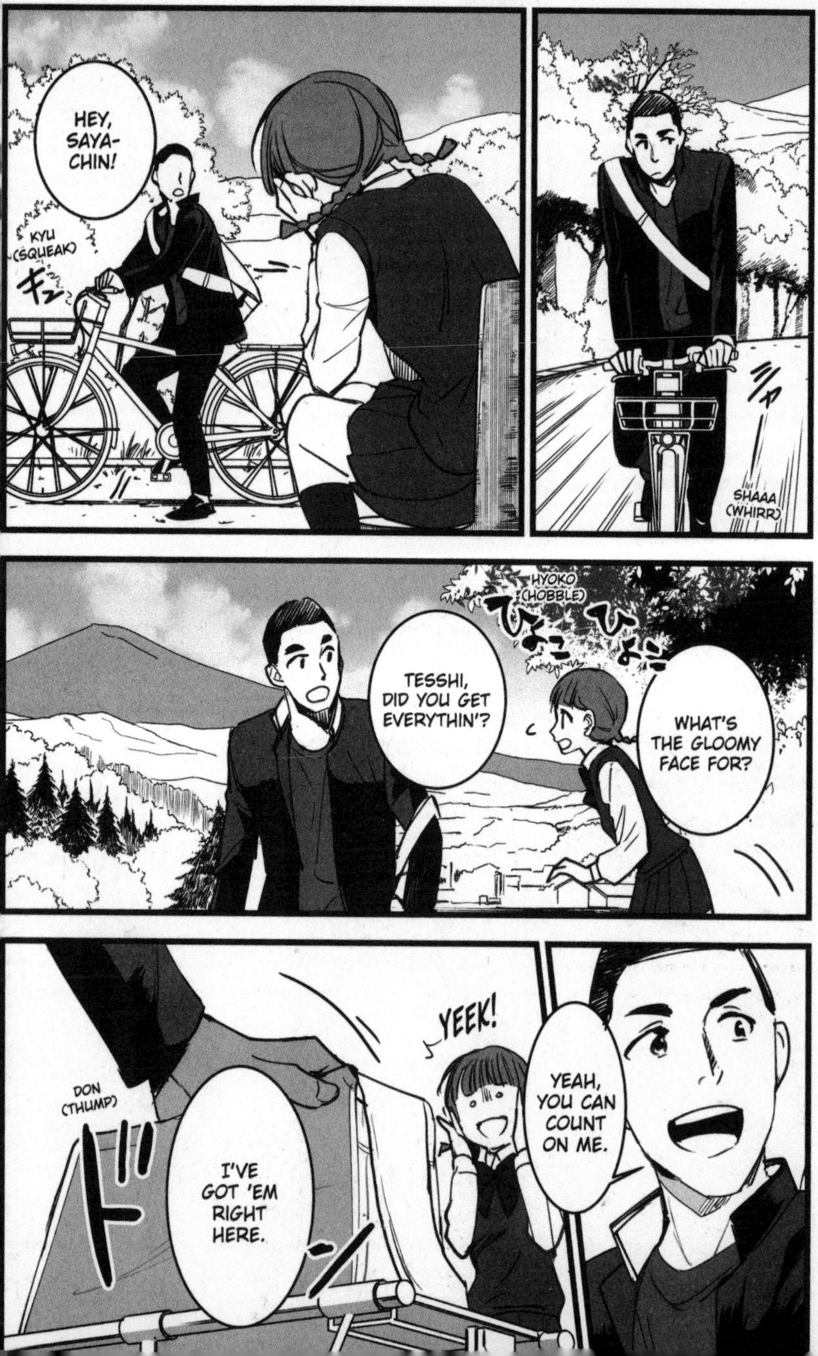
SHAAA (WHIRR)
HEY, SAYA-CHIN!
KYU (SQUEAK)
HYOKO (HOBBLE)
WHAT'S THE GLOOMY FACE FOR?
TESSHI, DID YOU GET EVERYTHIN'?
YEAH, YOU CAN COUNT ON ME.
YEEK!
I'VE GOT 'EM RIGHT HERE.
DON (THUMP)

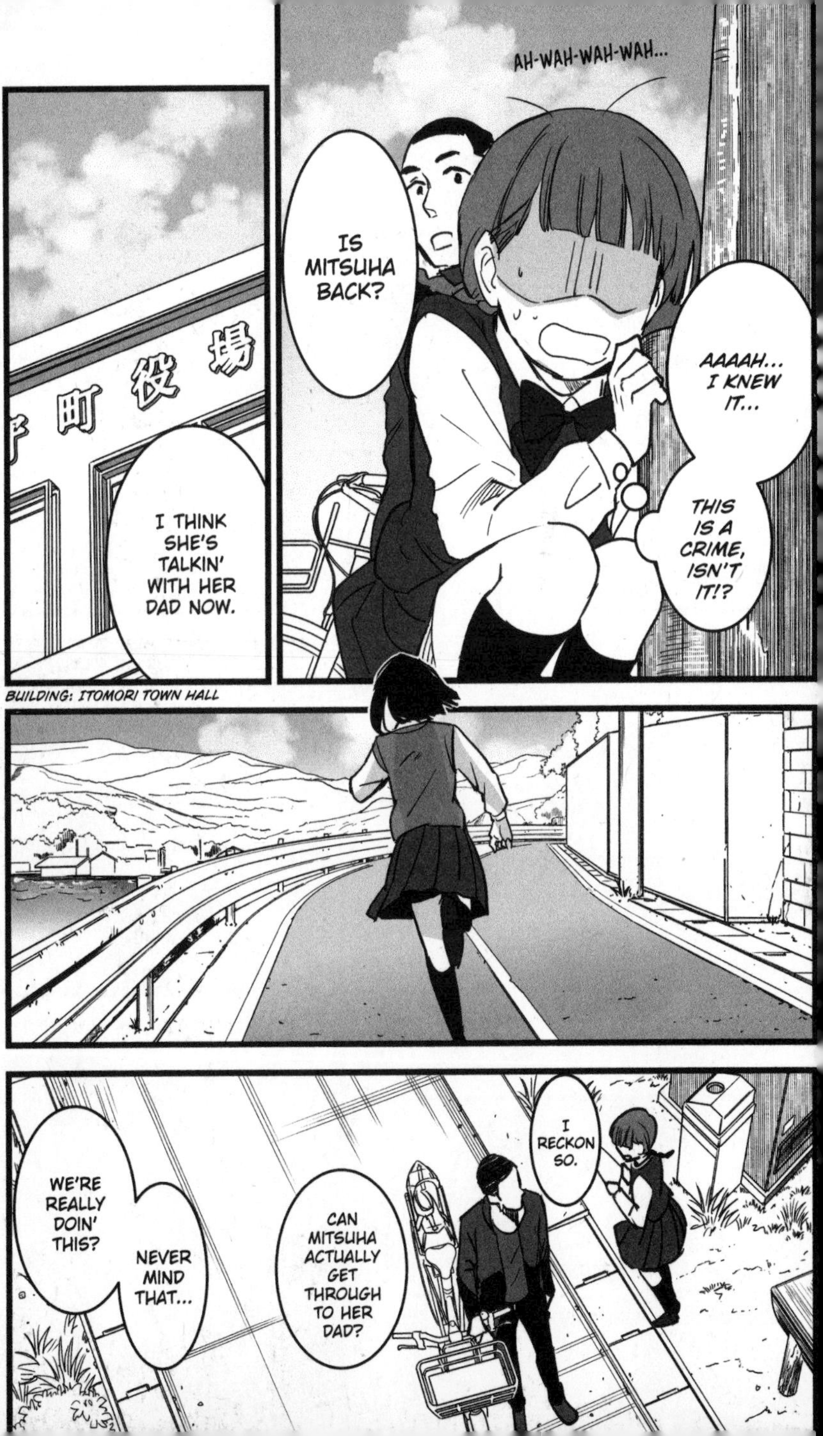
AH-WAH-WAH-WAH...
IS MITSUHA BACK?
AAAAH... I KNEW IT...
THIS IS A CRIME, ISN'T IT!?
町役場
I THINK SHE'S TALKIN' WITH HER DAD NOW.
BUILDING: ITOMORI TOWN HALL
WE'RE REALLY DOIN' THIS?
NEVER MIND THAT...
CAN MITSUHA ACTUALLY GET THROUGH TO HER DAD?
I RECKON SO.

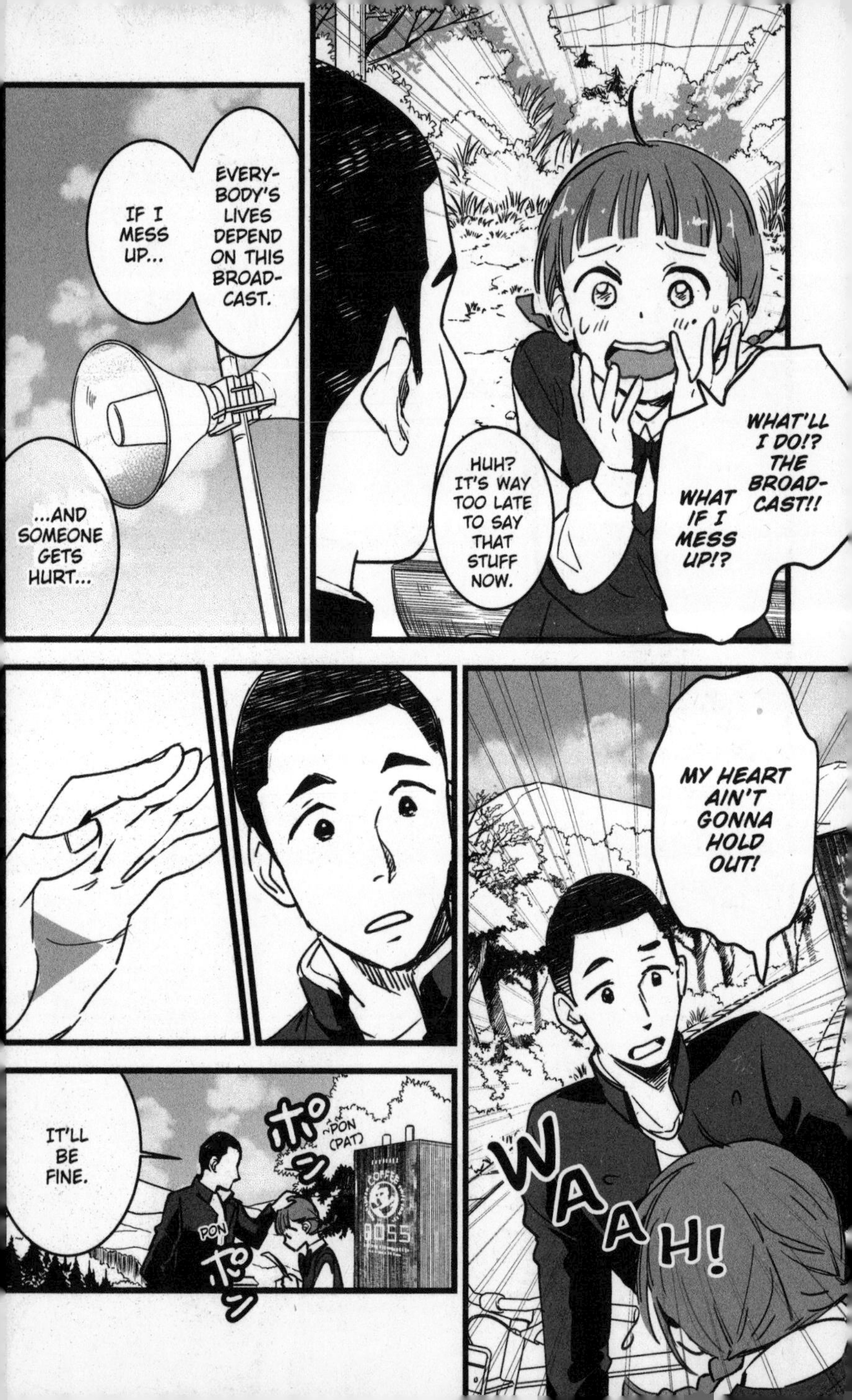
WHAT'LL I DO!? THE BROAD-CAST!!
WHAT IF I MESS UP!?
HUH? IT'S WAY TOO LATE TO SAY THAT STUFF NOW.
EVERY-BODY'S LIVES DEPEND ON THIS BROAD-CAST.
IF I MESS UP...
...AND SOMEONE GETS HURT...
MY HEART AIN'T GONNA HOLD OUT!
WAAH!
IT'LL BE FINE.
PON (PAT)
PON

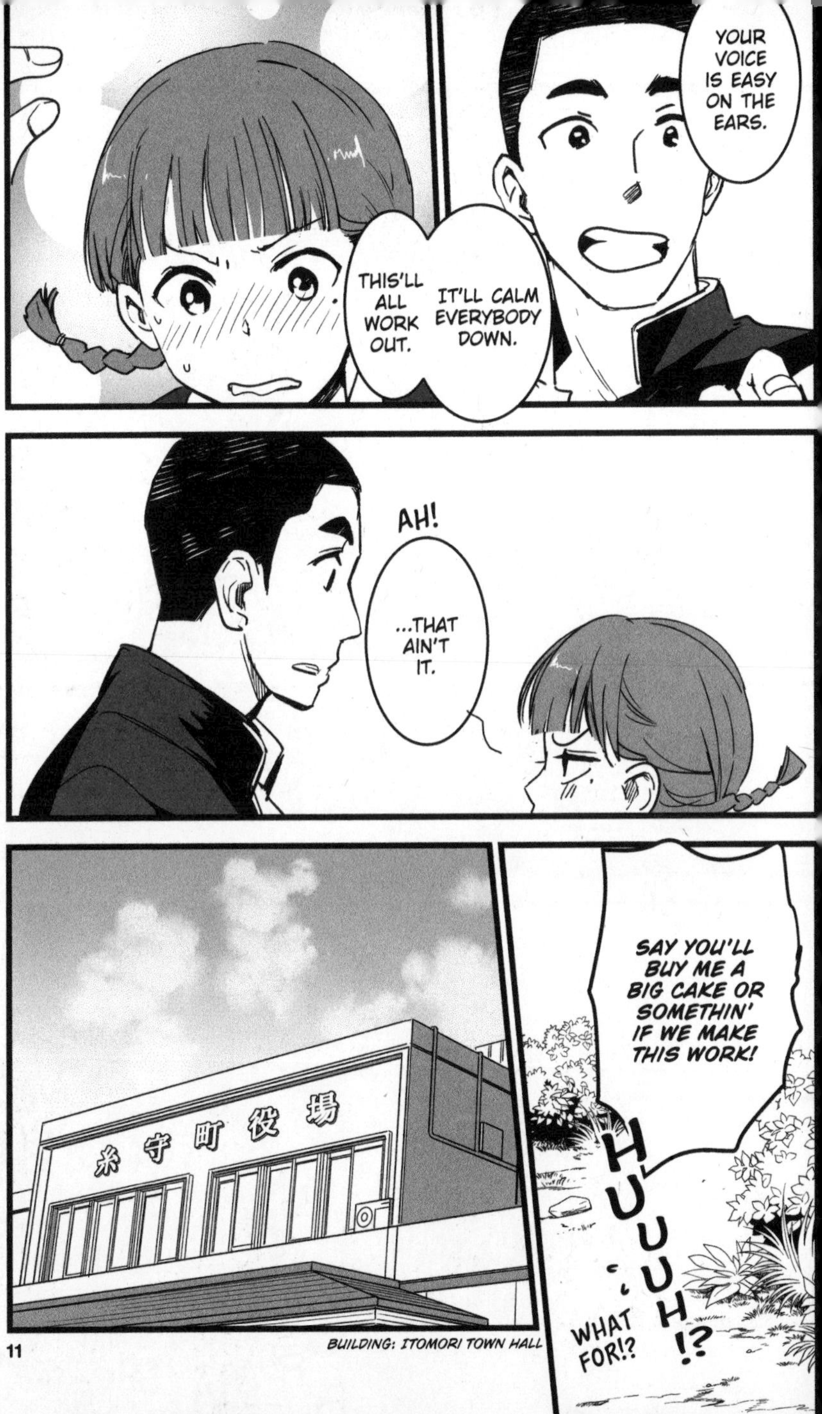
YOUR VOICE IS EASY ON THE EARS.
IT'LL CALM EVERYBODY DOWN.
THIS'LL ALL WORK OUT.
AH!
...THAT AIN'T IT.
SAY YOU'LL BUY ME A BIG CAKE OR SOMETHIN' IF WE MAKE THIS WORK!
HUUUUH!?
WHAT FOR!?
糸守町役場
BUILDING: ITOMORI TOWN HALL

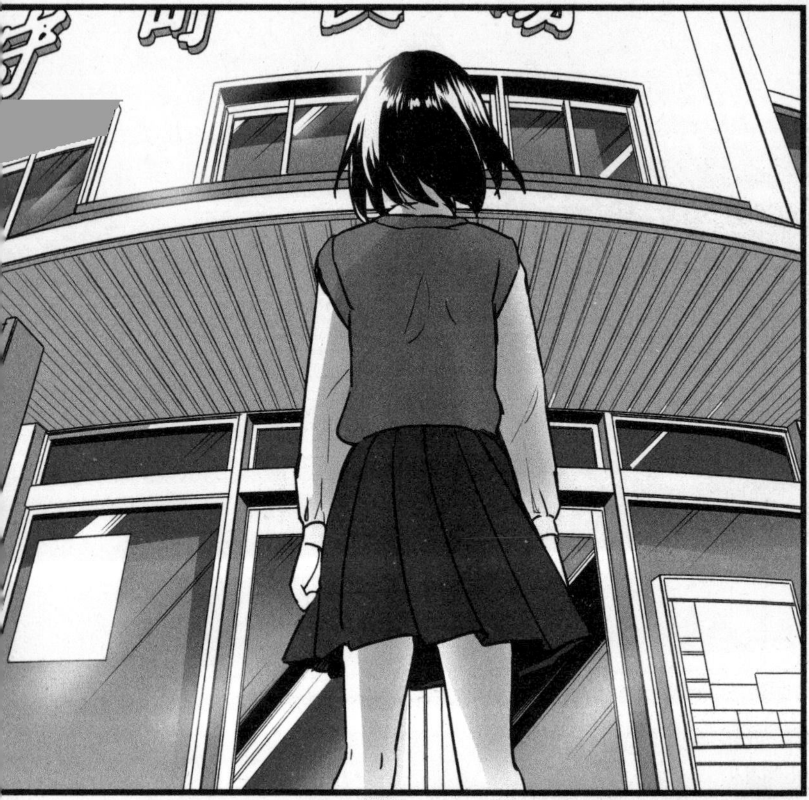

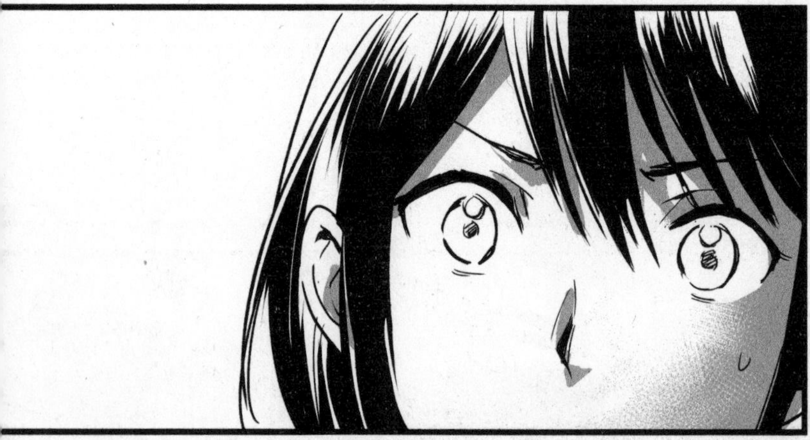

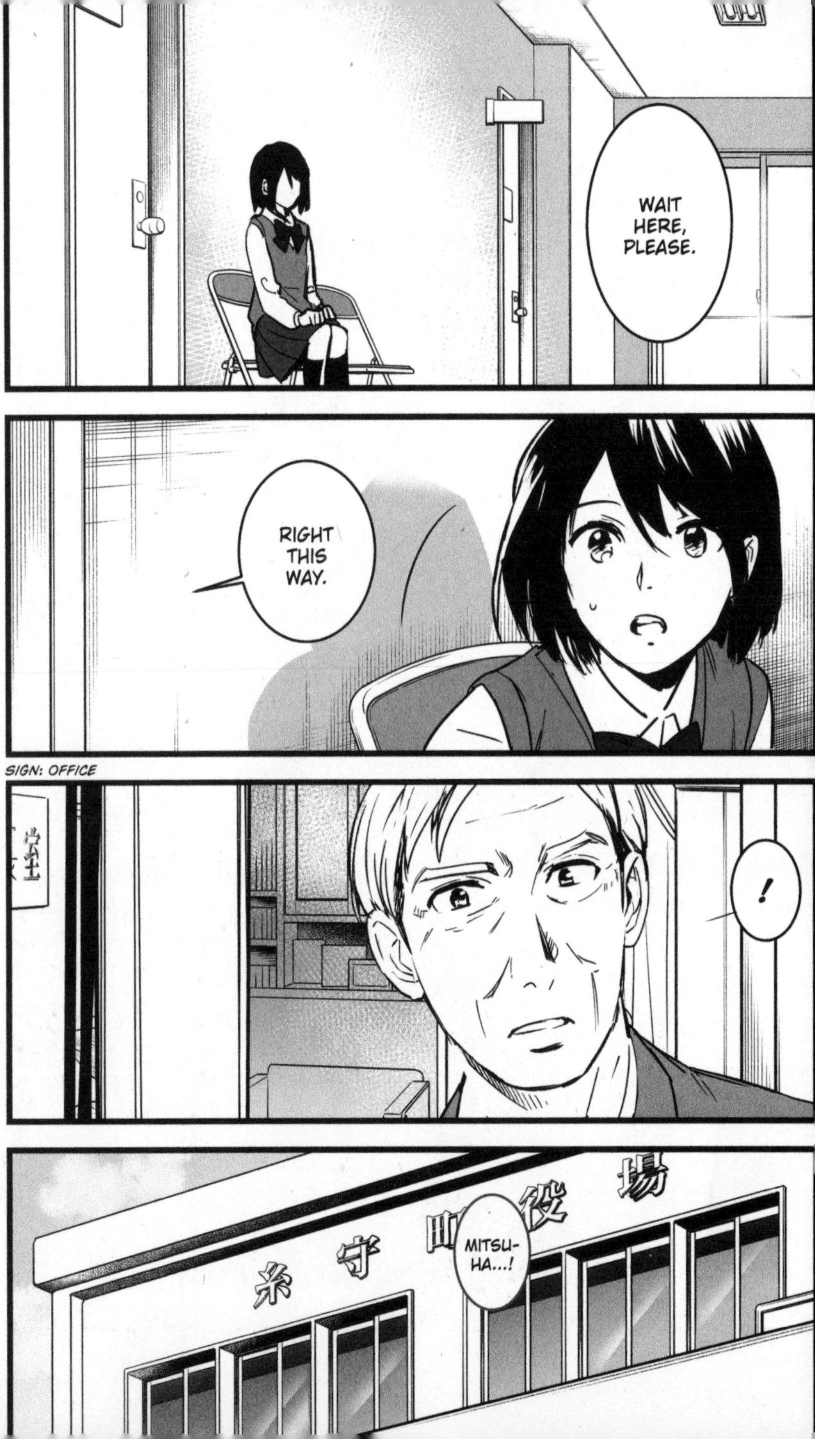
WAIT HERE, PLEASE.
RIGHT THIS WAY.
SIGN: OFFICE
!
糸守町役場
MITSU-HA...!

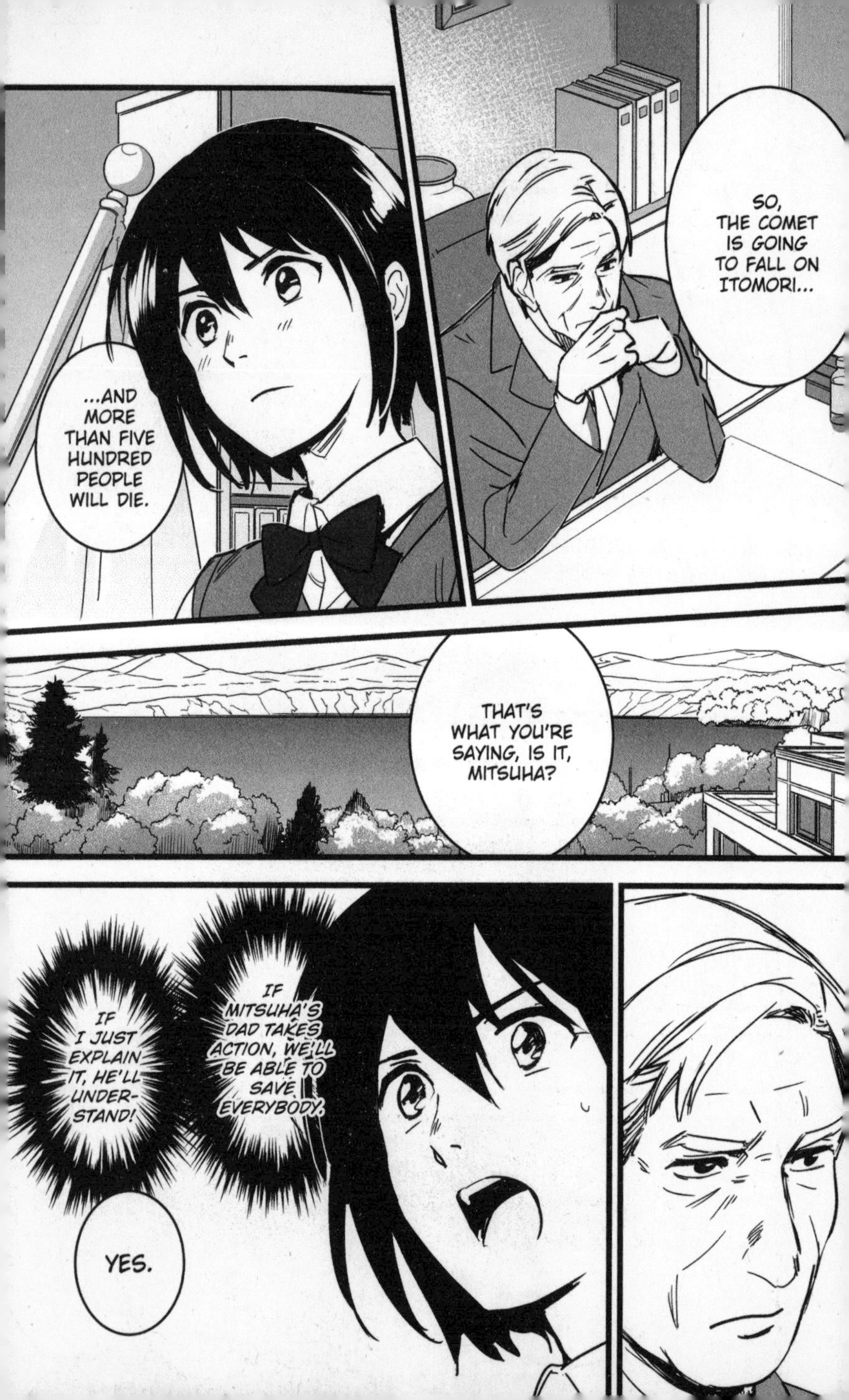
SO, THE COMET IS GOING TO FALL ON ITOMORI...
...AND MORE THAN FIVE HUNDRED PEOPLE WILL DIE.
THAT'S WHAT YOU'RE SAYING, IS IT, MITSUHA?
IF MITSUHA'S DAD TAKES ACTION, WE'LL BE ABLE TO SAVE EVERYBODY.
IF I JUST EXPLAIN IT, HE'LL UNDERSTAND!
YES.

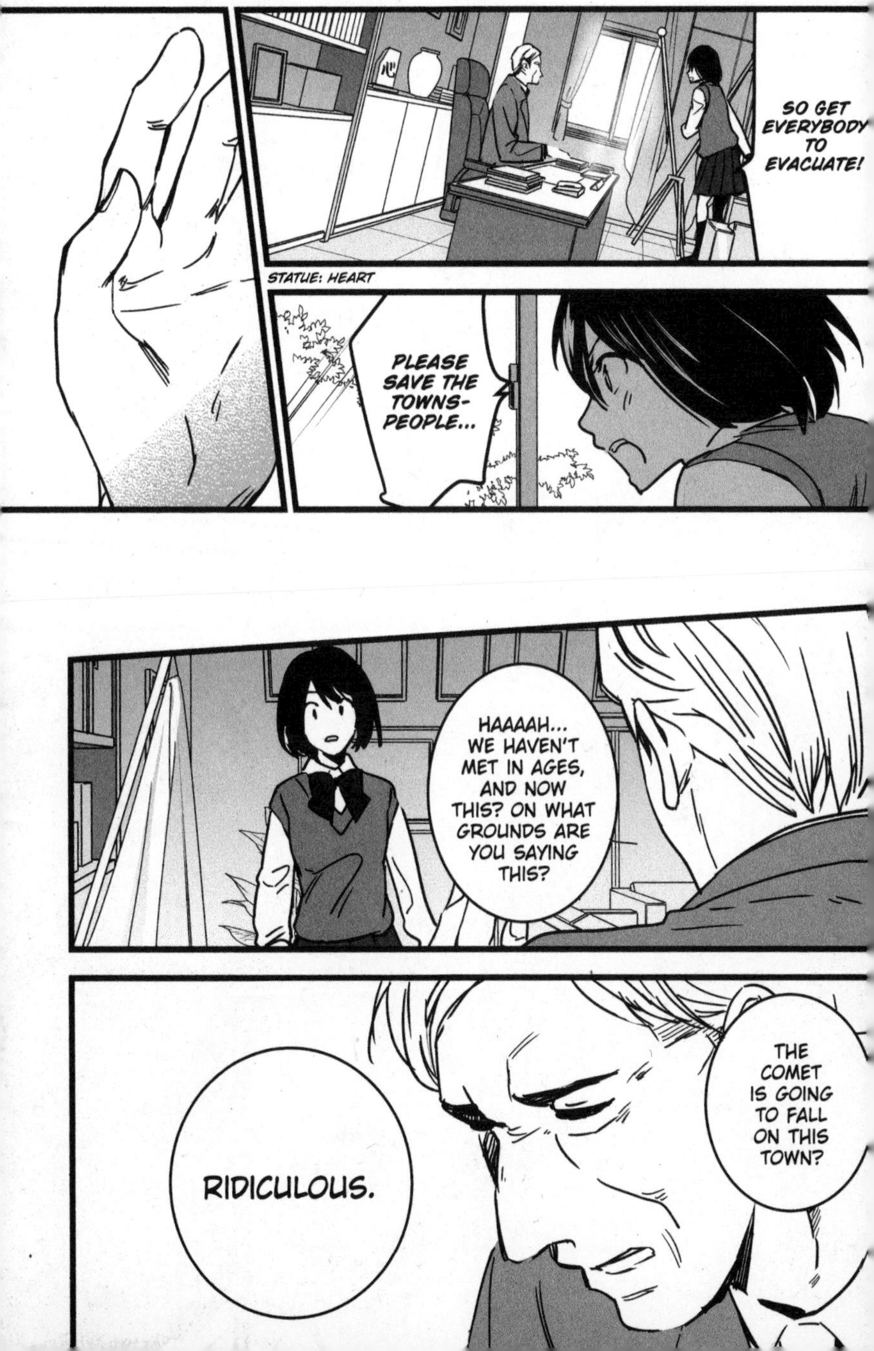
SO GET EVERYBODY TO EVACUATE!
STATUE: HEART
PLEASE SAVE THE TOWNS-PEOPLE...
HAAAAH... WE HAVEN'T MET IN AGES, AND NOW THIS? ON WHAT GROUNDS ARE YOU SAYING THIS?
THE COMET IS GOING TO FALL ON THIS TOWN?
RIDICULOUS.

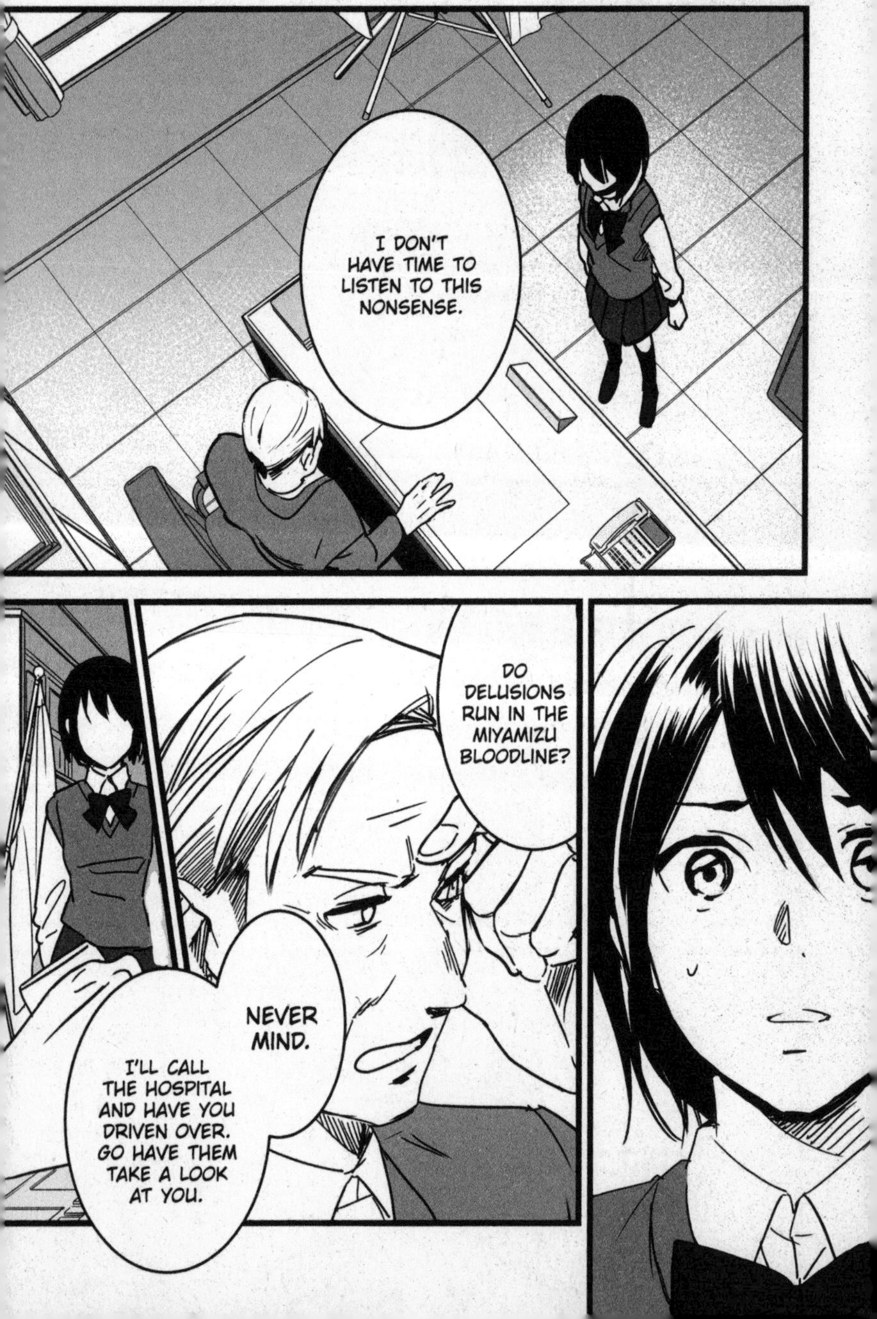
I DON'T HAVE TIME TO LISTEN TO THIS NONSENSE.
DO DELUSIONS RUN IN THE MIYAMIZU BLOODLINE?
NEVER MIND.
I'LL CALL THE HOSPITAL AND HAVE YOU DRIVEN OVER. GO HAVE THEM TAKE A LOOK AT YOU.

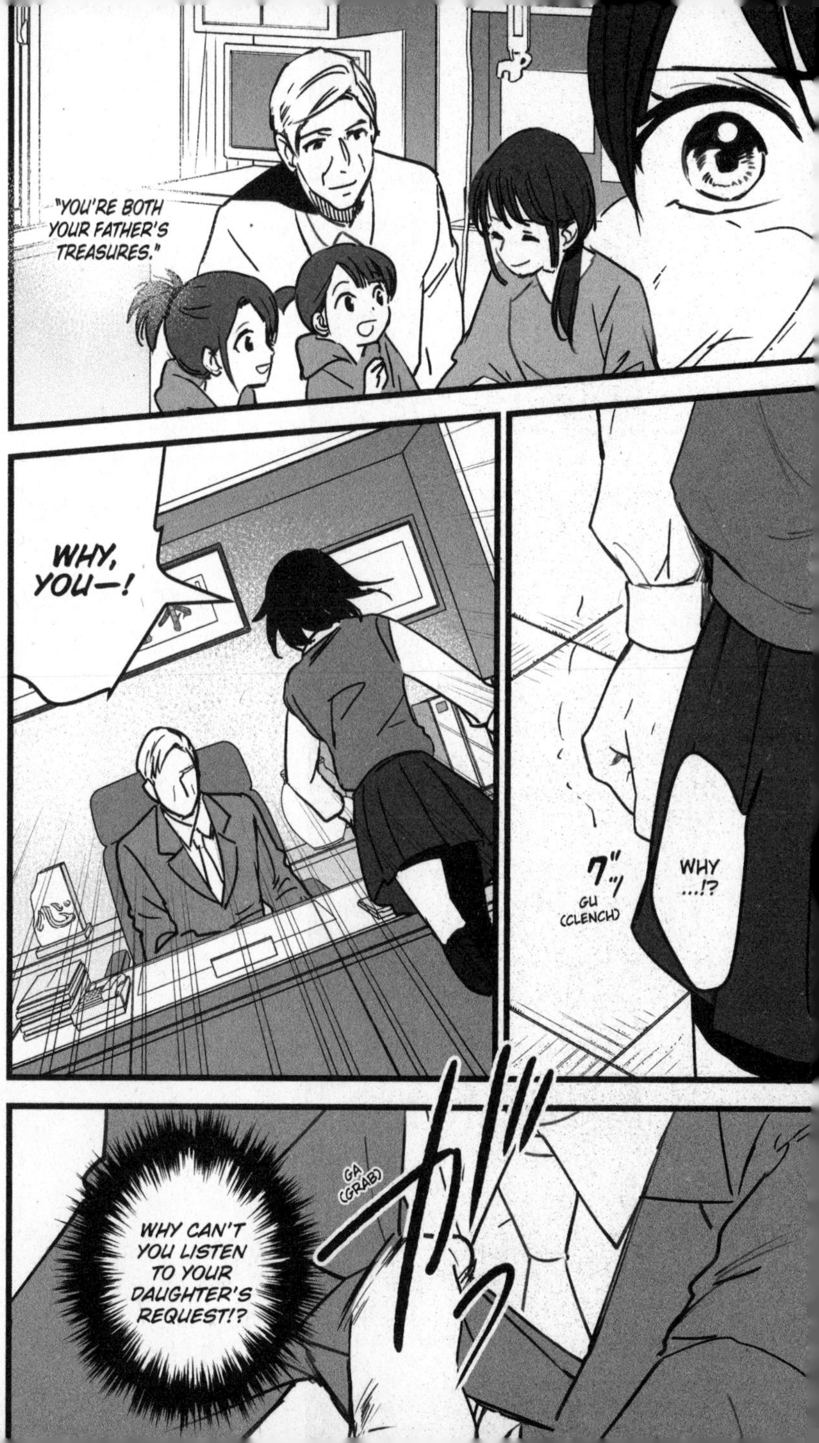
"YOU'RE BOTH YOUR FATHER'S TREASURES."
WHY ...!?
グッ
GU (CLENCH)
WHY, YOU—!
ガッ
GA (GRAB)
WHY CAN'T YOU LISTEN TO YOUR DAUGHTER'S REQUEST!?

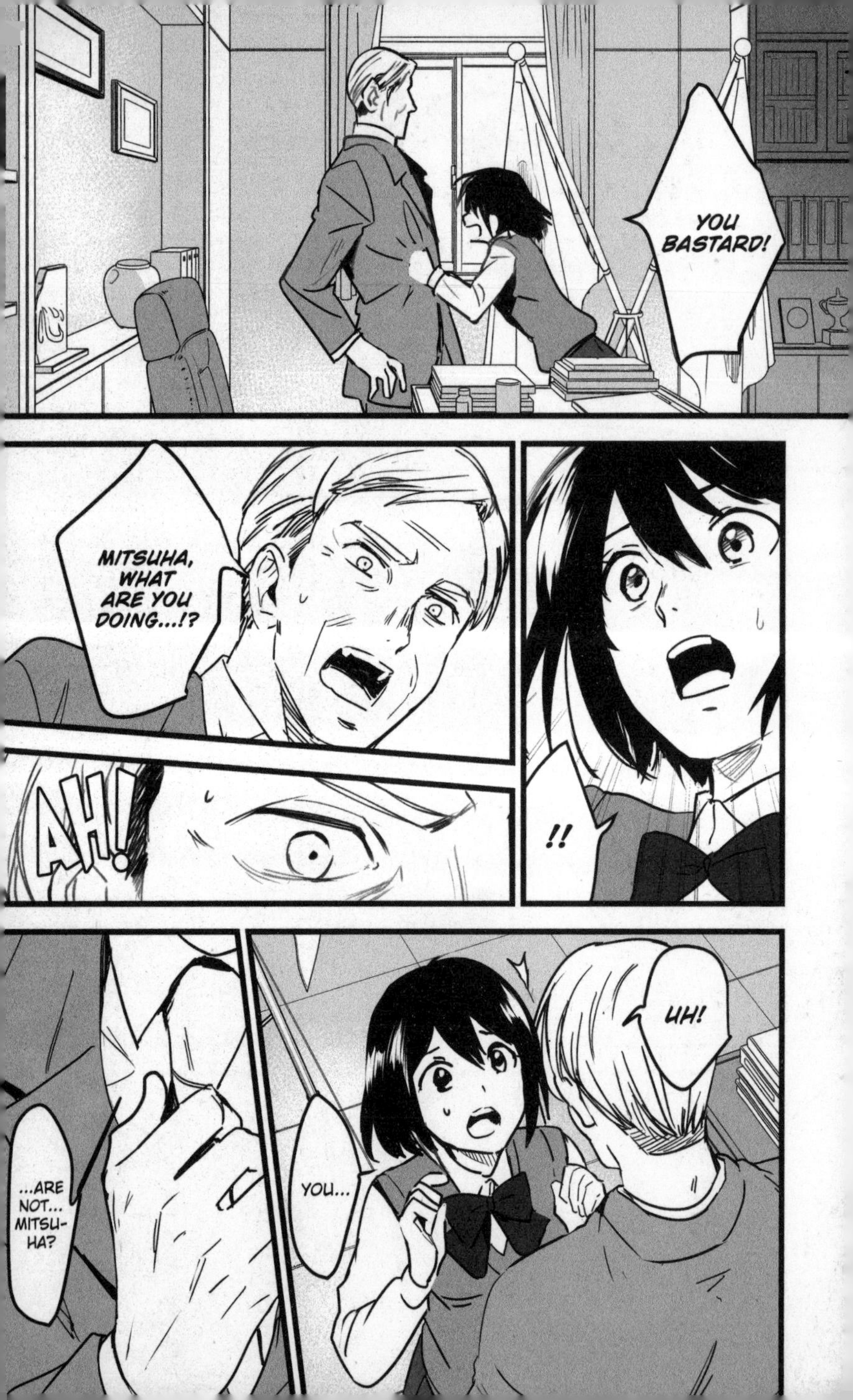
YOU BASTARD!
!!
MITSUHA, WHAT ARE YOU DOING...!?
AH!
UH!
YOU...
...ARE NOT... MITSU-HA?

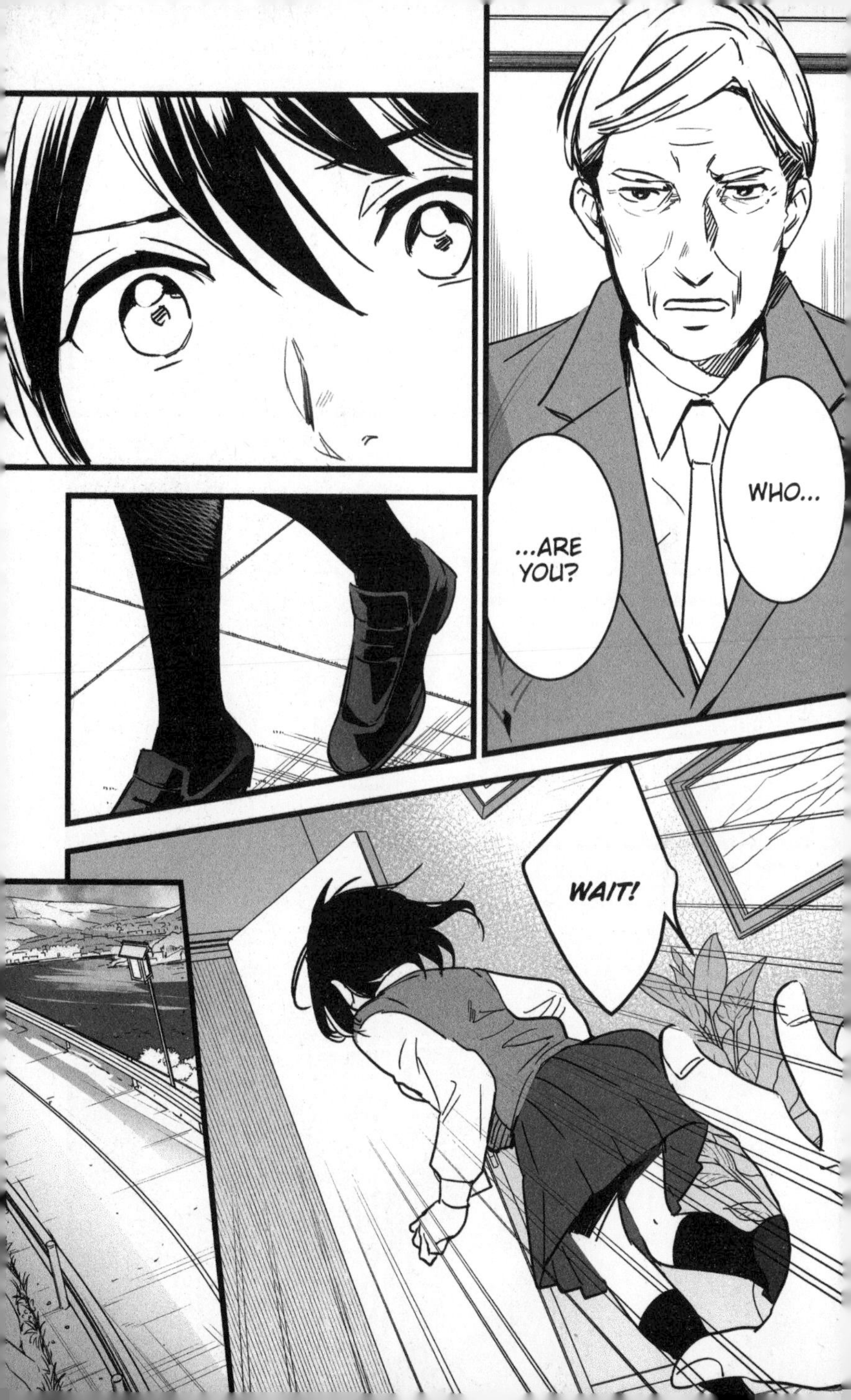
WHO...
...ARE YOU?
WAIT!

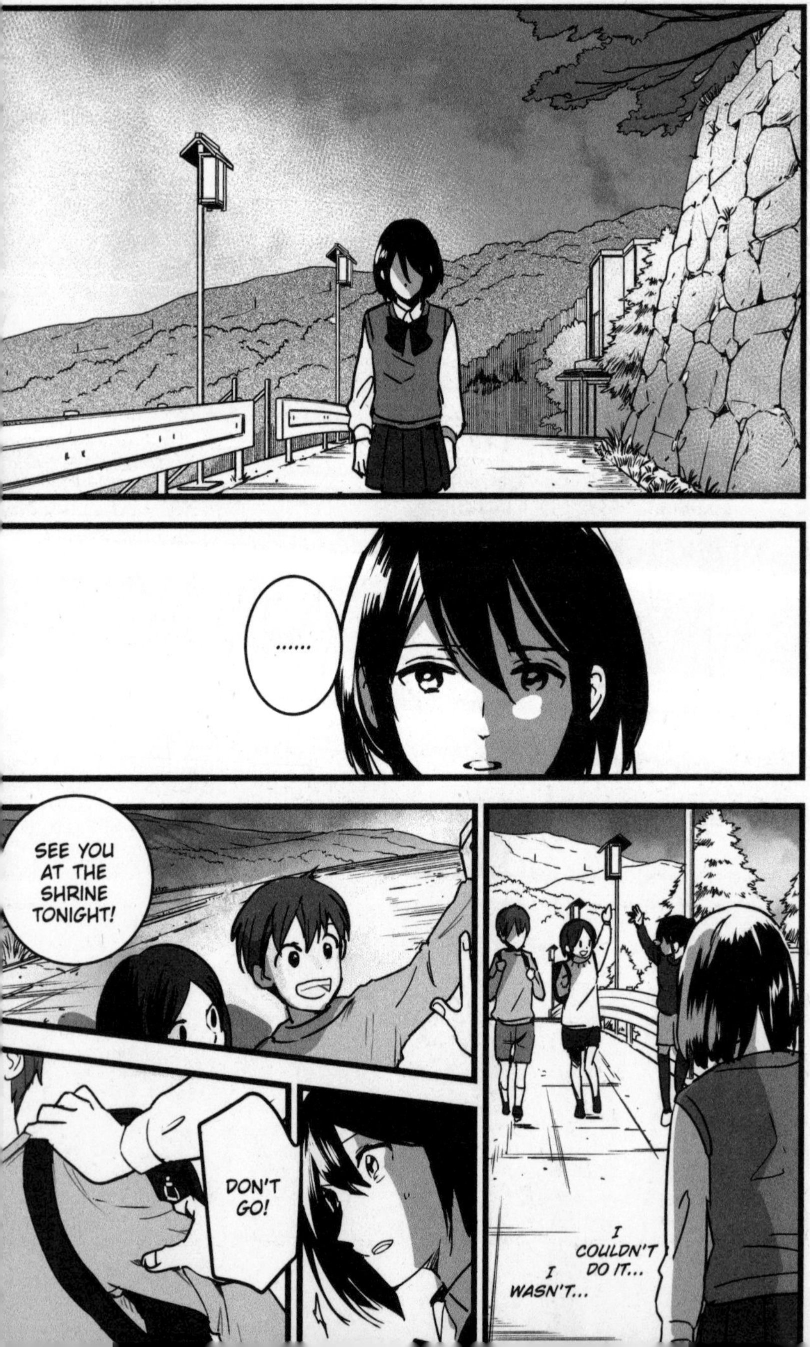
......
I COULDN'T DO IT...
I WASN'T...
SEE YOU AT THE SHRINE TONIGHT!
DON'T GO!

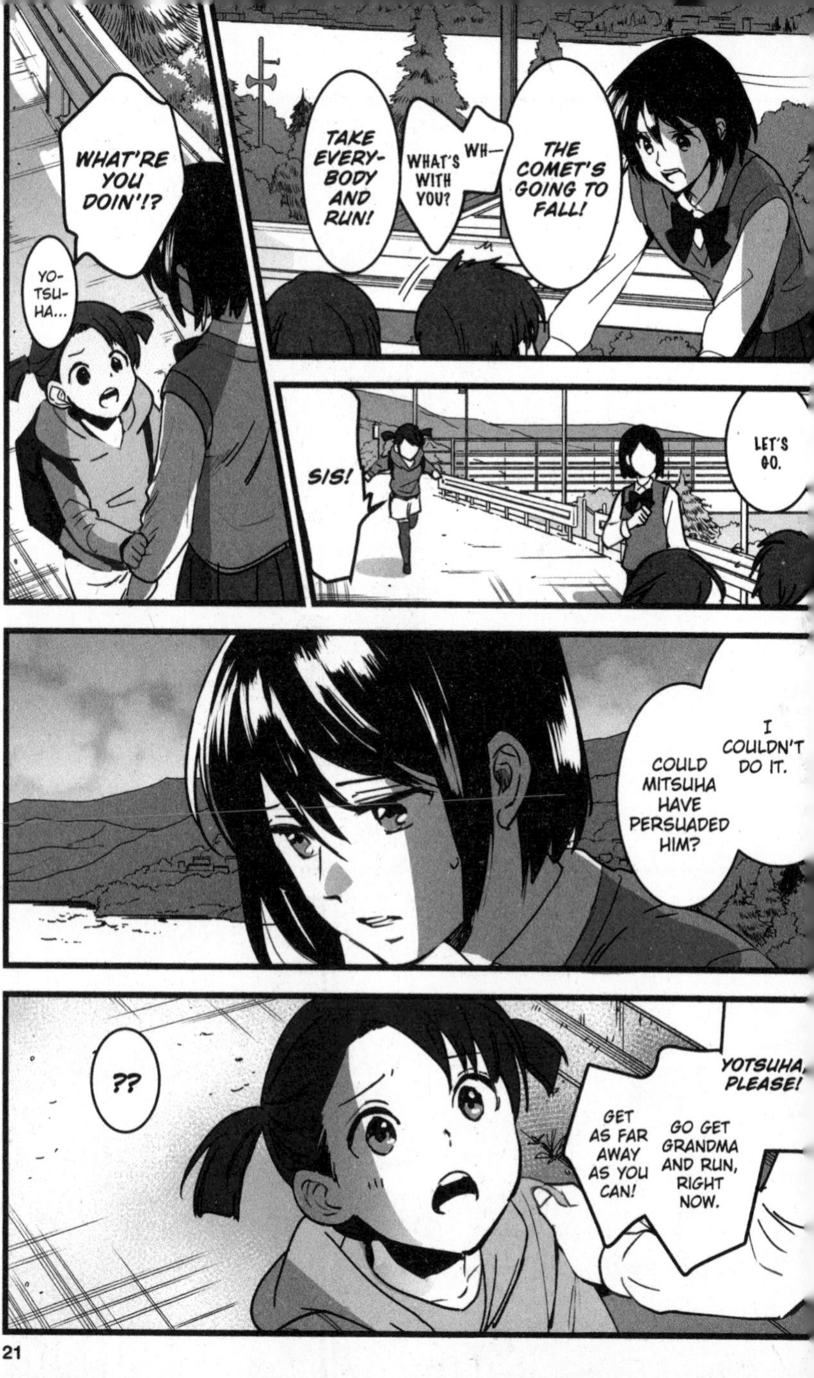
THE COMET'S GOING TO FALL!
WH—
WHAT'S WITH YOU?
TAKE EVERY-BODY AND RUN!
LET'S GO.
SIS!
WHAT'RE YOU DOIN'!?
YO-TSU-HA...
I COULDN'T DO IT.
COULD MITSUHA HAVE PERSUADED HIM?
YOTSUHA, PLEASE!
GO GET GRANDMA AND RUN, RIGHT NOW.
GET AS FAR AWAY AS YOU CAN!
??

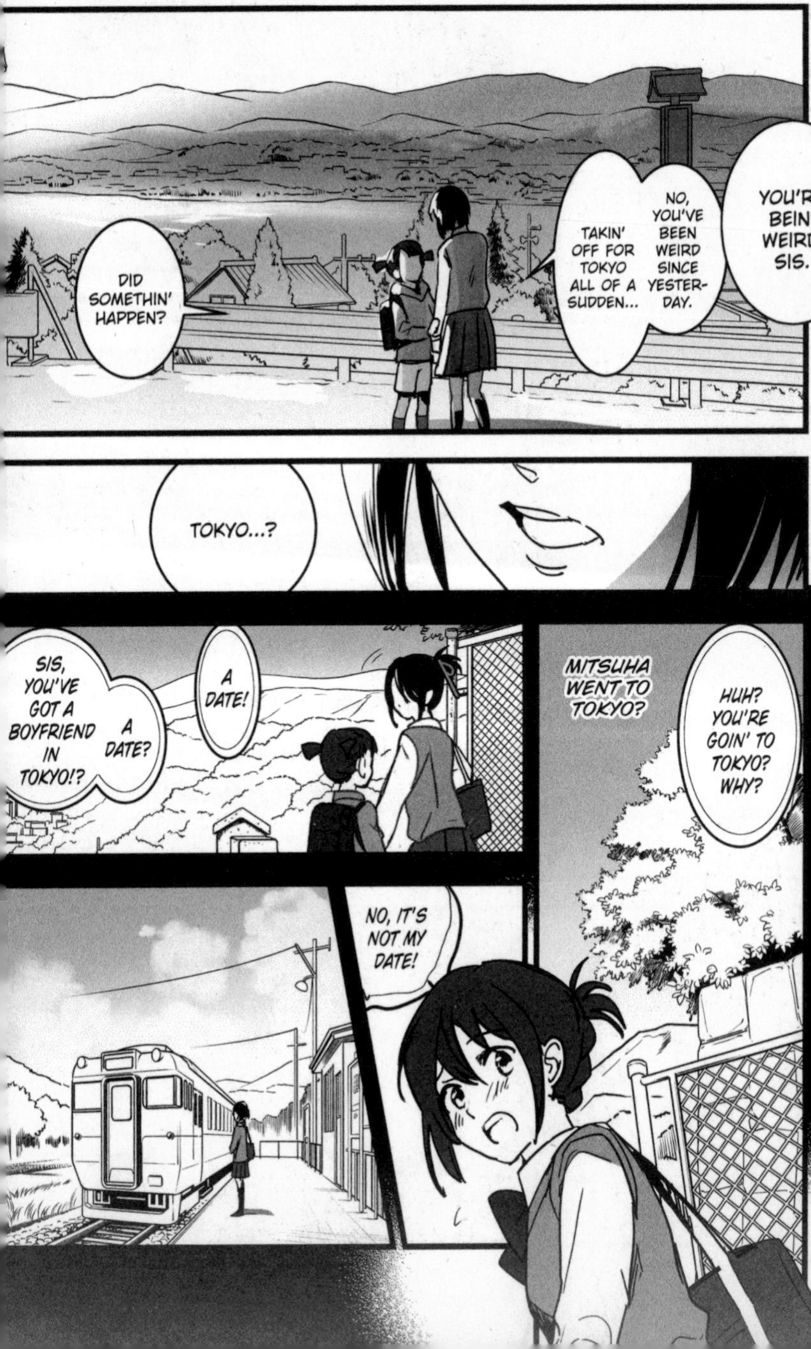
YOU'RE BEIN' WEIRD, SIS.
NO, YOU'VE BEEN WEIRD SINCE YESTER-DAY.
TAKIN' OFF FOR TOKYO ALL OF A SUDDEN...
DID SOMETHIN' HAPPEN?
TOKYO...?
HUH? YOU'RE GOIN' TO TOKYO? WHY?
MITSUHA WENT TO TOKYO?
A DATE!
A DATE?
SIS, YOU'VE GOT A BOYFRIEND IN TOKYO!?
NO, IT'S NOT MY DATE!

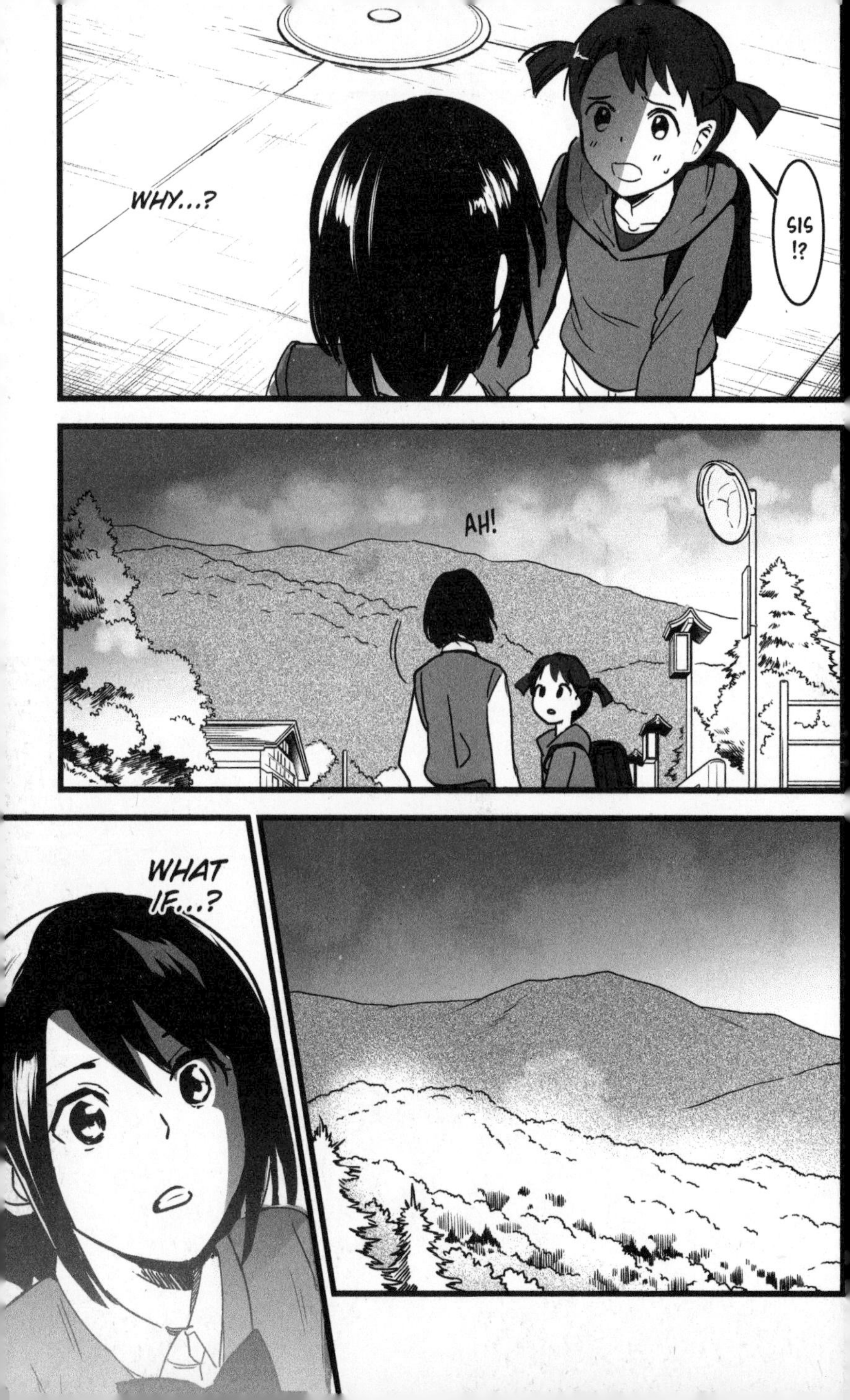
SIS !?
WHY...?
AH!
WHAT IF...?

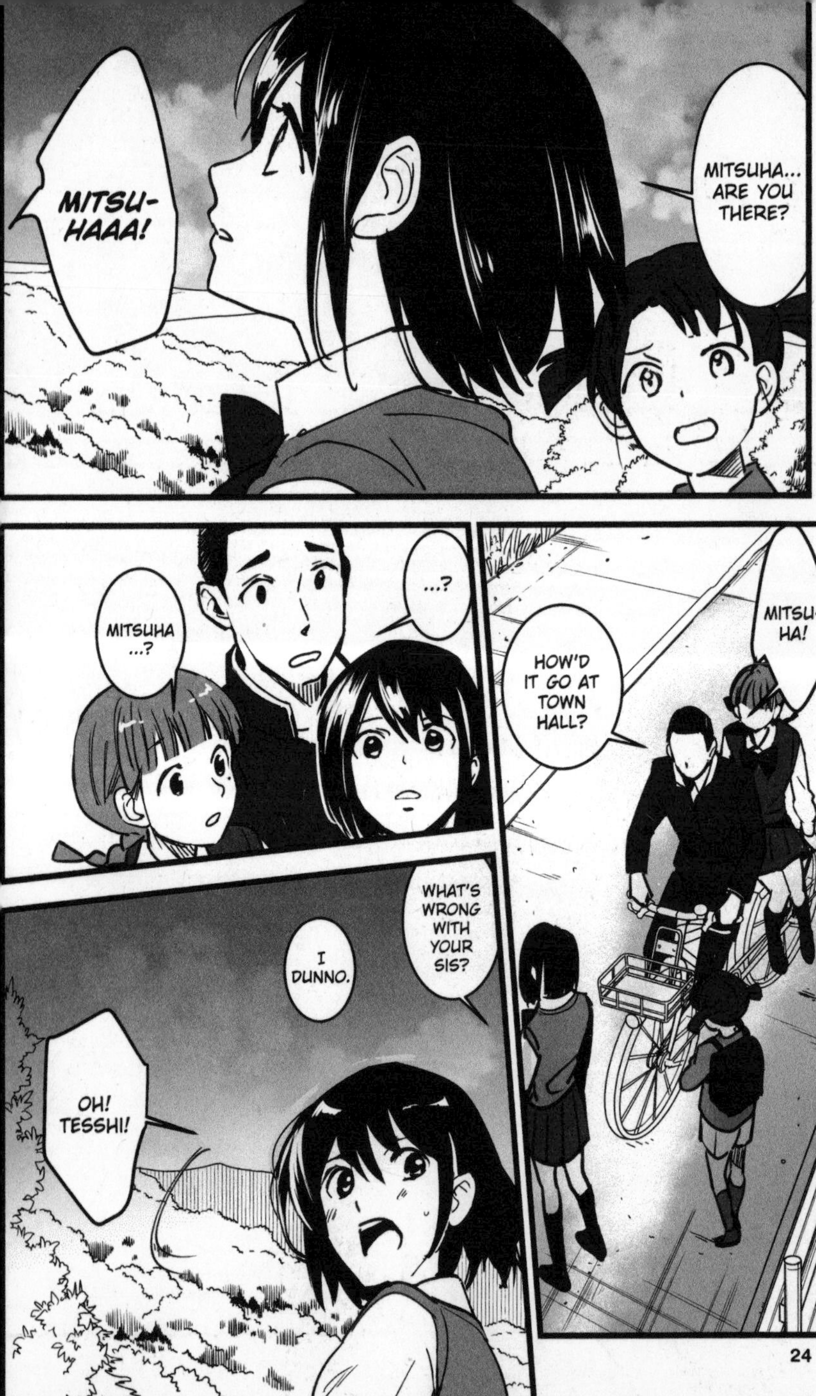
MITSUHA... ARE YOU THERE?
MITSU-HAAA!
MITSU-HA!
HOW'D IT GO AT TOWN HALL?
...?
MITSUHA ...?
WHAT'S WRONG WITH YOUR SIS?
I DUNNO.
OH! TESSHI!

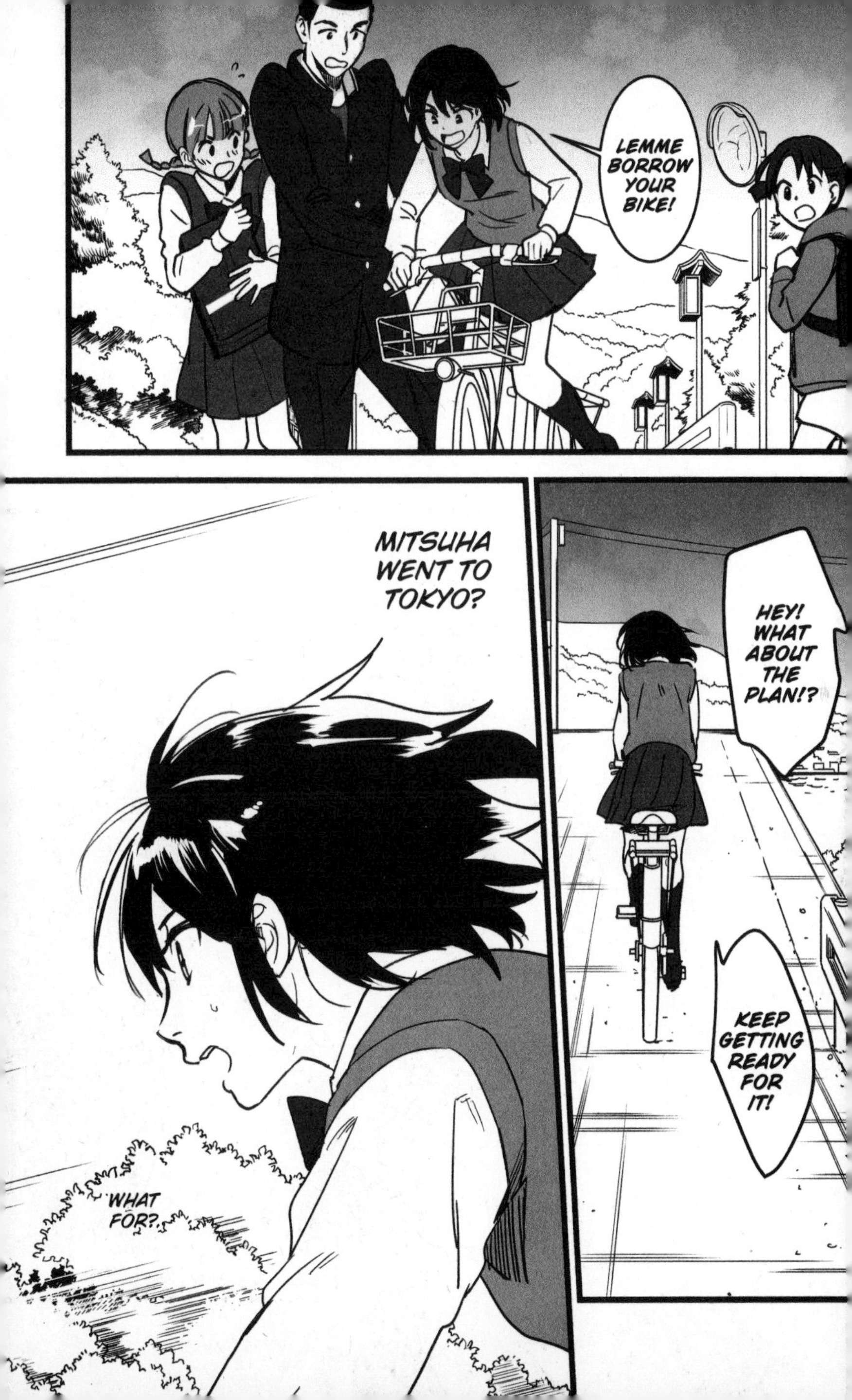
LEMME BORROW YOUR BIKE!
HEY! WHAT ABOUT THE PLAN!?
KEEP GETTING READY FOR IT!
MITSUHA WENT TO TOKYO?
WHAT FOR?

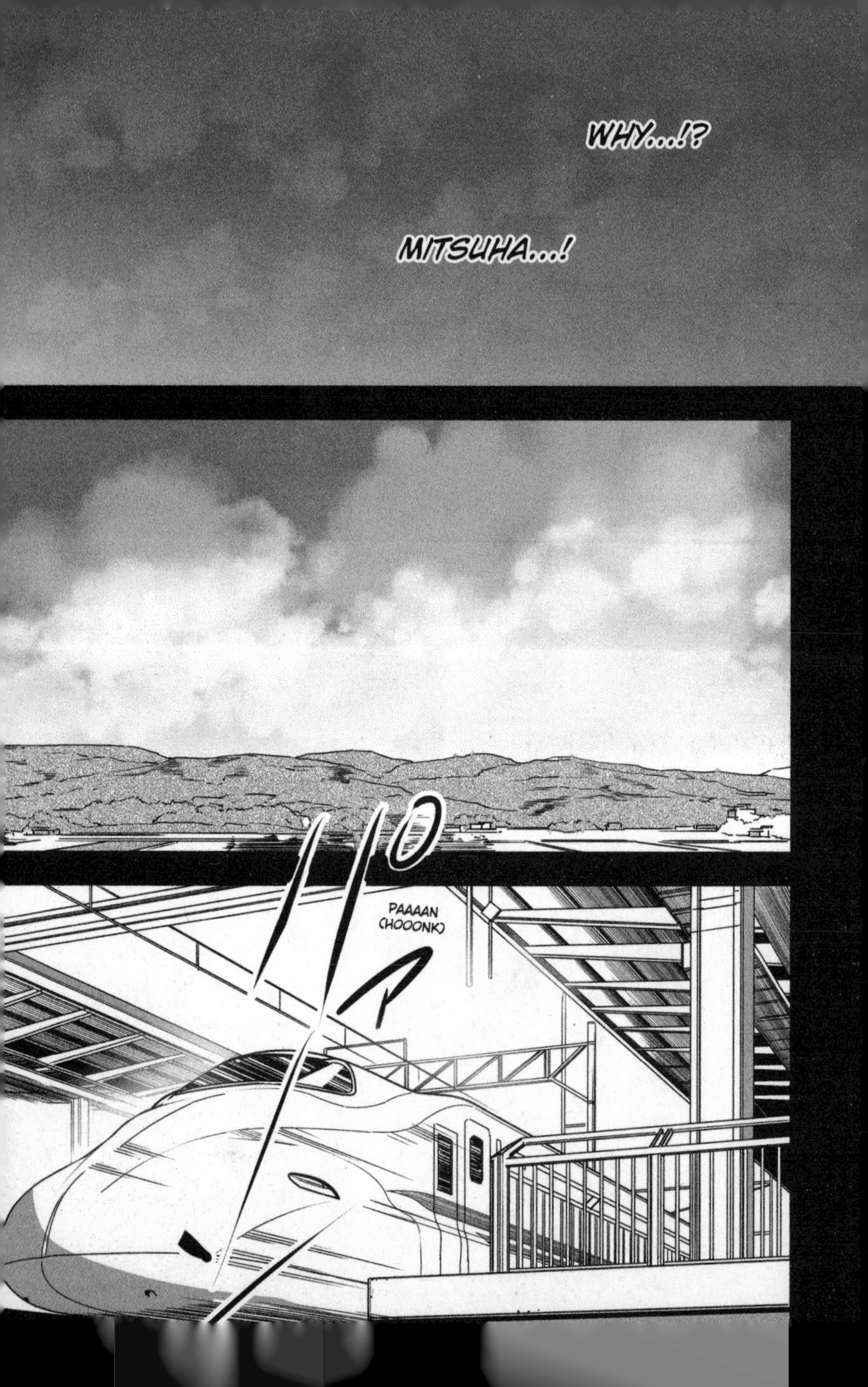
WHY...!?
MITSUHA...!
PAAAAN
(HOOONK)

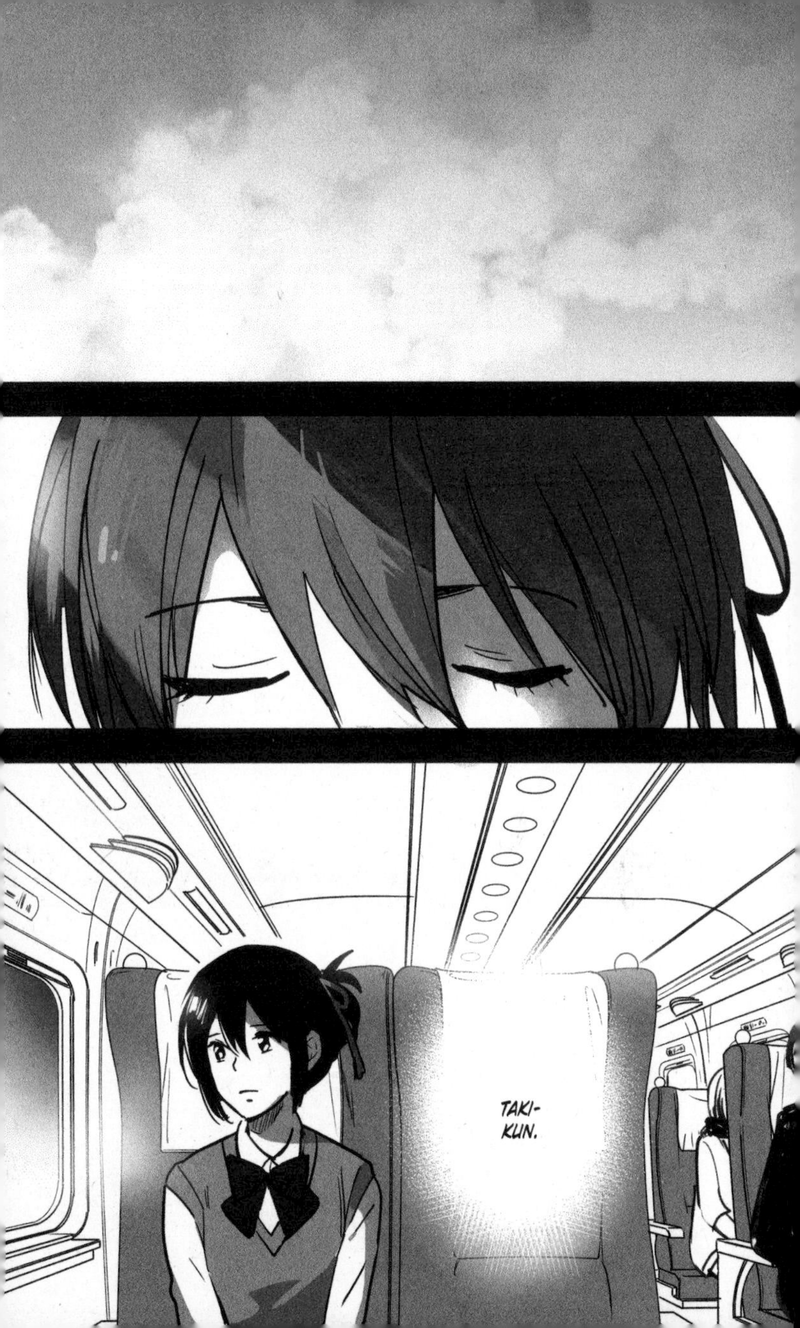
TAKI-KUN.

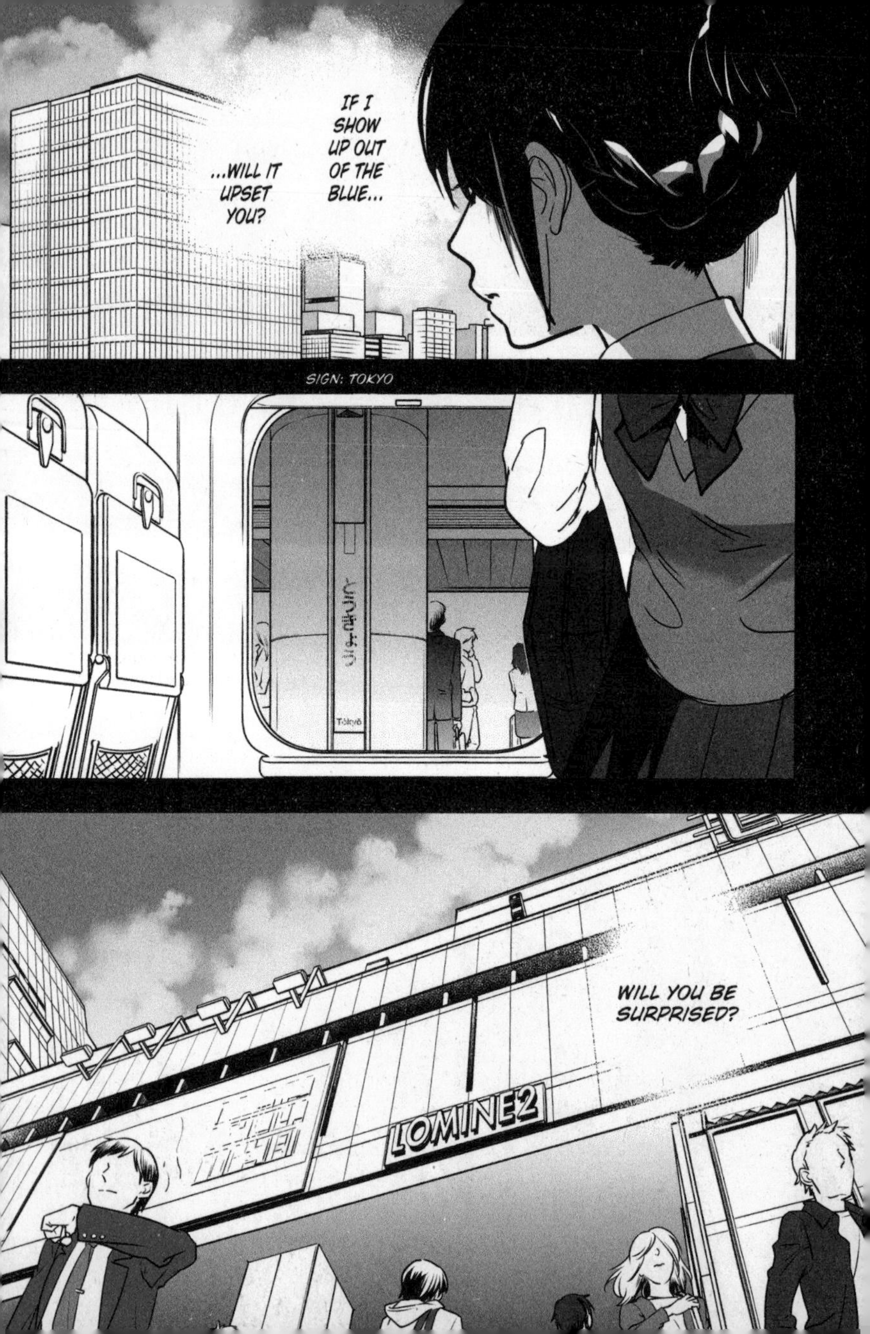
IF I SHOW UP OUT OF THE BLUE...
...WILL IT UPSET YOU?
SIGN: TOKYO
Tōkyō
WILL YOU BE SURPRISED?
LOMINE2

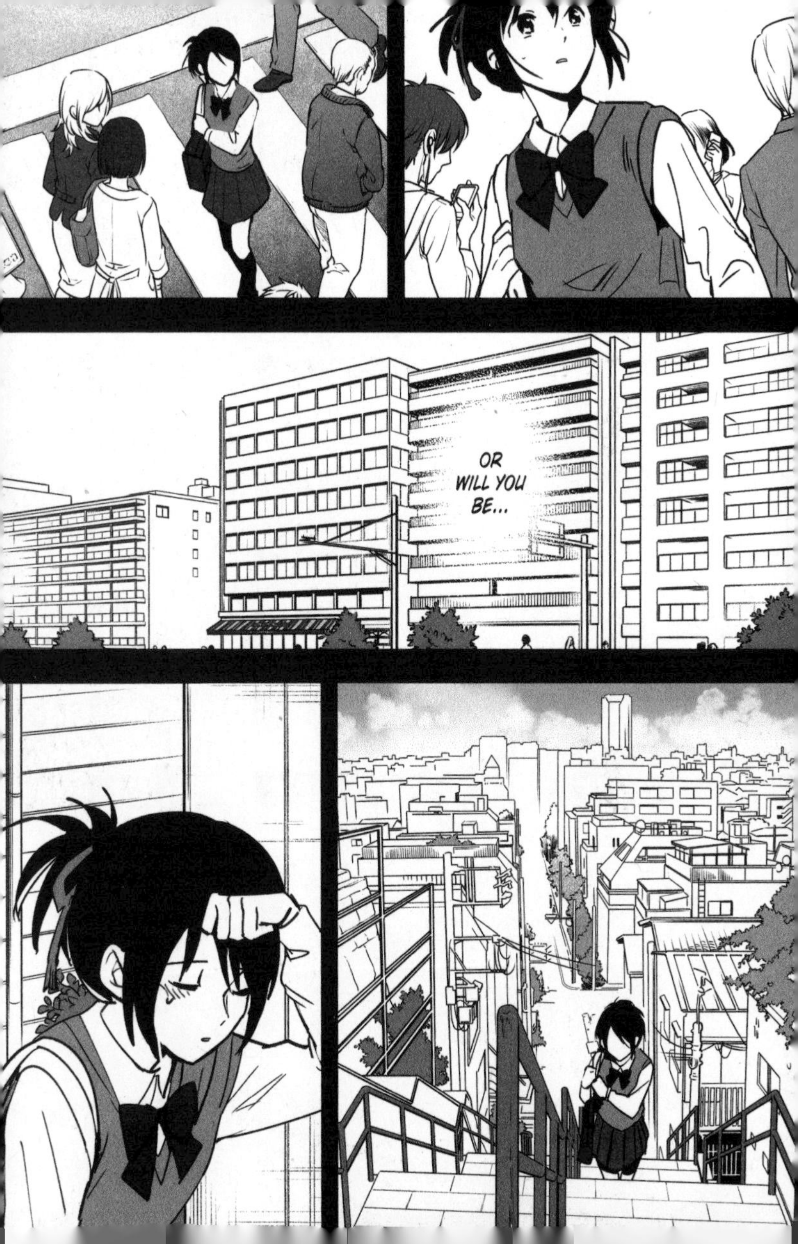
OR WILL YOU BE...

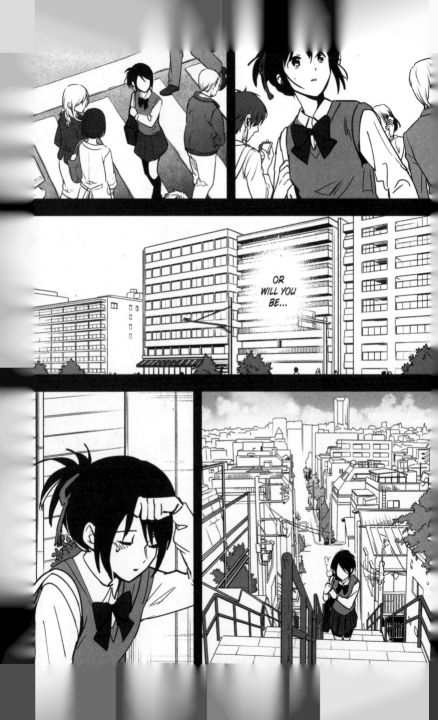

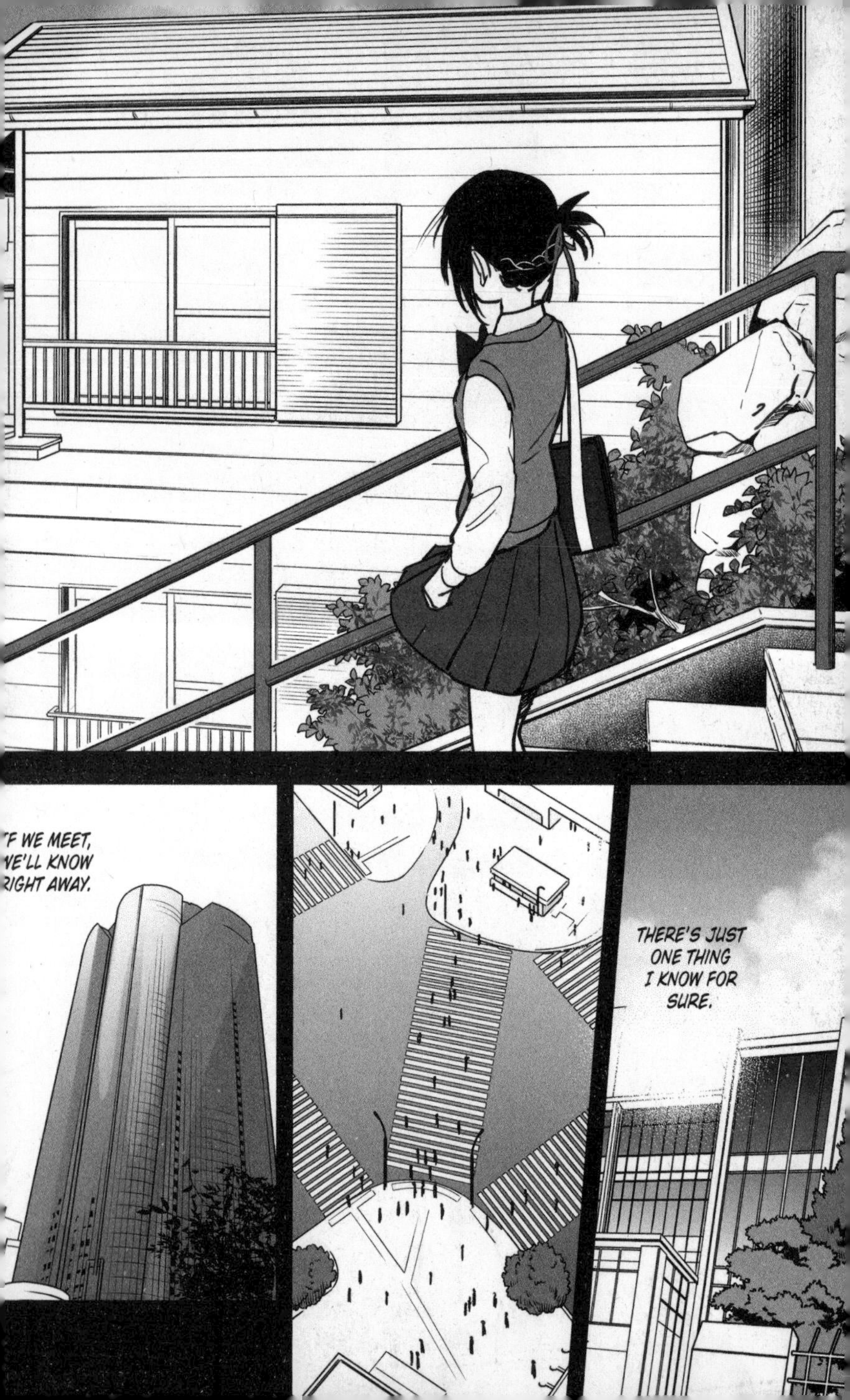
THERE'S JUST ONE THING I KNOW FOR SURE.
F WE MEET, E'LL KNOW RIGHT AWAY.

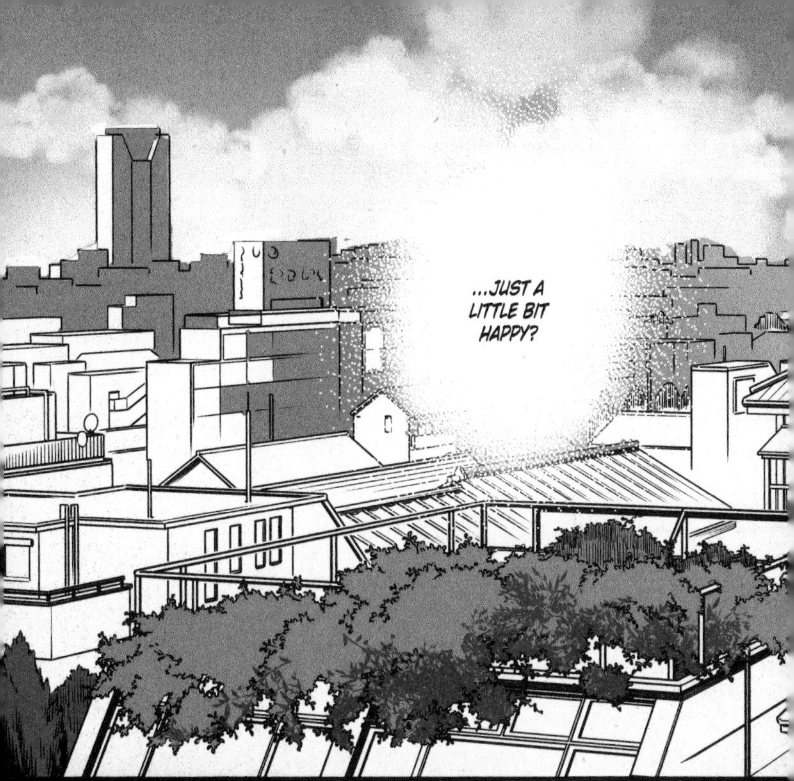
...JUST A LITTLE BIT HAPPY?
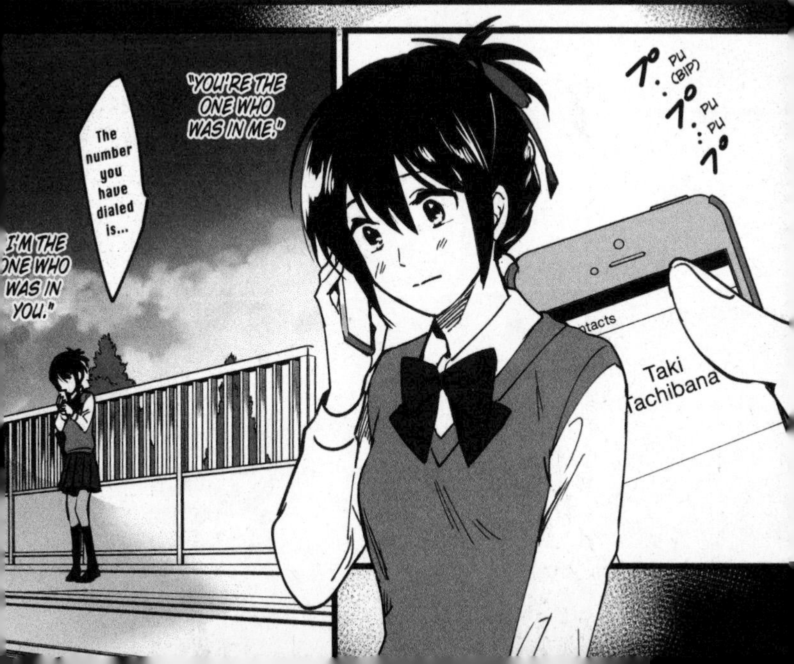
プ PU (BIP)
プ PU
PU プ
Taki Tachibana
"YOU'RE THE ONE WHO WAS IN ME."
The number you have dialed is...
"I'M THE ONE WHO WAS IN YOU."

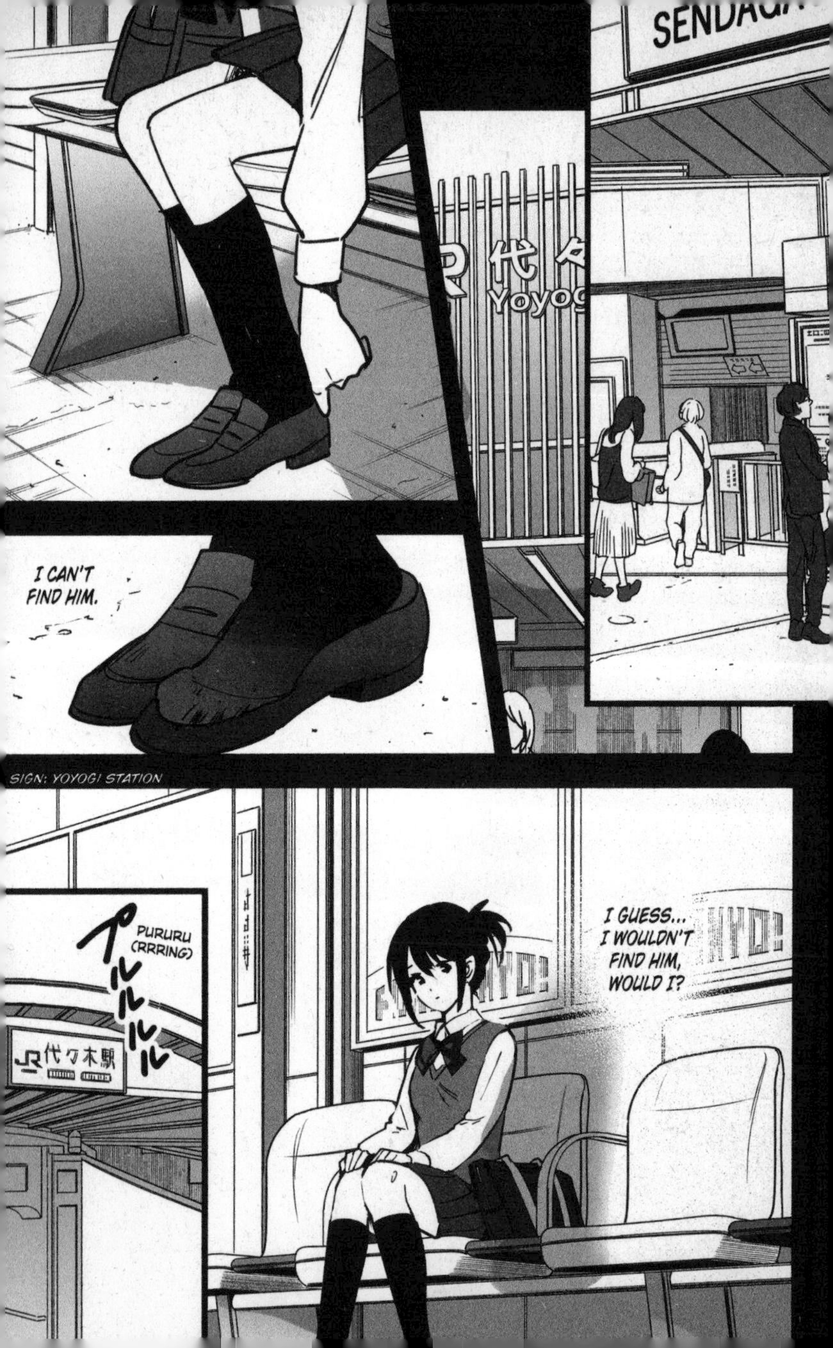
I CAN'T FIND HIM.
SIGN: YOYOGI STATION
I GUESS... I WOULDN'T FIND HIM, WOULD I?
プルルルル
PURURU (RRRING)
代々木駅

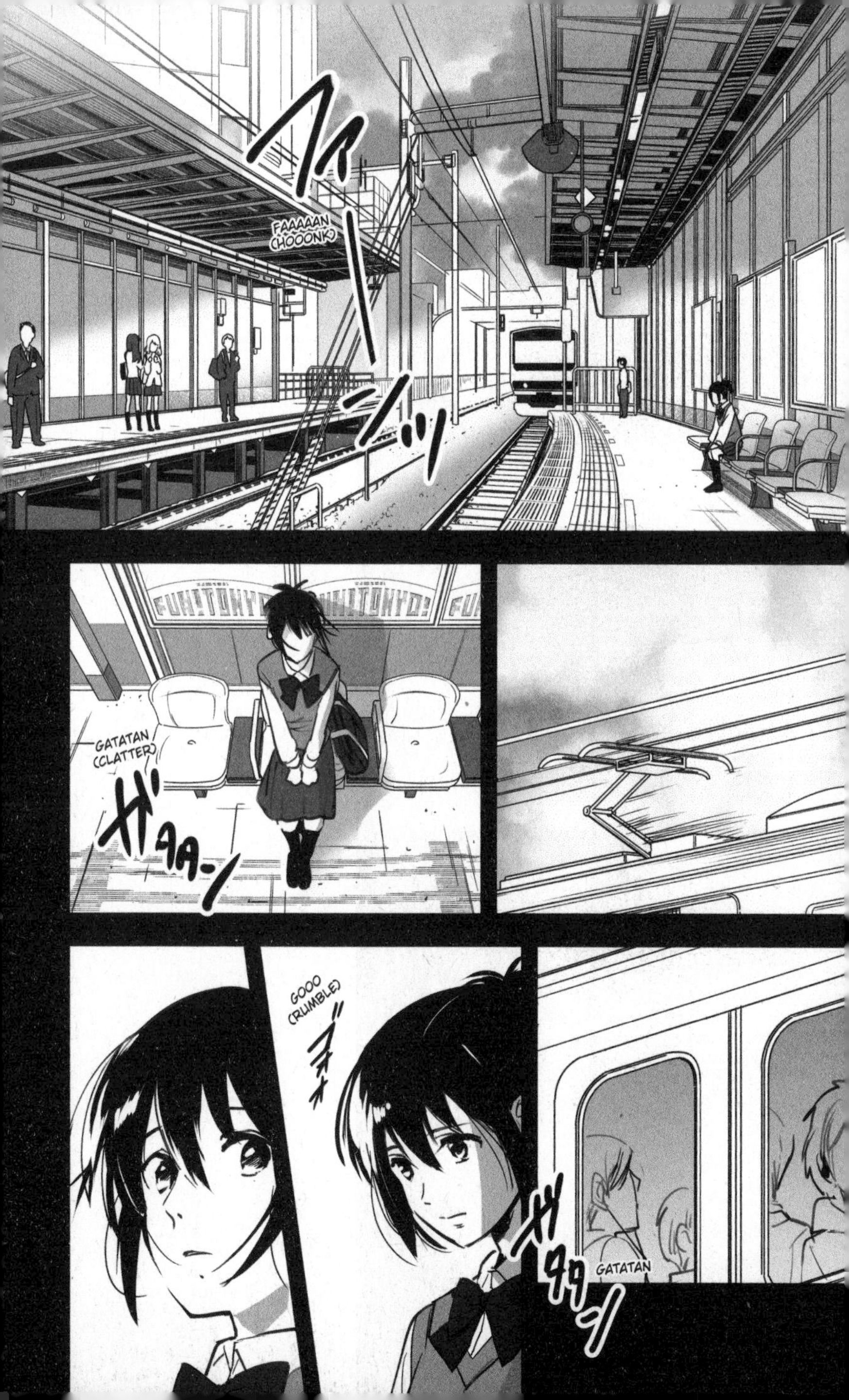
FAAAAAN (HOOONK)
GATATAN (CLATTER)
GATATAN
GOOO (RUMBLE)

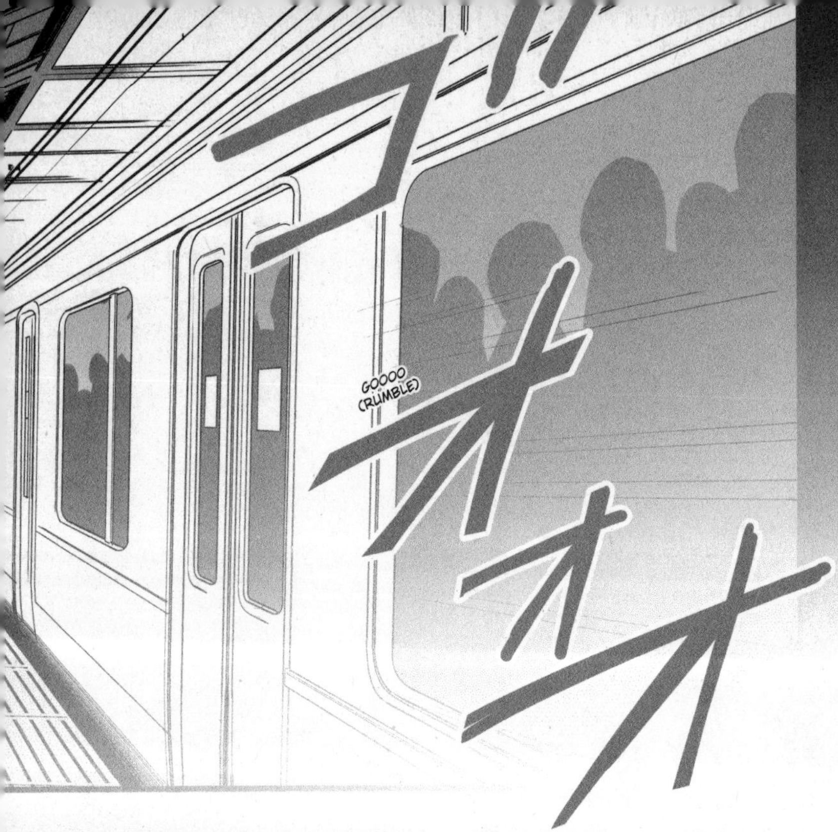
GOOOO
(RUMBLE)

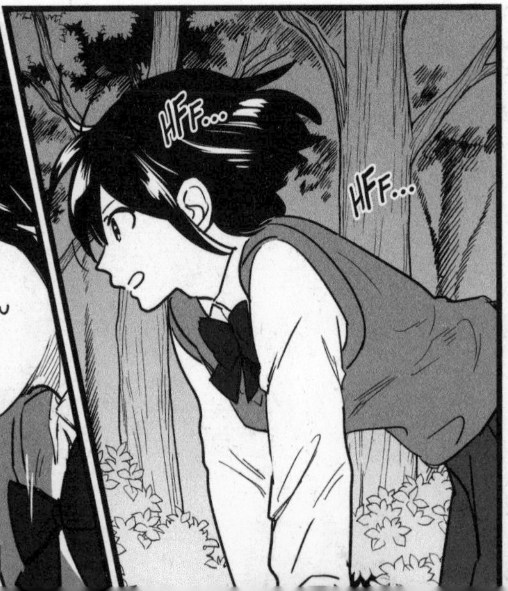
HFF...
HFF...

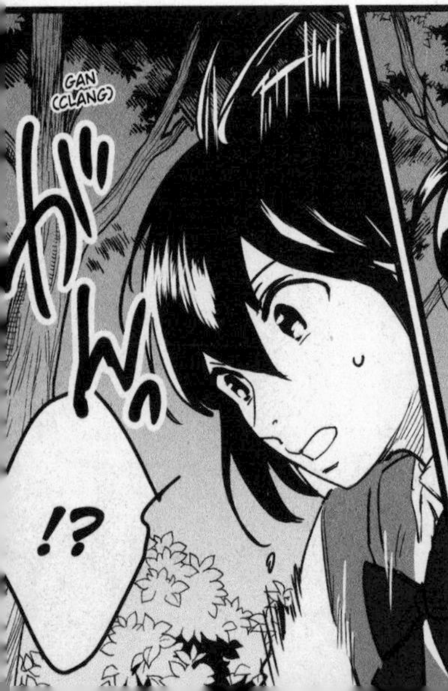
GAN
(CLANG)
!?

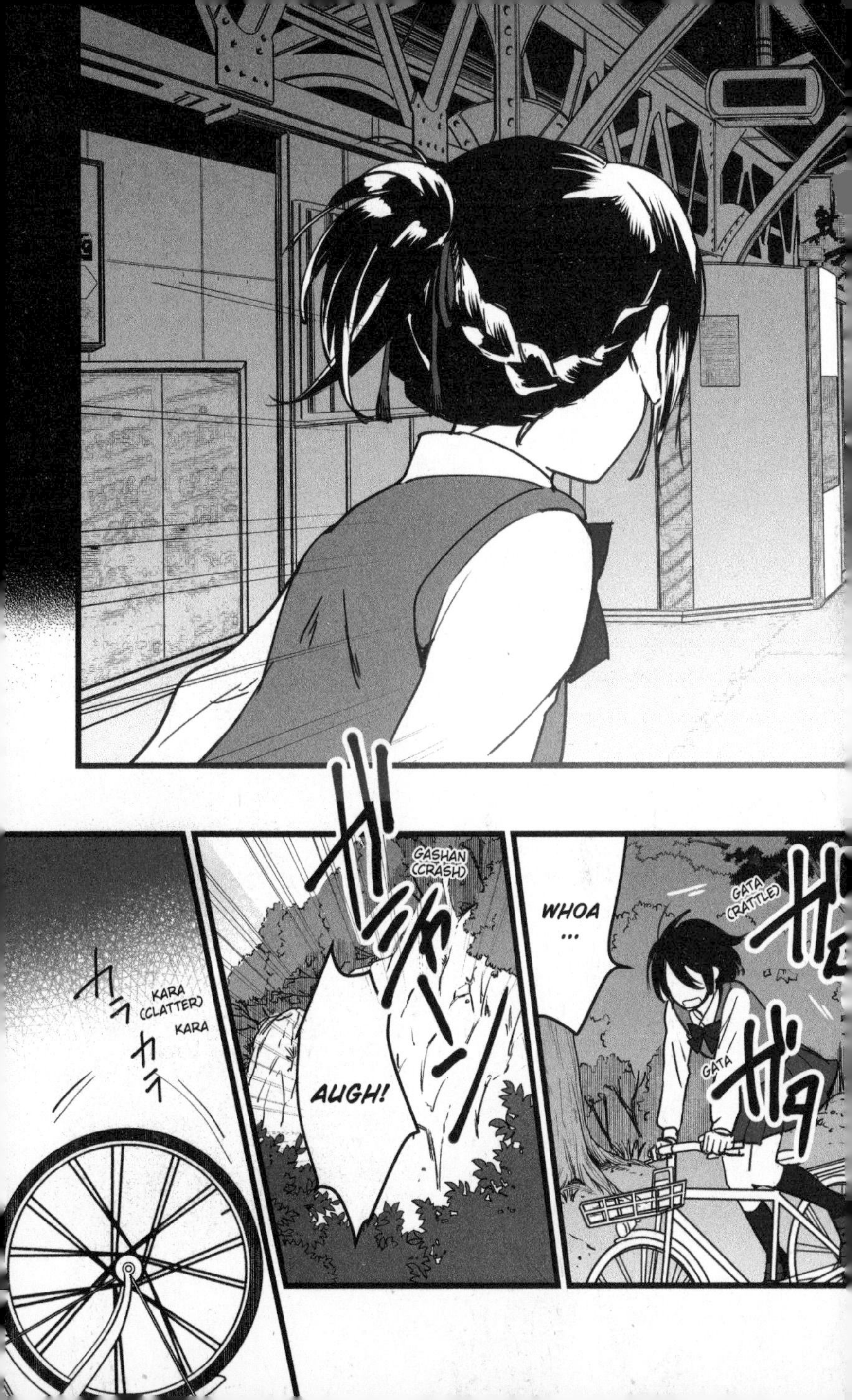
GATA (RATTLE)
GATA
WHOA ...
GASHAN (CRASH)
AUGH!
KARA (CLATTER) KARA

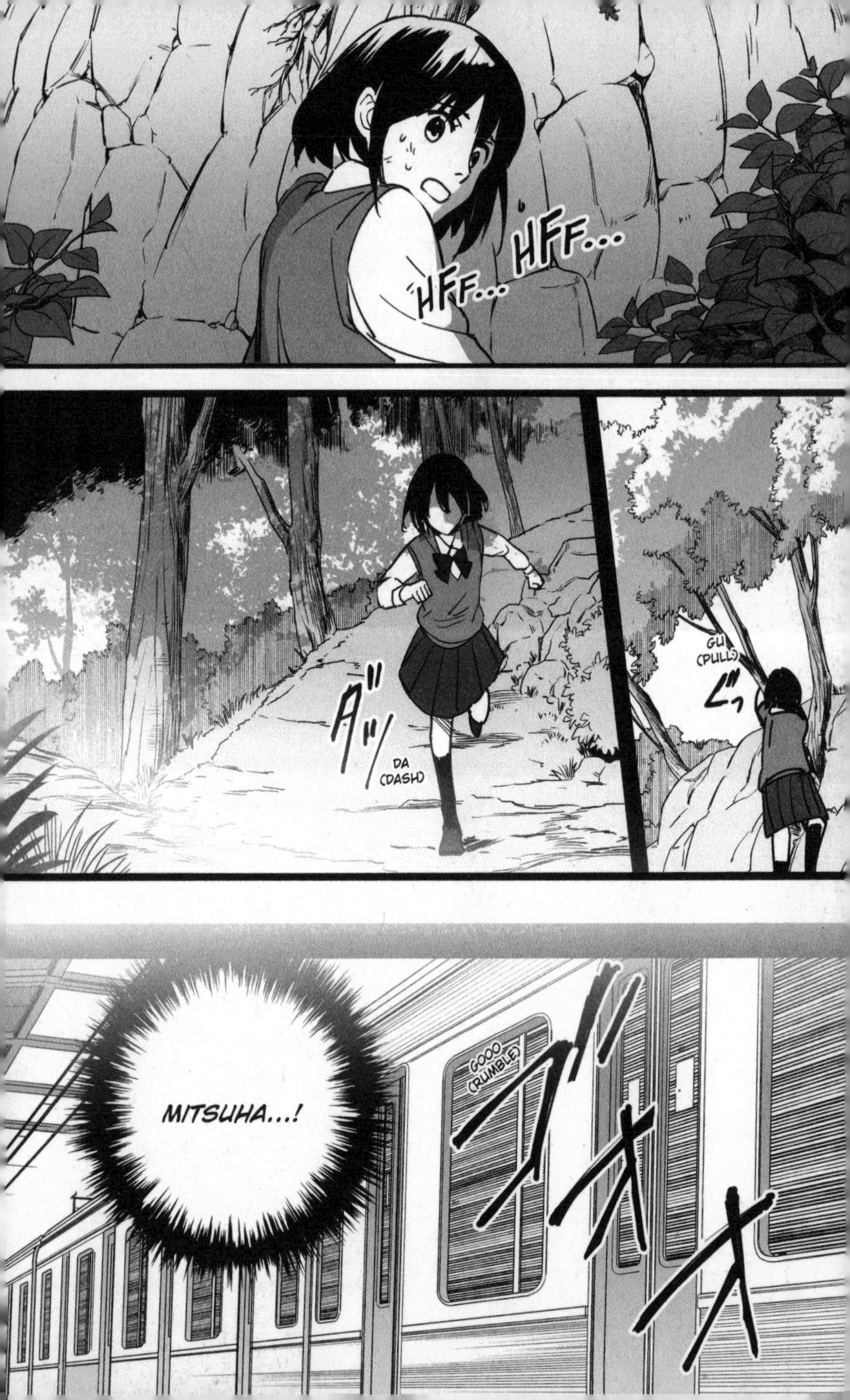
HFF... HFF...
GU (PULL)
DA (DASH)
MITSUHA...!
GOOO (RUMBLE)

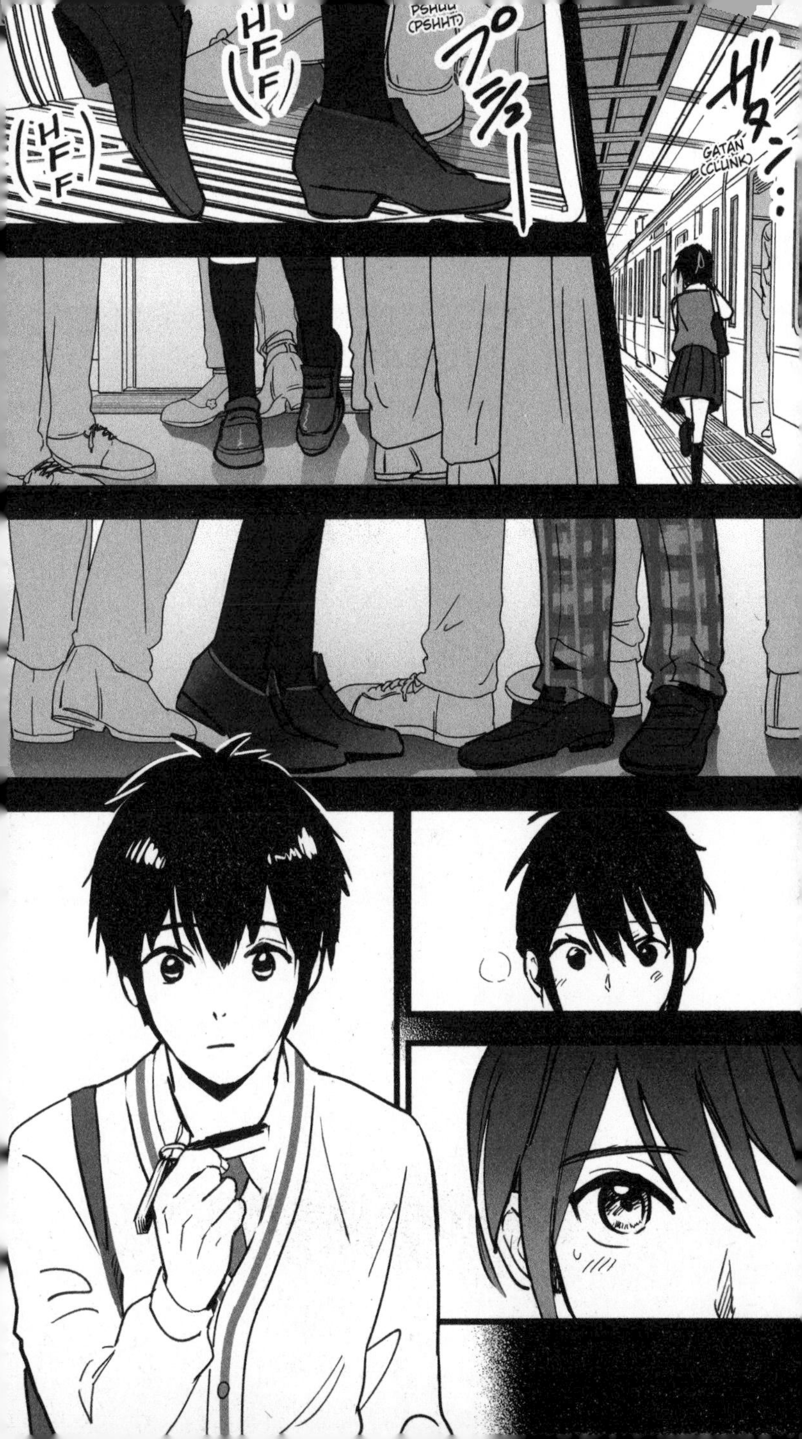
ガタン…
GATAN (CLUNK)
プシュー
PSHUU (PSHHT)
HFF
HFF

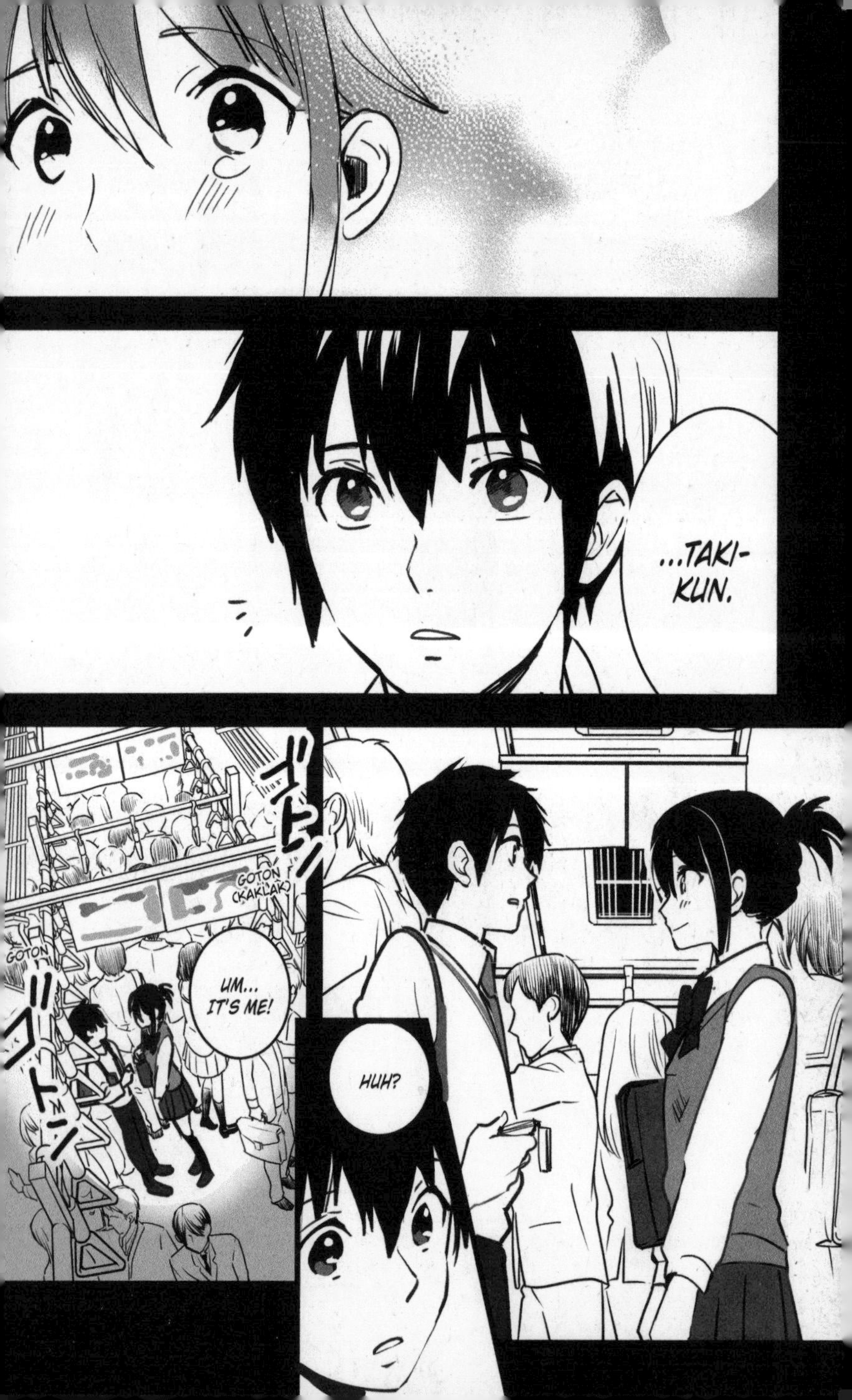
...TAKI-KUN.
GOTON (KAKLAK)
GOTON
UM... IT'S ME!
HUH?

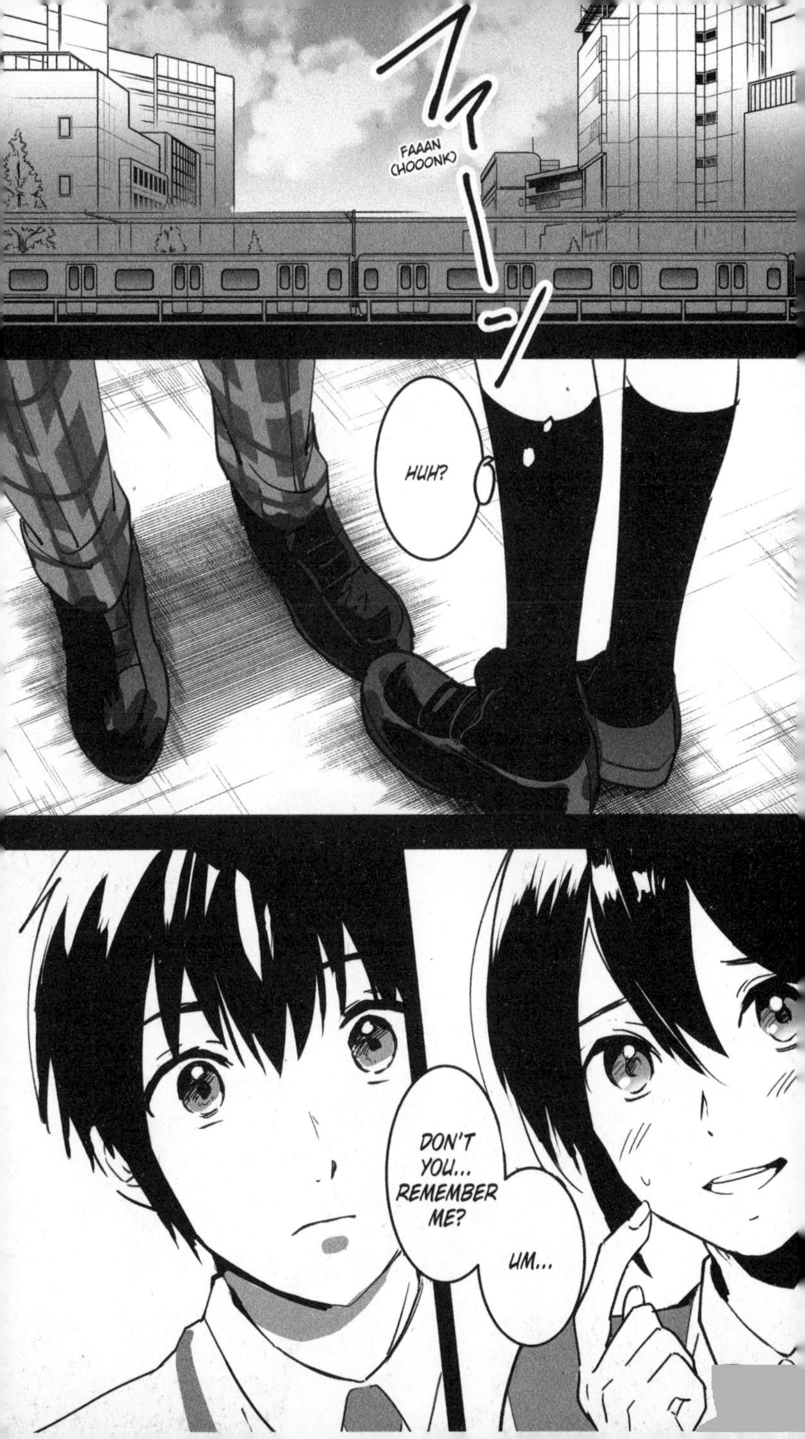
FAAAN (HOOONK)
HUH?
DON'T YOU... REMEMBER ME?
UM...

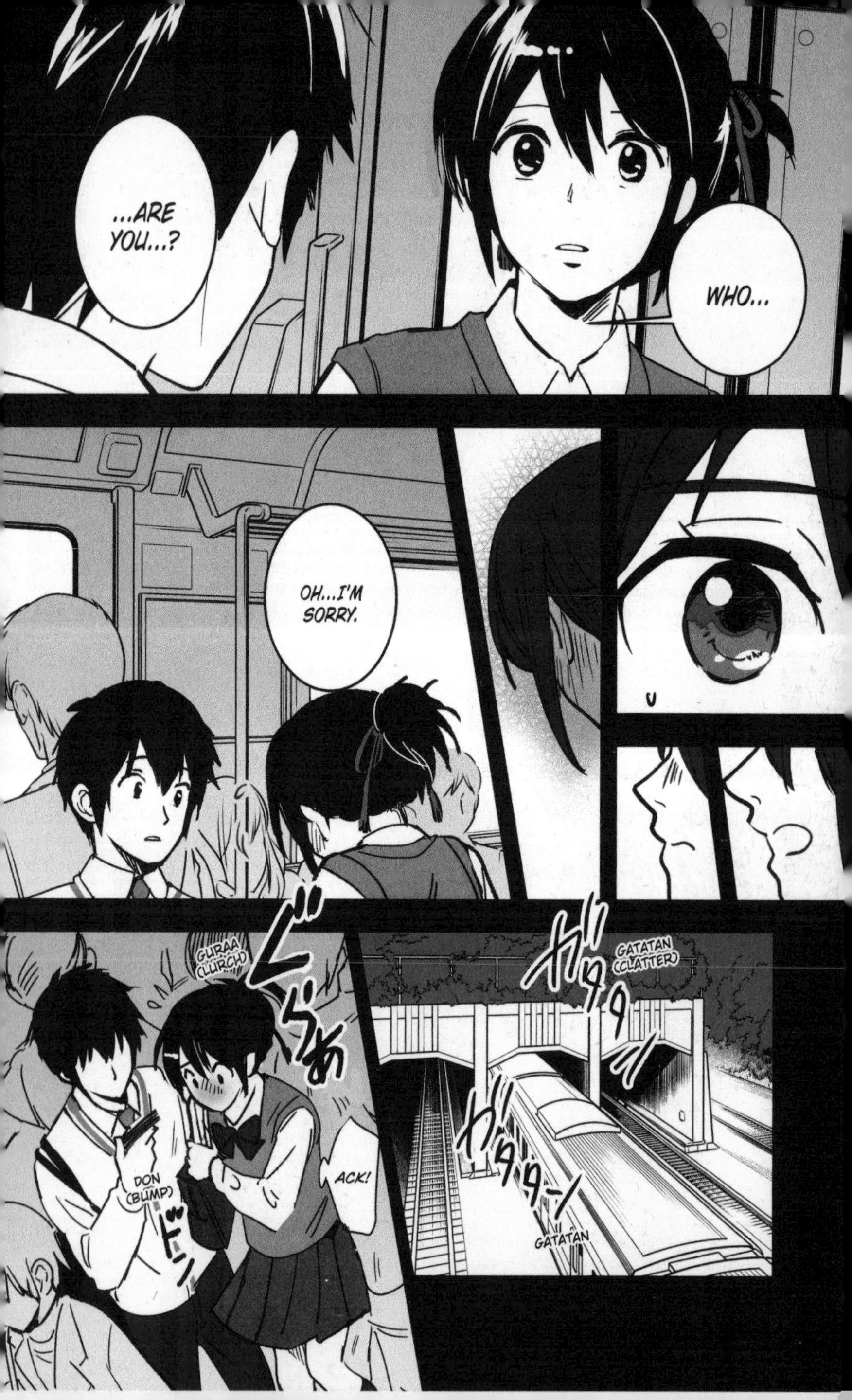
WHO...
...ARE YOU...?
OH...I'M SORRY.
GATATAN (CLATTER)
GATATAN
GURAA (LURCH)
ACK!
DON (BUMP)

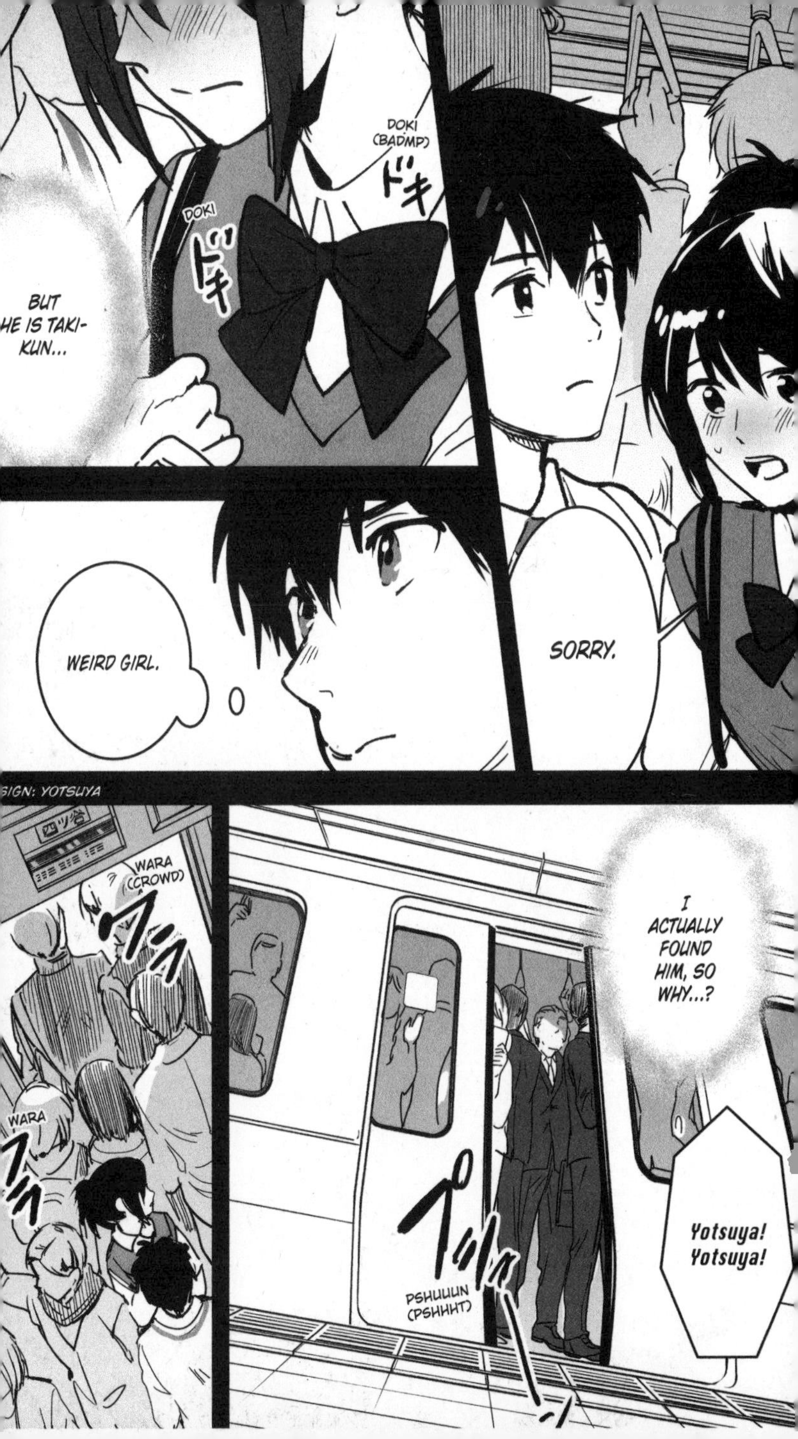
SORRY.
DOKI (BADMP)
DOKI
BUT HE IS TAKI-KUN...
WEIRD GIRL.
SIGN: YOTSUYA
I ACTUALLY FOUND HIM, SO WHY...?
Yotsuya! Yotsuya!
PSHUUUN (PSHHHT)
WARA (CROWD)
WARA

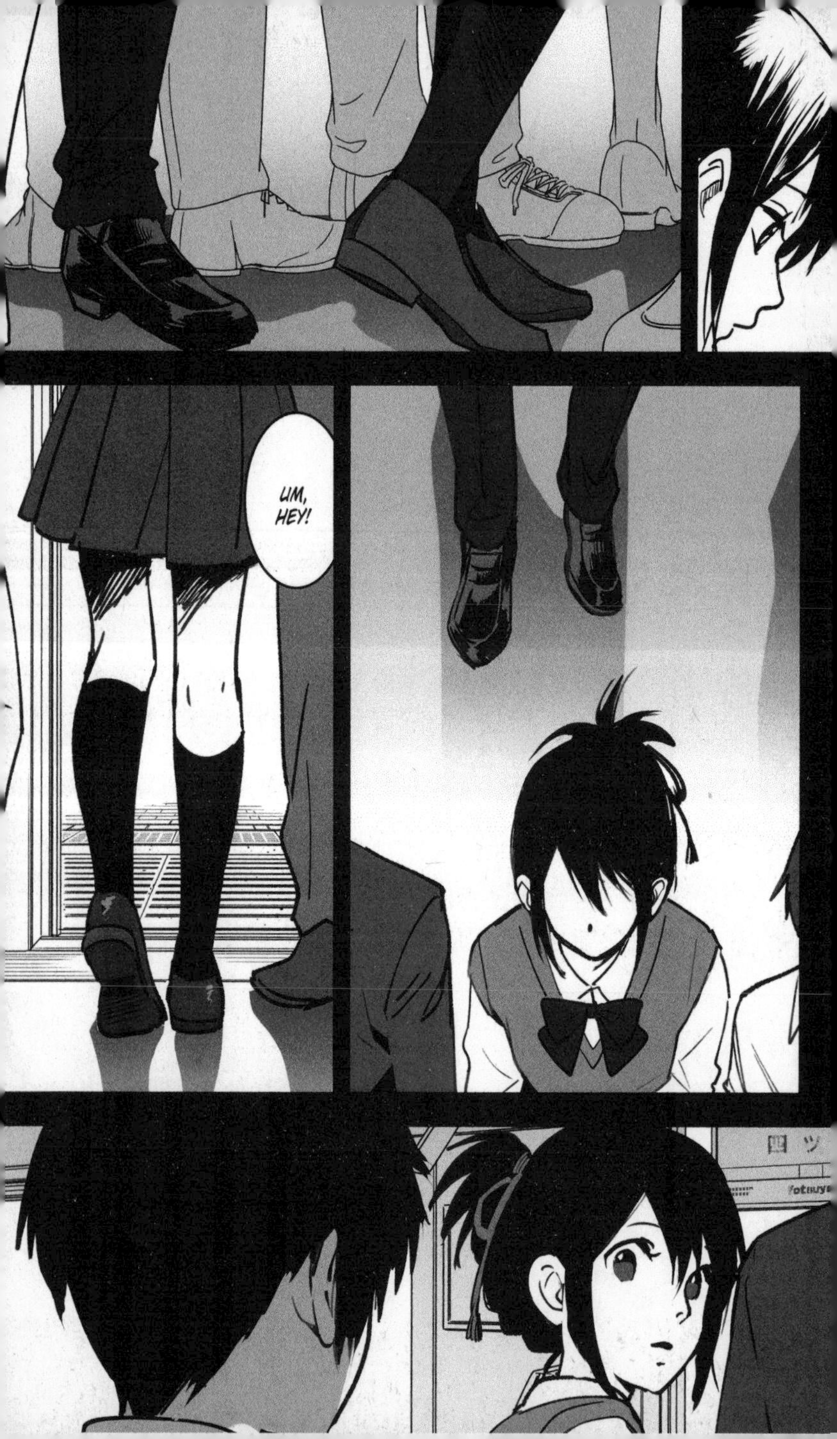
UM, HEY!

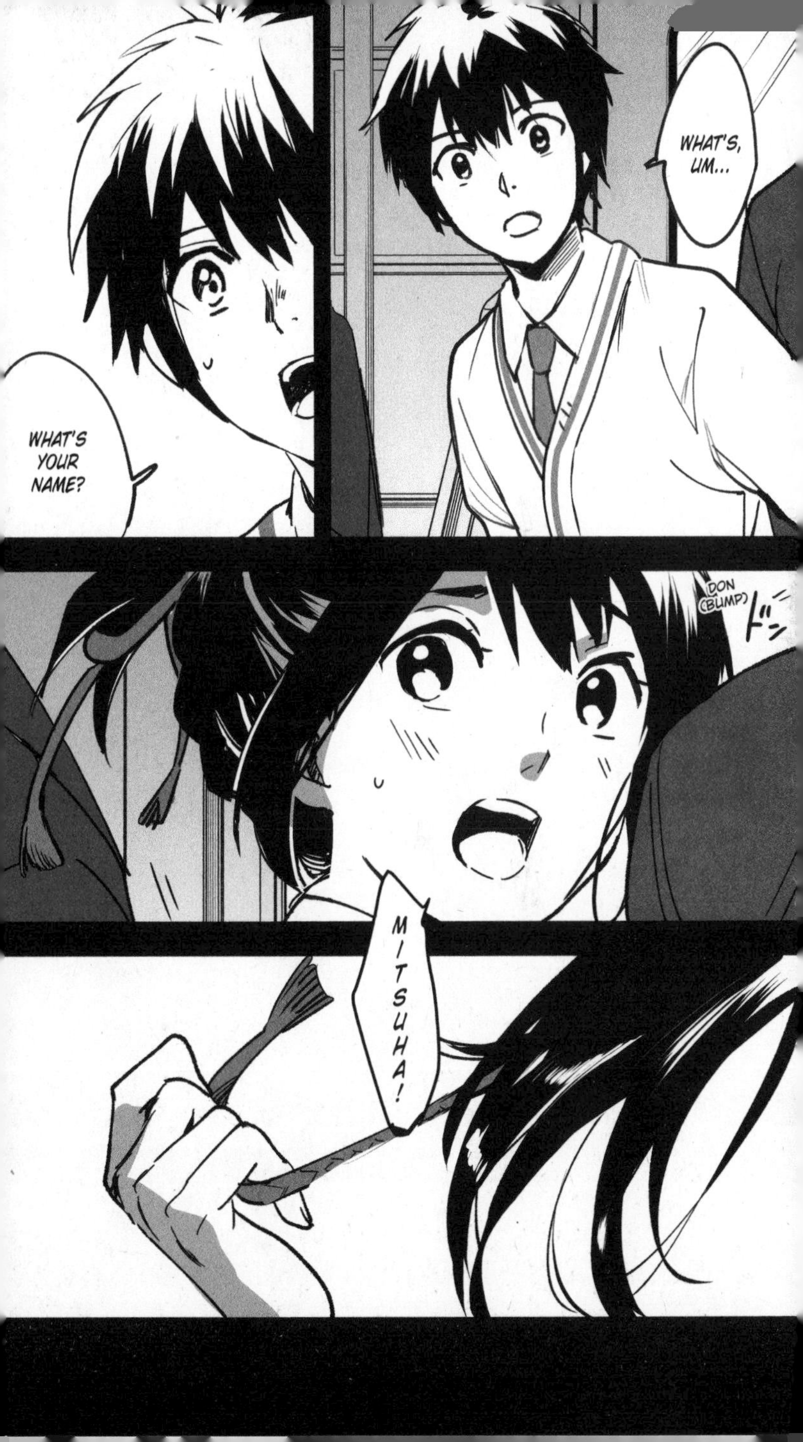
WHAT'S, UM...
WHAT'S YOUR NAME?
DON (BUMP)
MITSUHA!

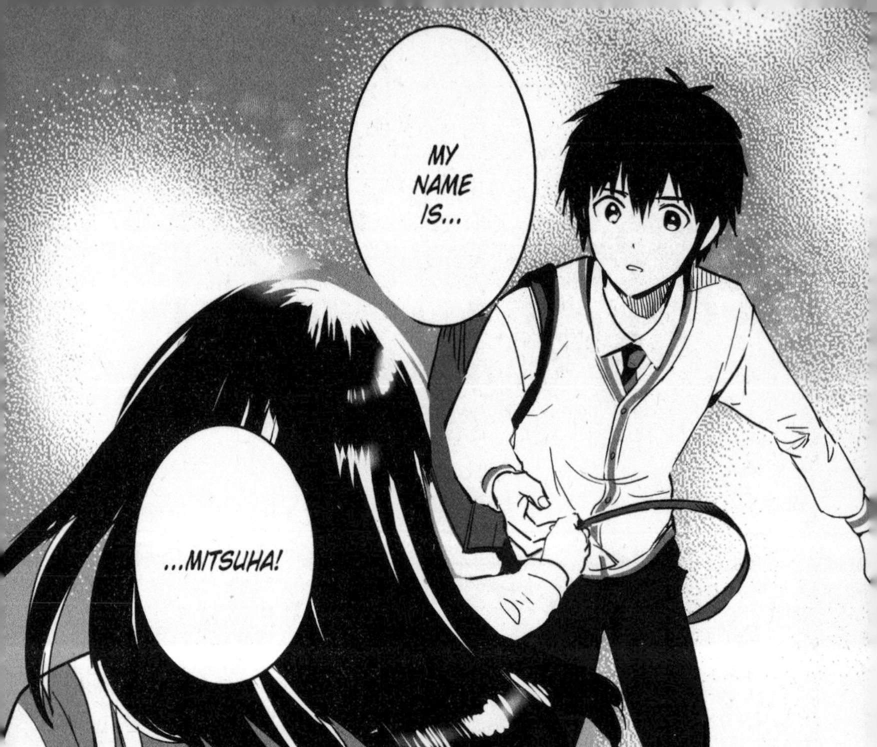
MY NAME IS...
...MITSUHA!

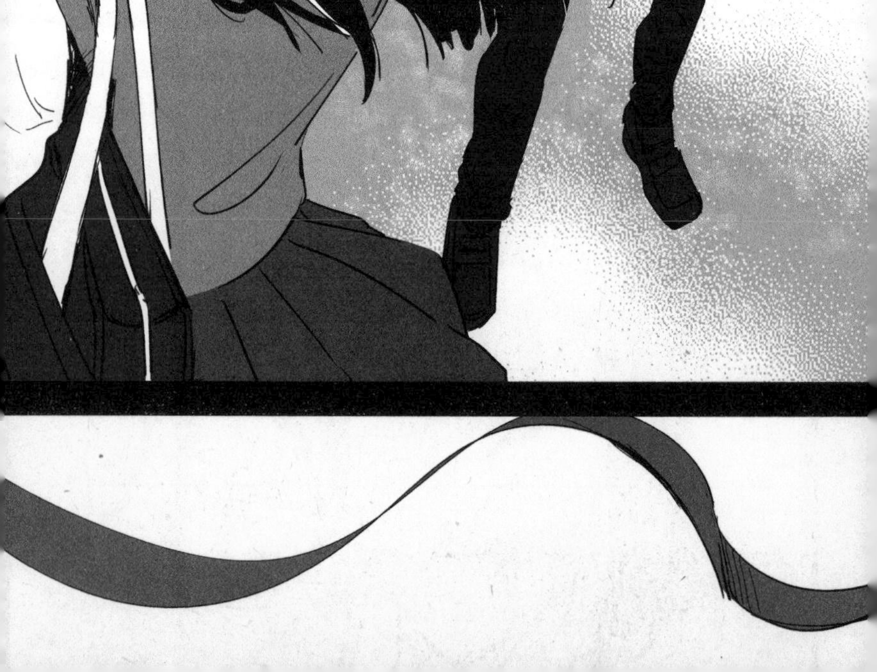

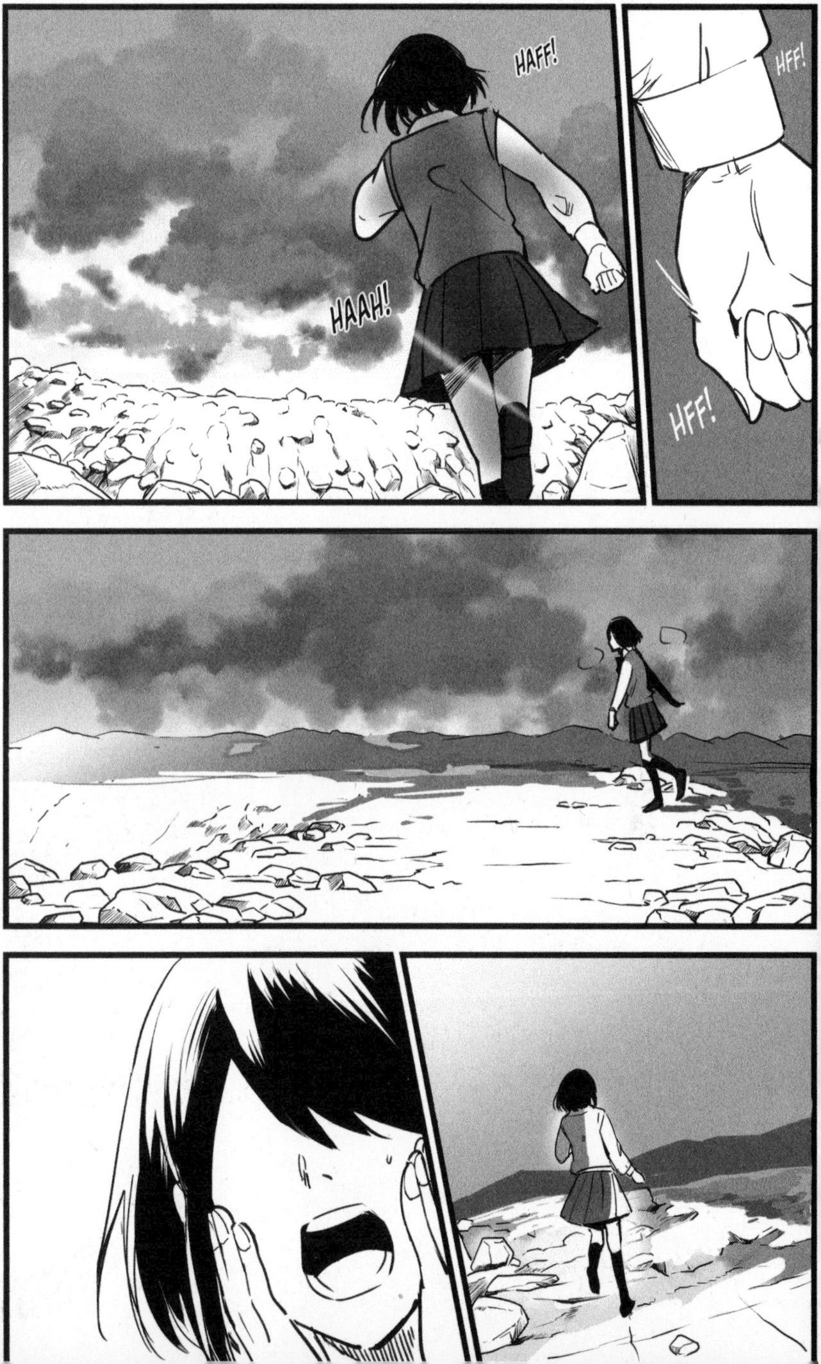
HFF!
HFF!
HAFF!
HAAH!

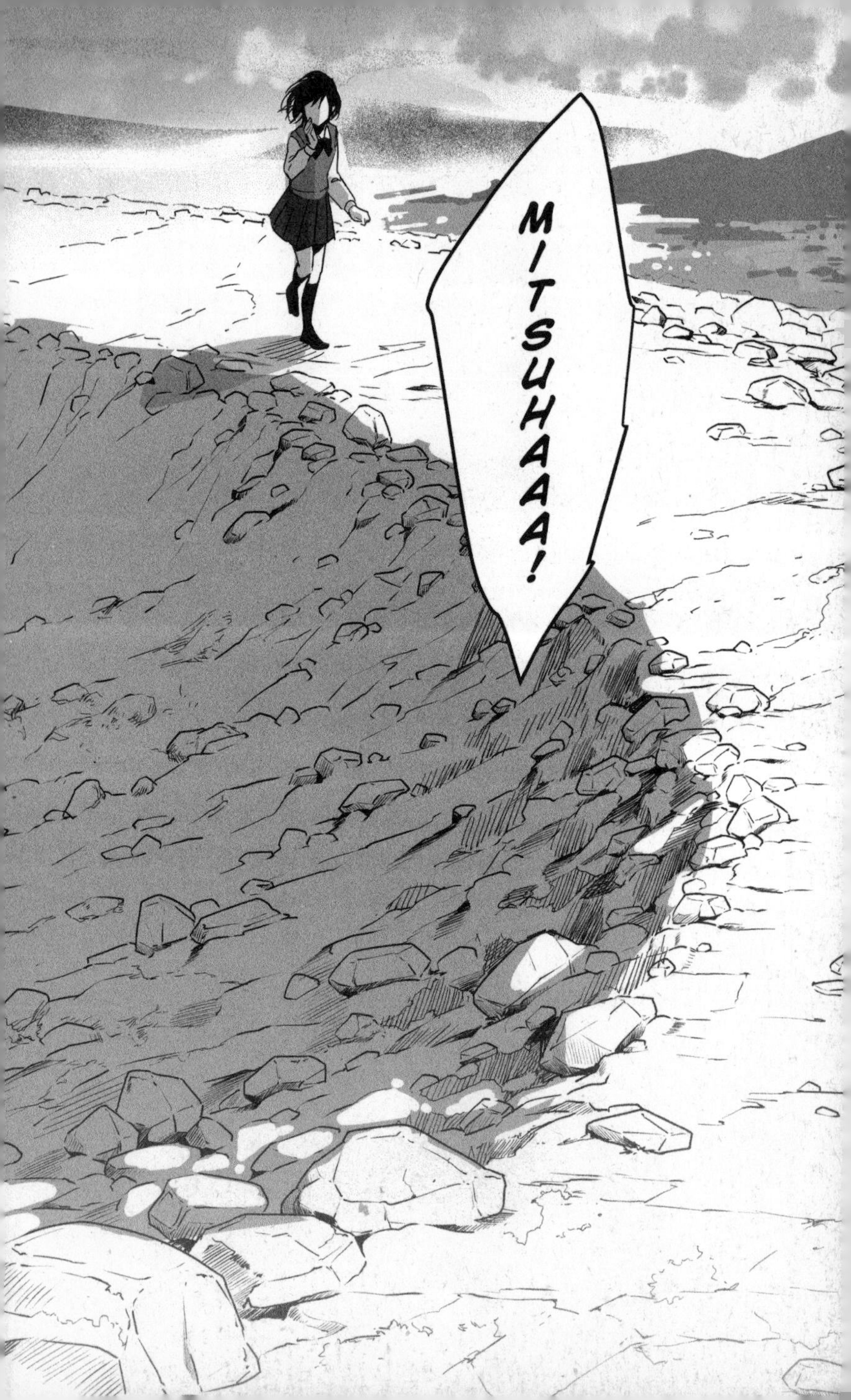
MITSUHAAAA!

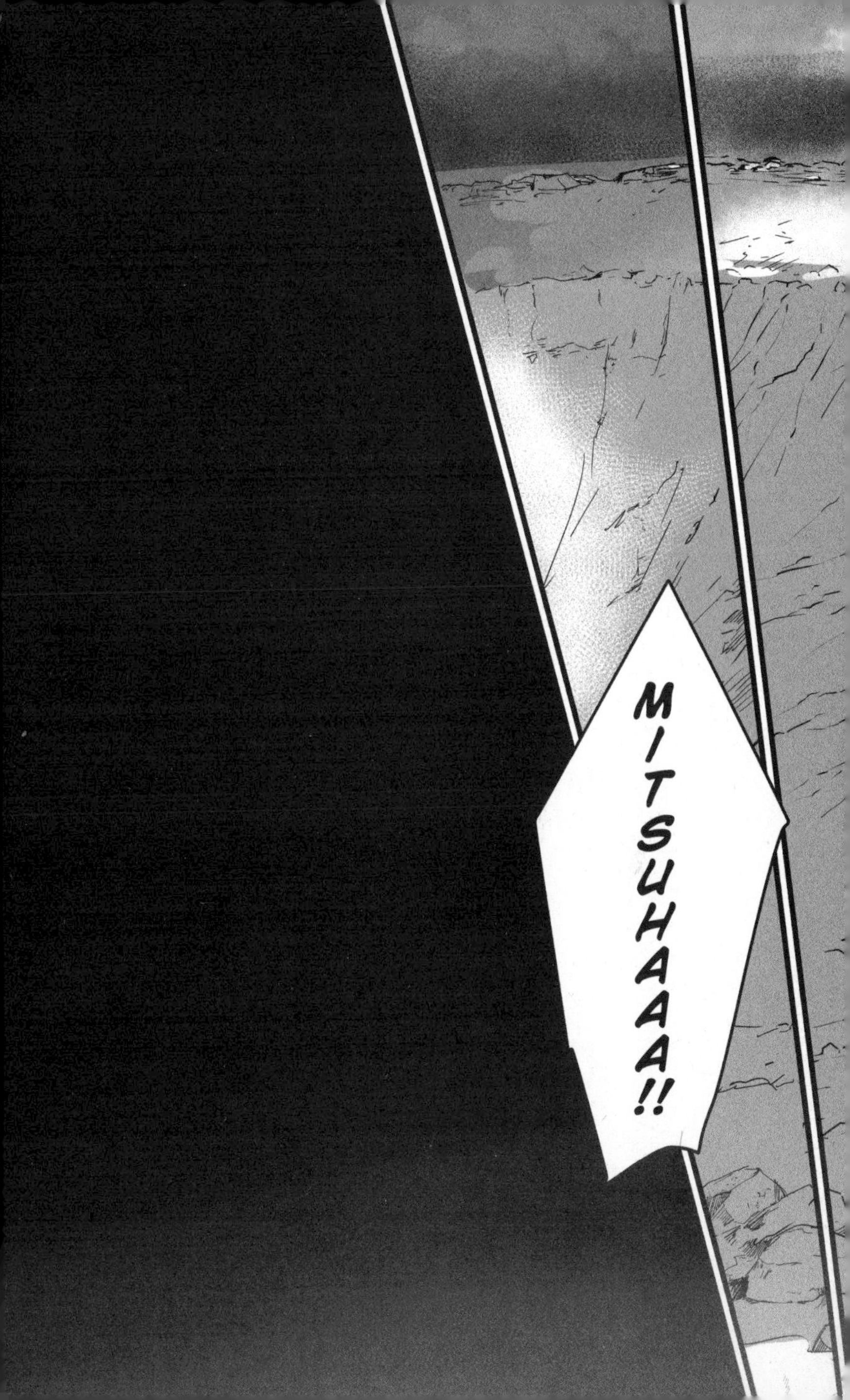
MITSUHAAAA!!

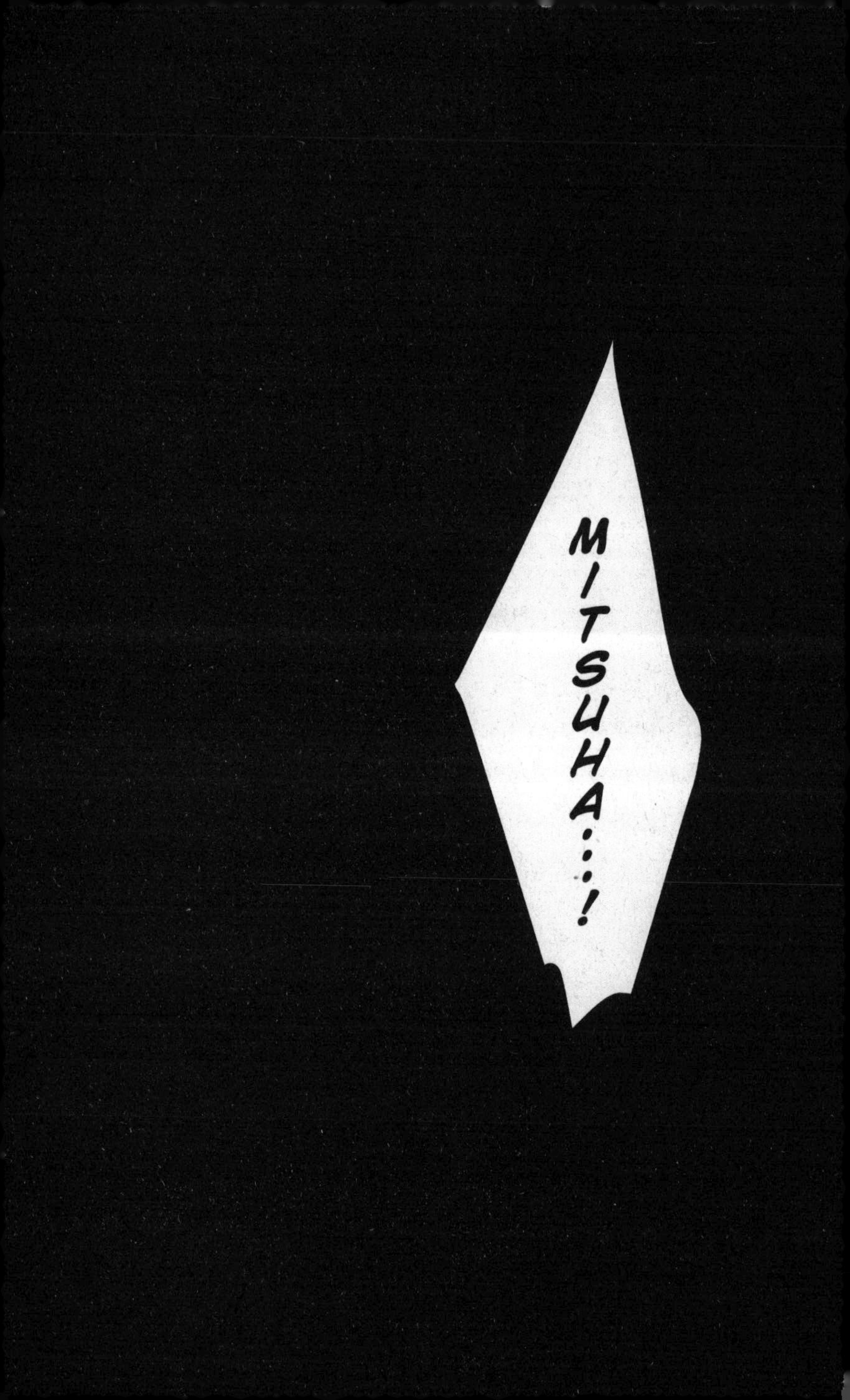
MITSUHA...!

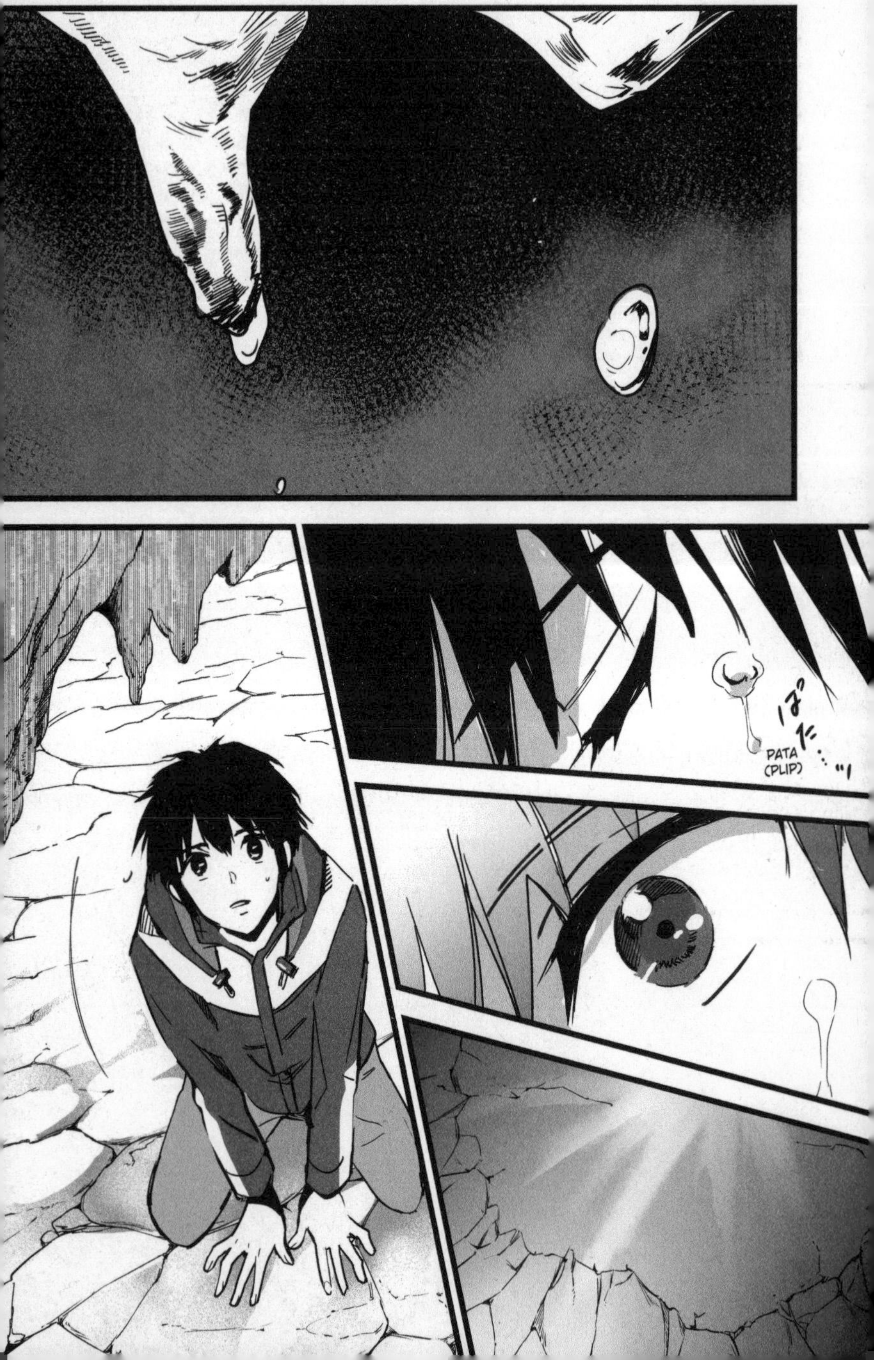
ぱた…ッ
PATA
(PLIP)

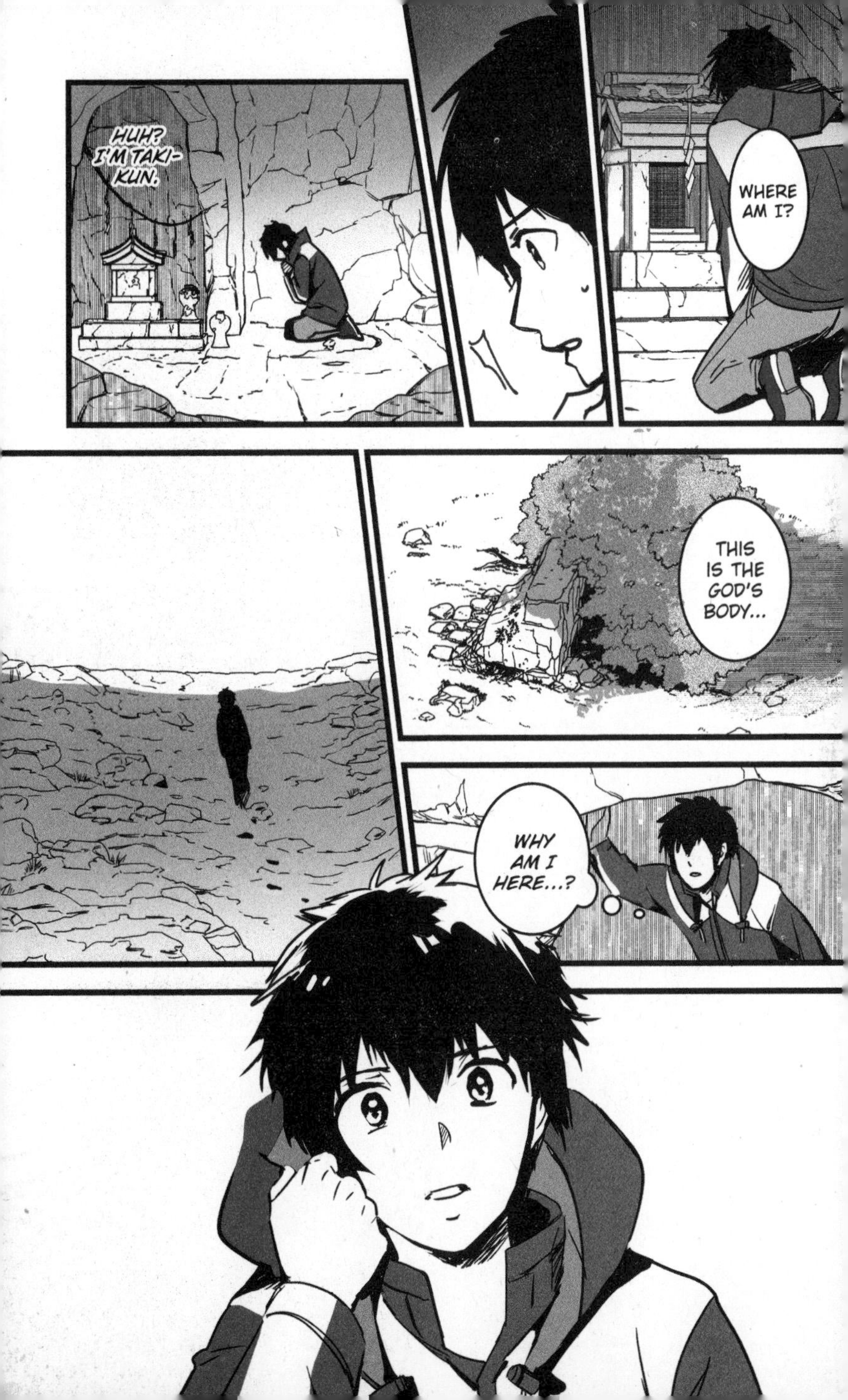
WHERE AM I?
HUH? I'M TAKI-KUN.
THIS IS THE GOD'S BODY...
WHY AM I HERE...?

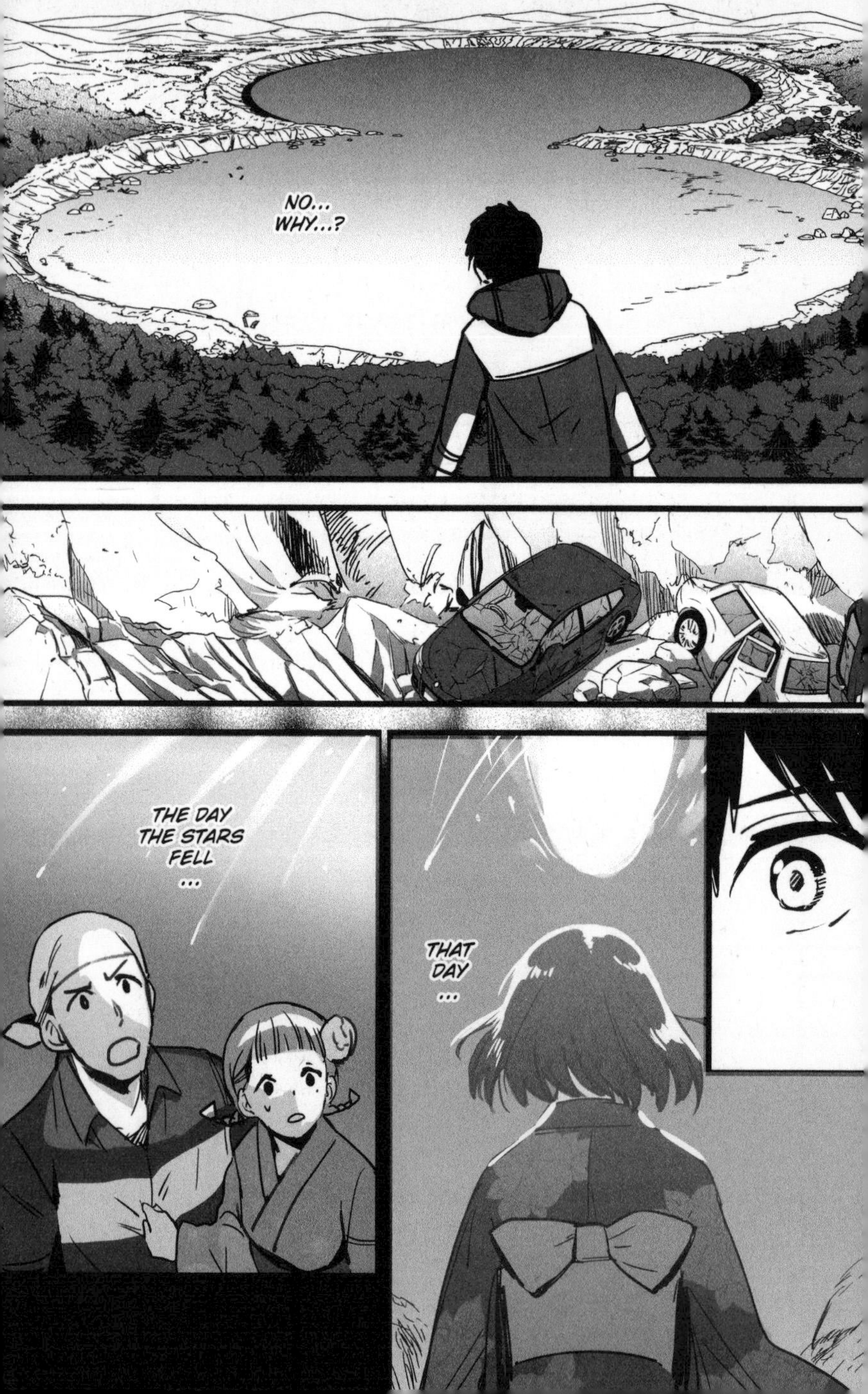
NO... WHY...?
THAT DAY ...
THE DAY THE STARS FELL ...

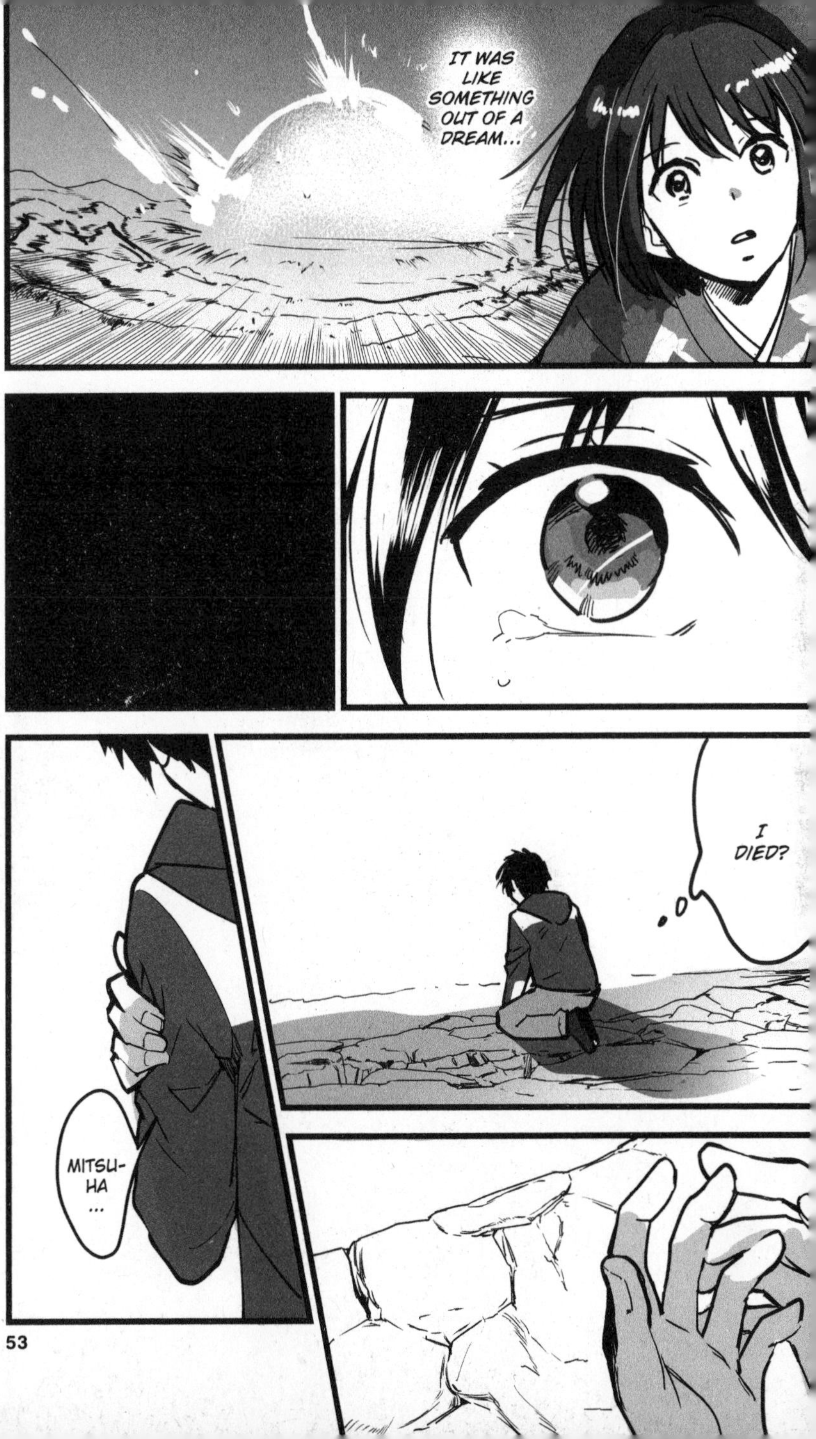
IT WAS LIKE SOMETHING OUT OF A DREAM...
I DIED?
MITSU-HA ...

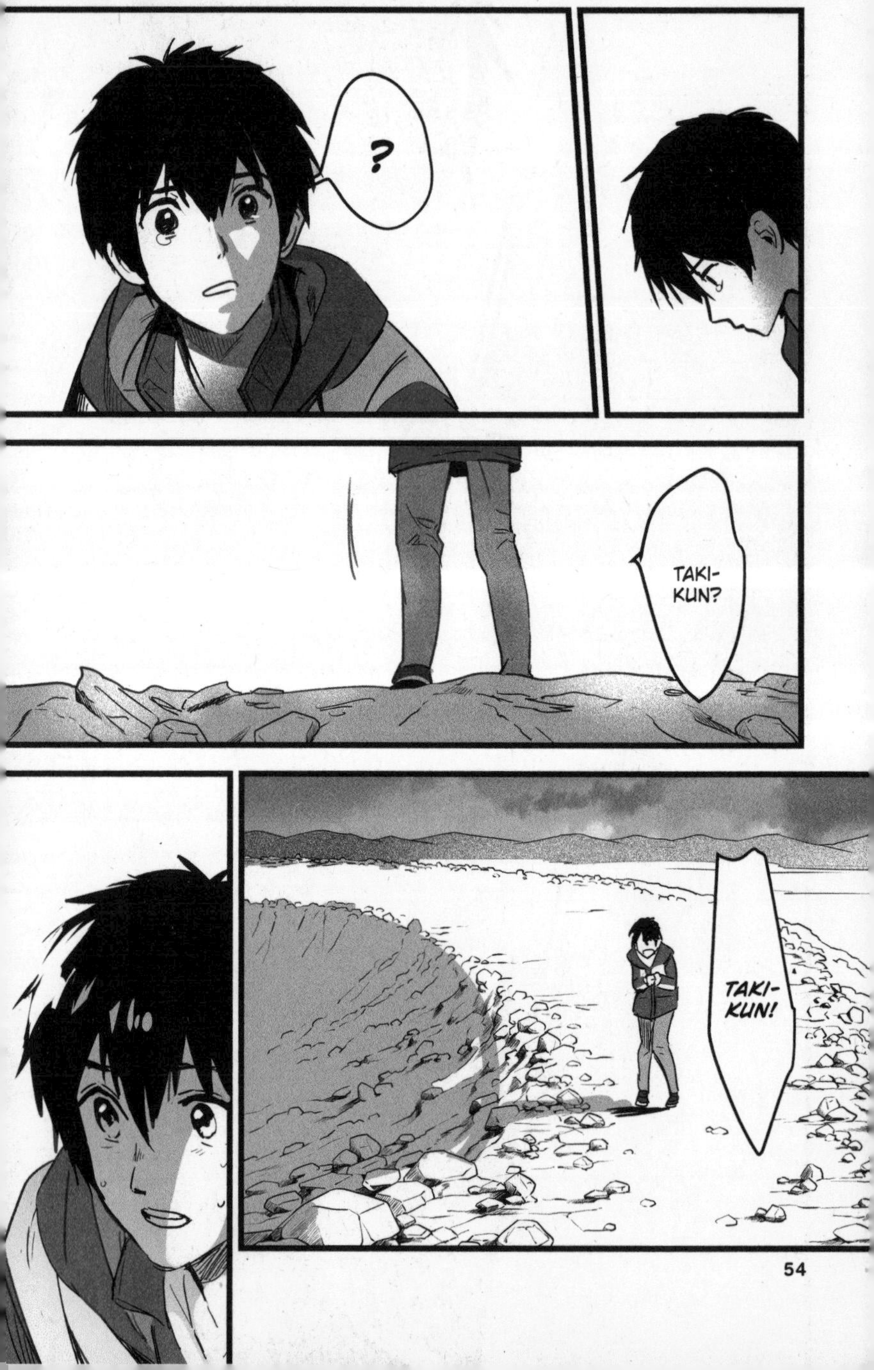
?
TAKI-KUN?
TAKI-KUN!

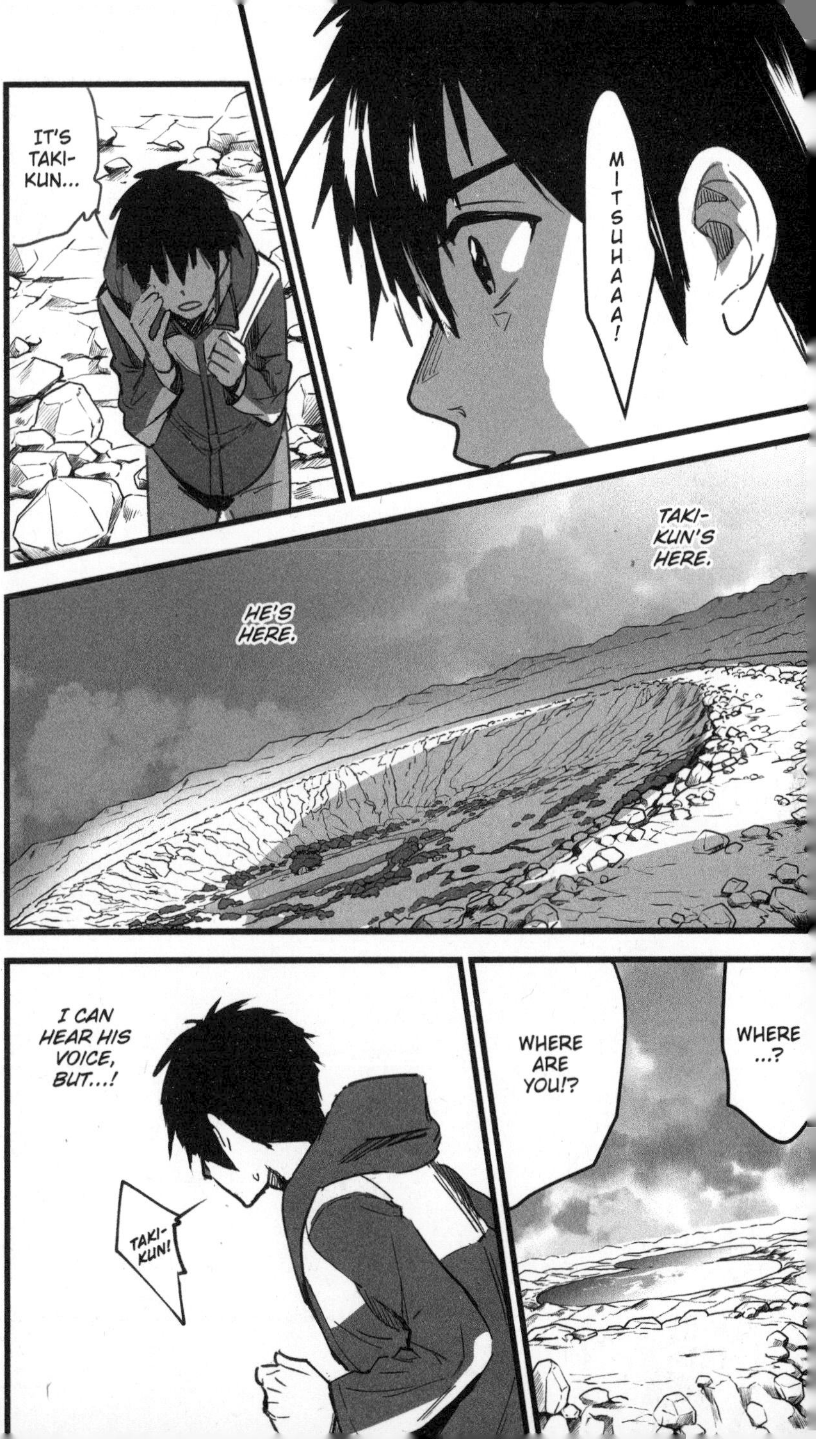
MITSUHAAAA!
IT'S TAKI-KUN...
TAKI-KUN'S HERE.
HE'S HERE.
WHERE ...?
WHERE ARE YOU!?
I CAN HEAR HIS VOICE, BUT...!
TAKI-KUN!

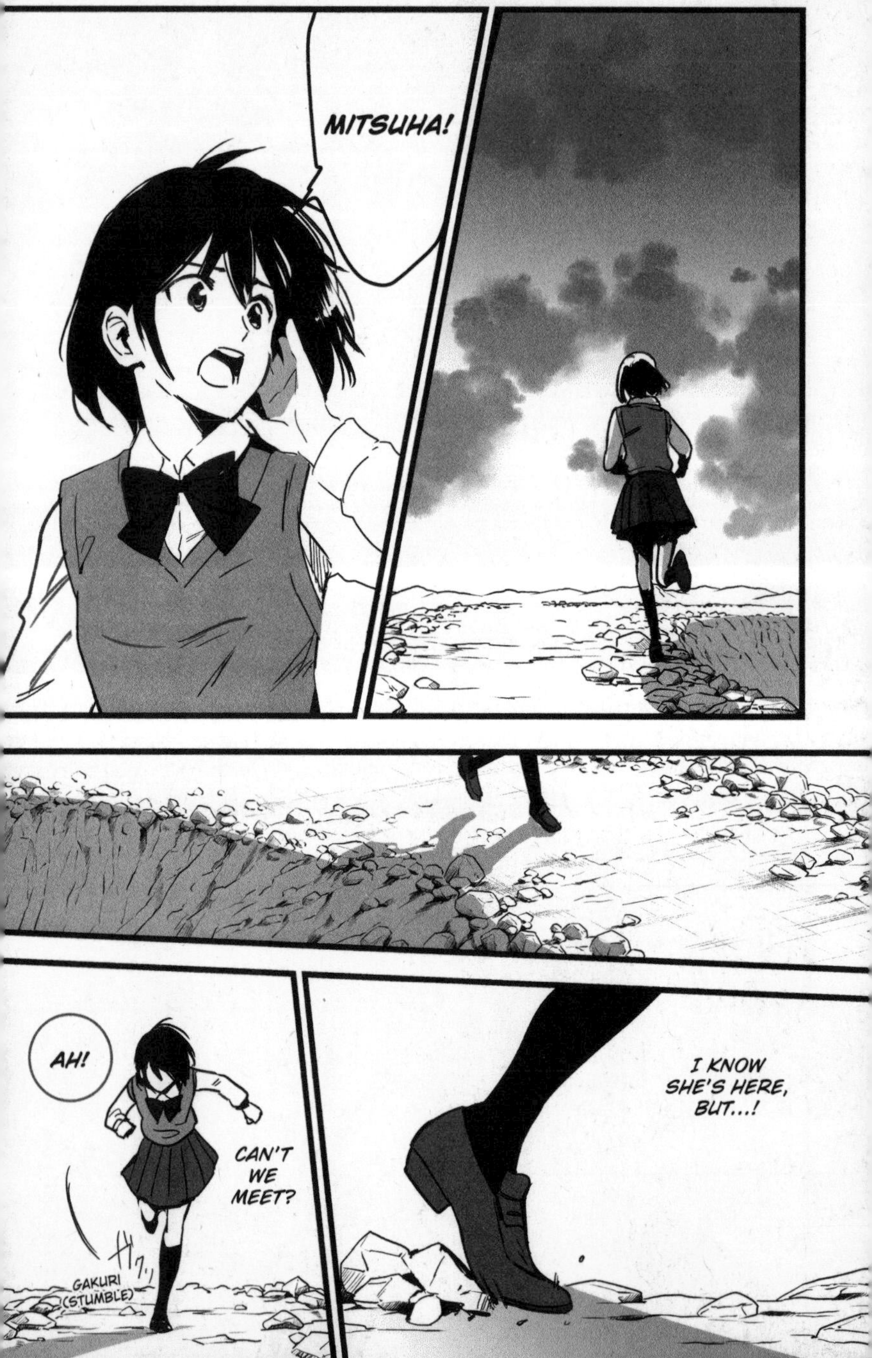
MITSUHA!
I KNOW SHE'S HERE, BUT...!
CAN'T WE MEET?
AH!
GAKURI (STUMBLE)

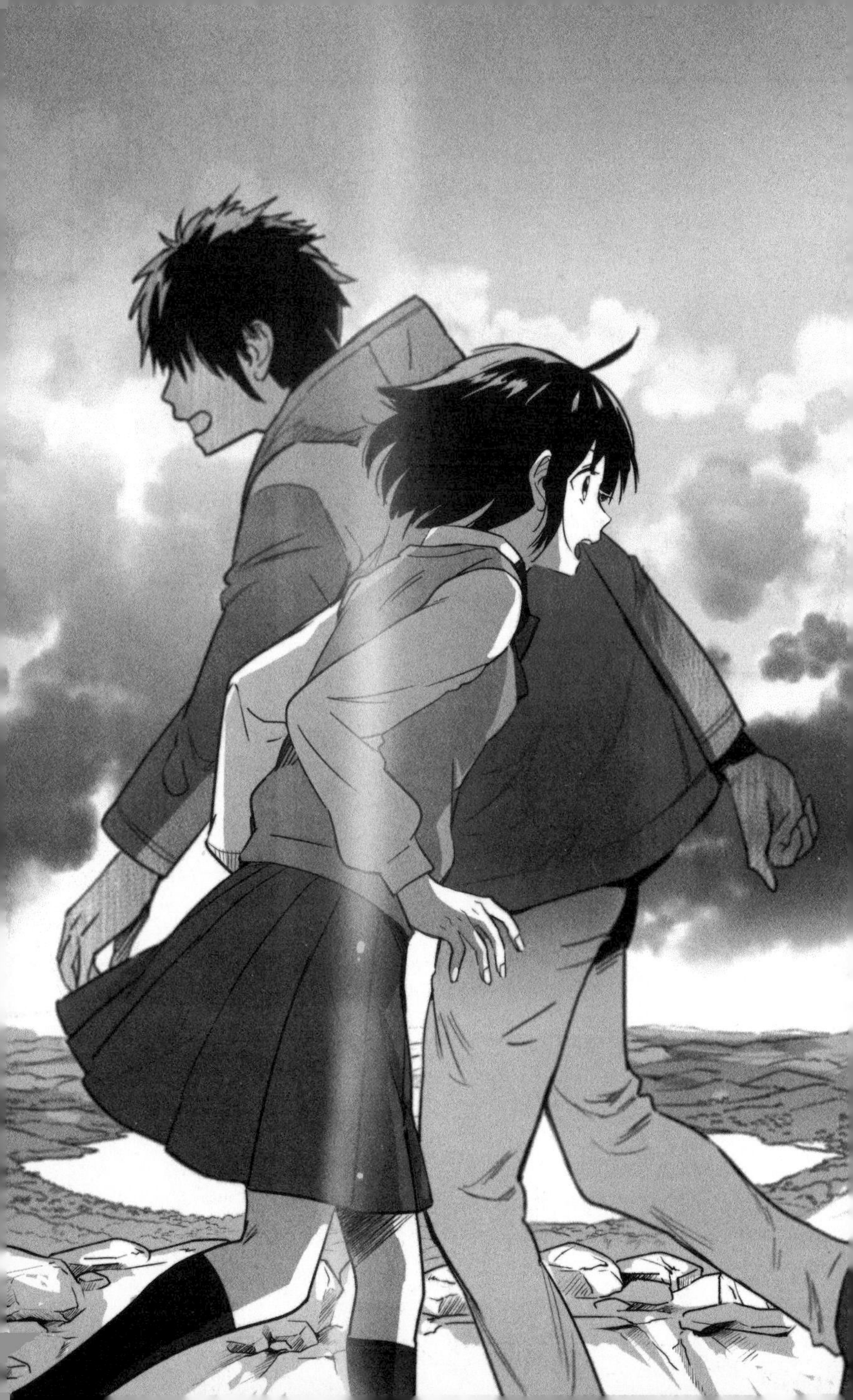

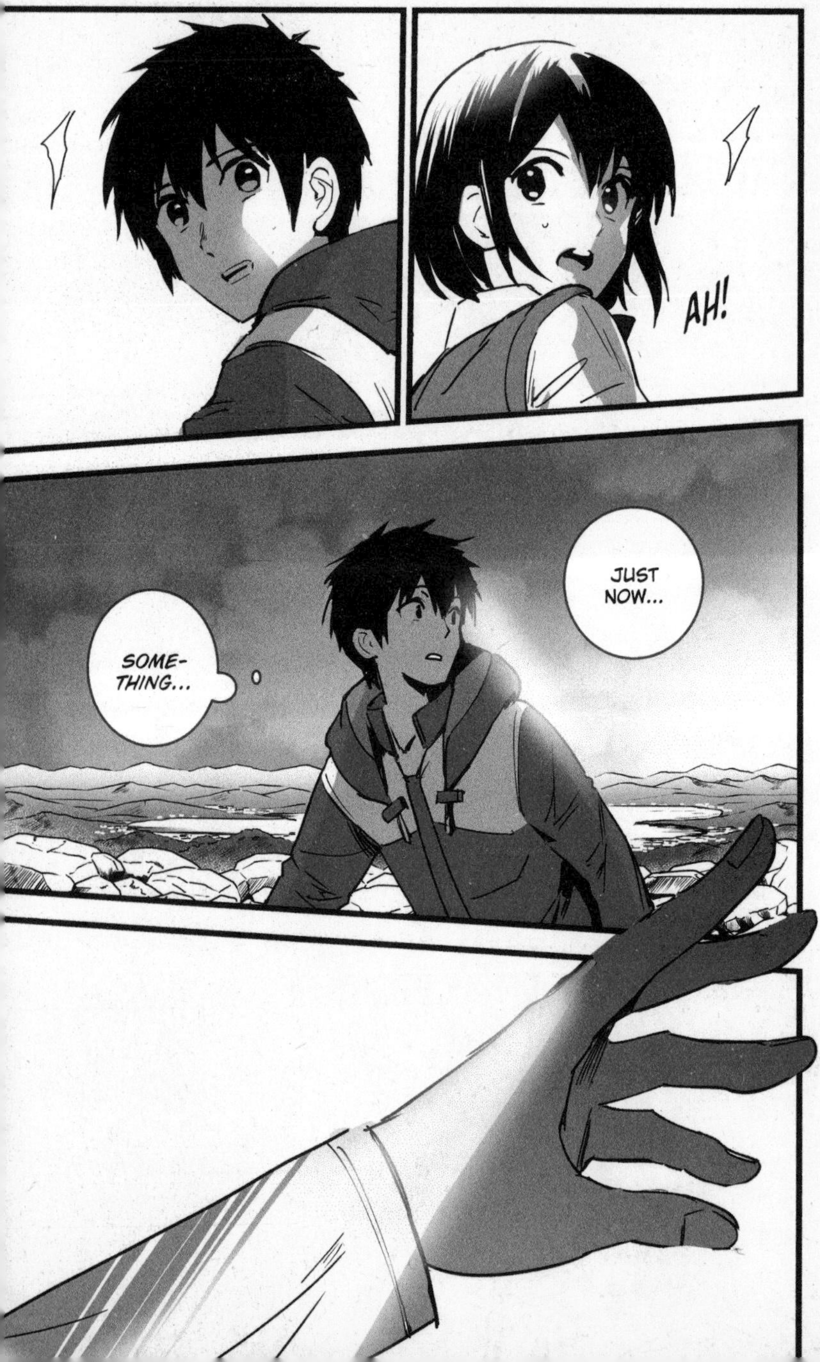
AH!
JUST NOW...
SOME-THING...

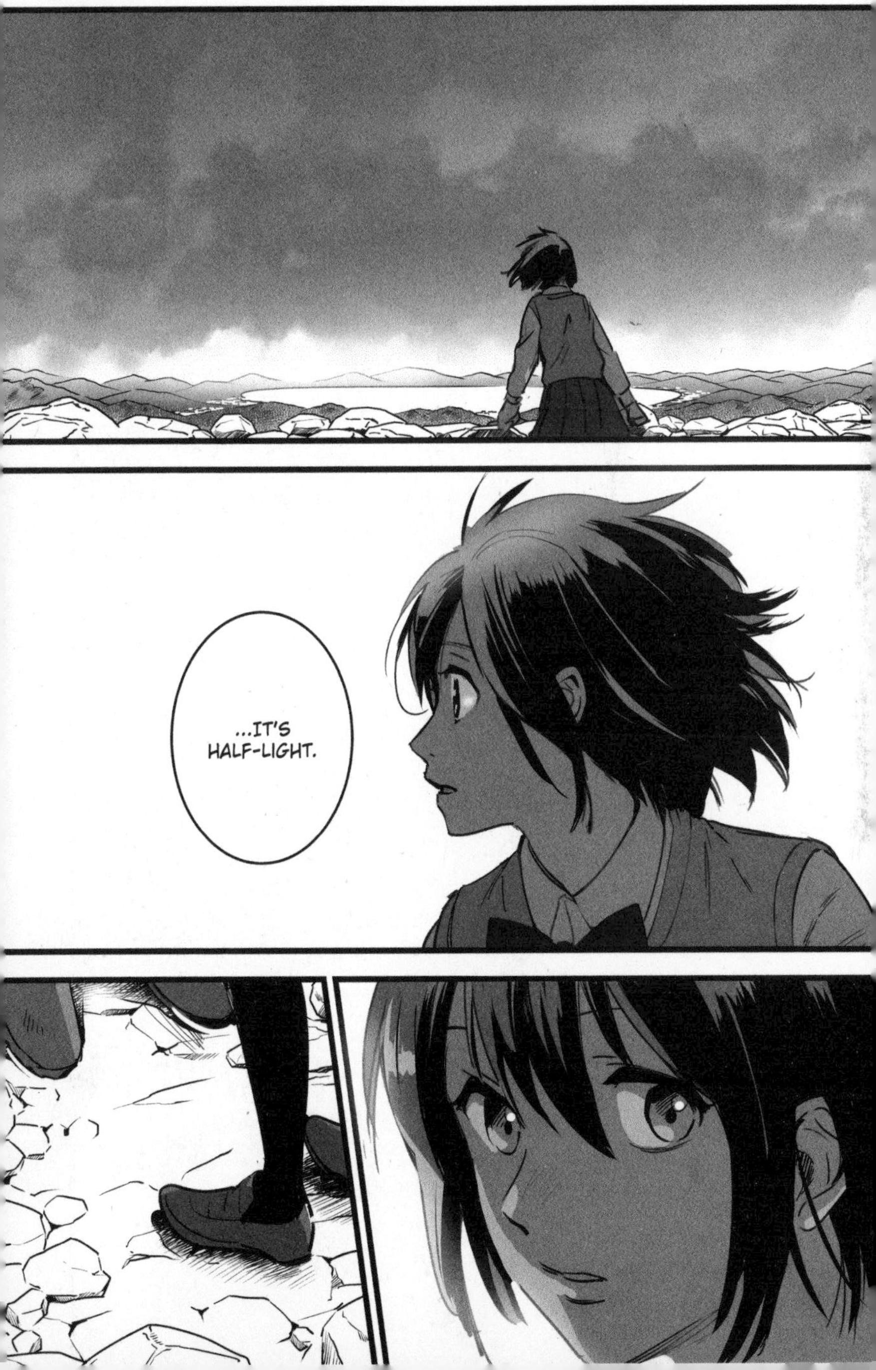
...IT'S HALF-LIGHT.

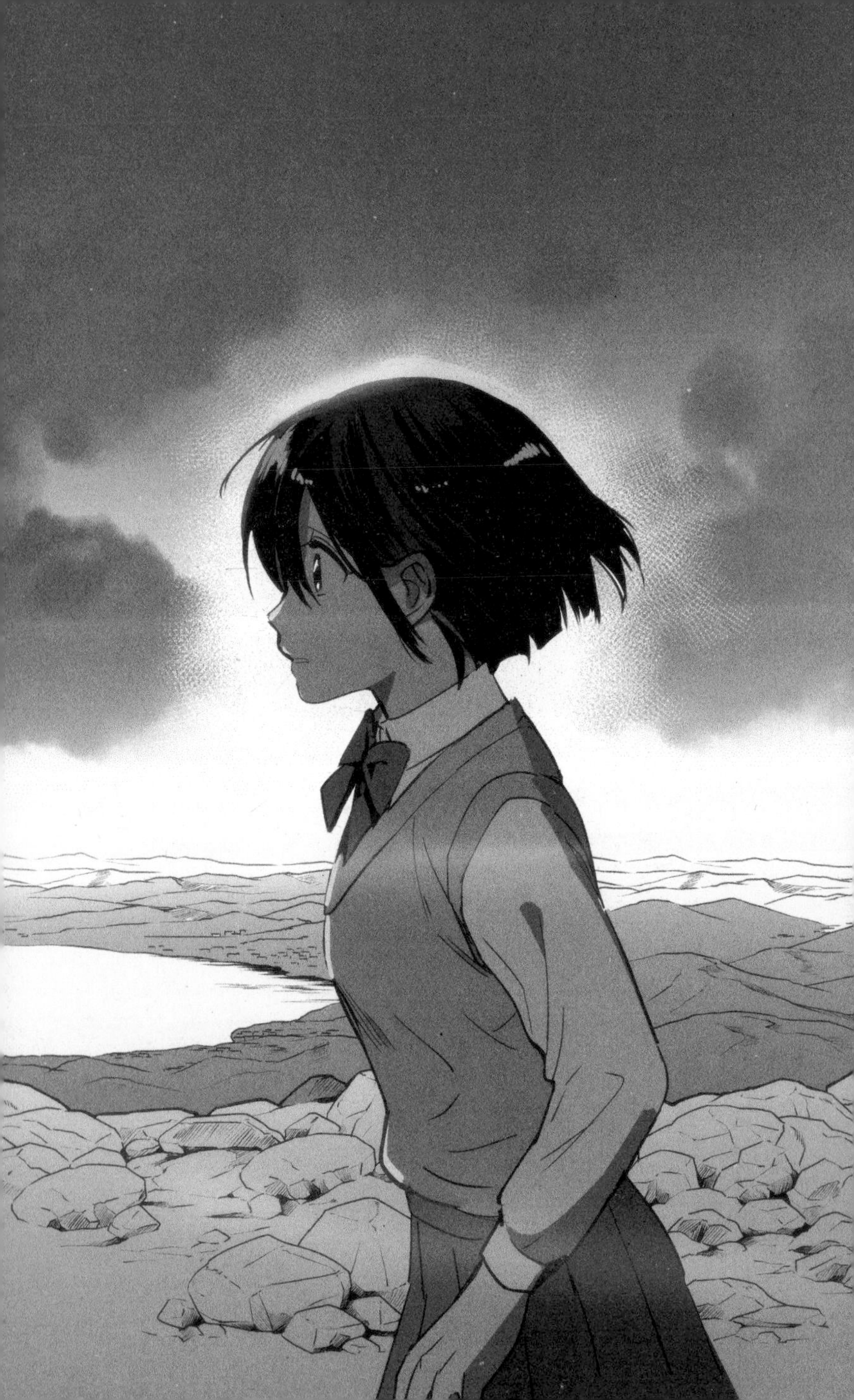

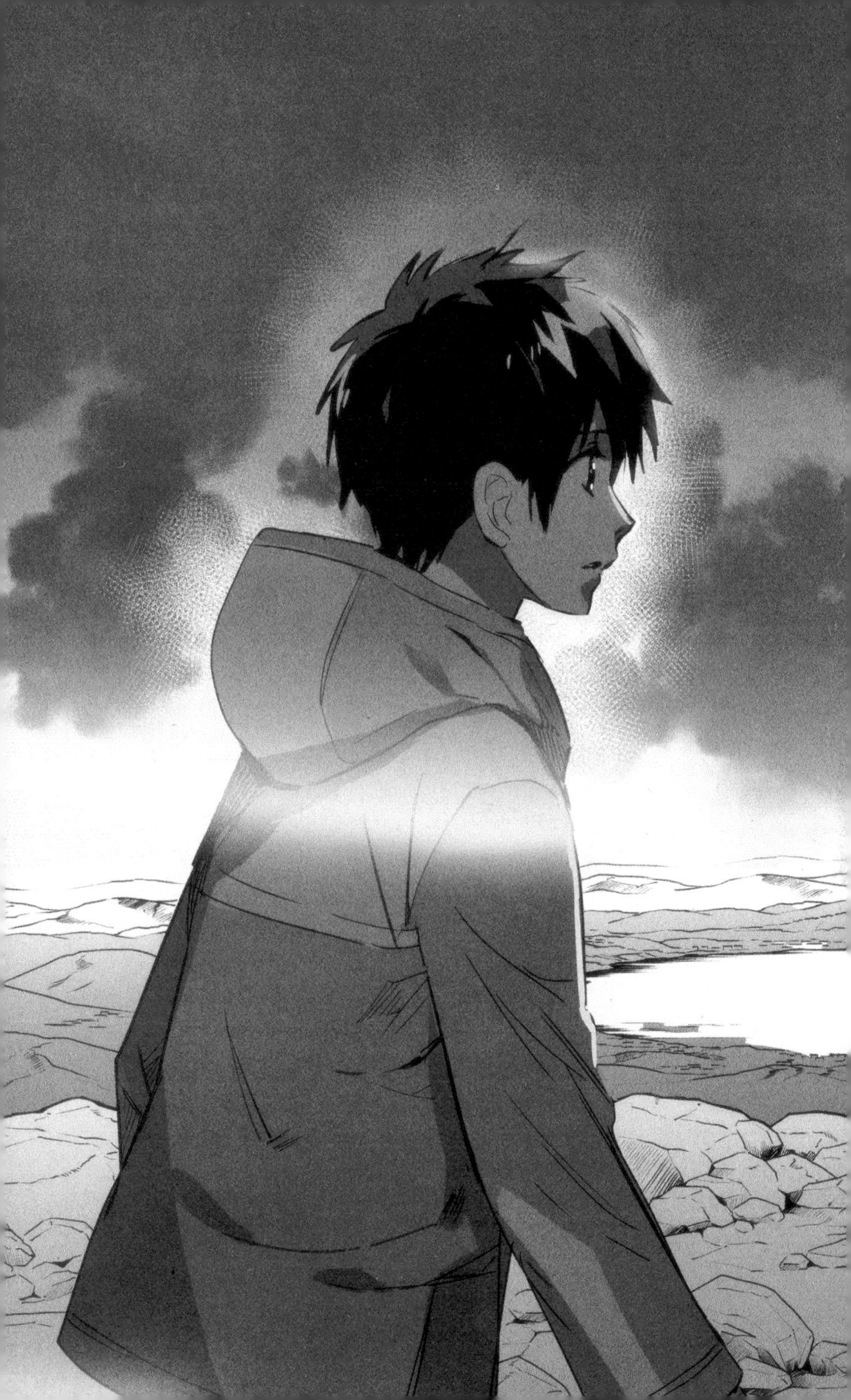

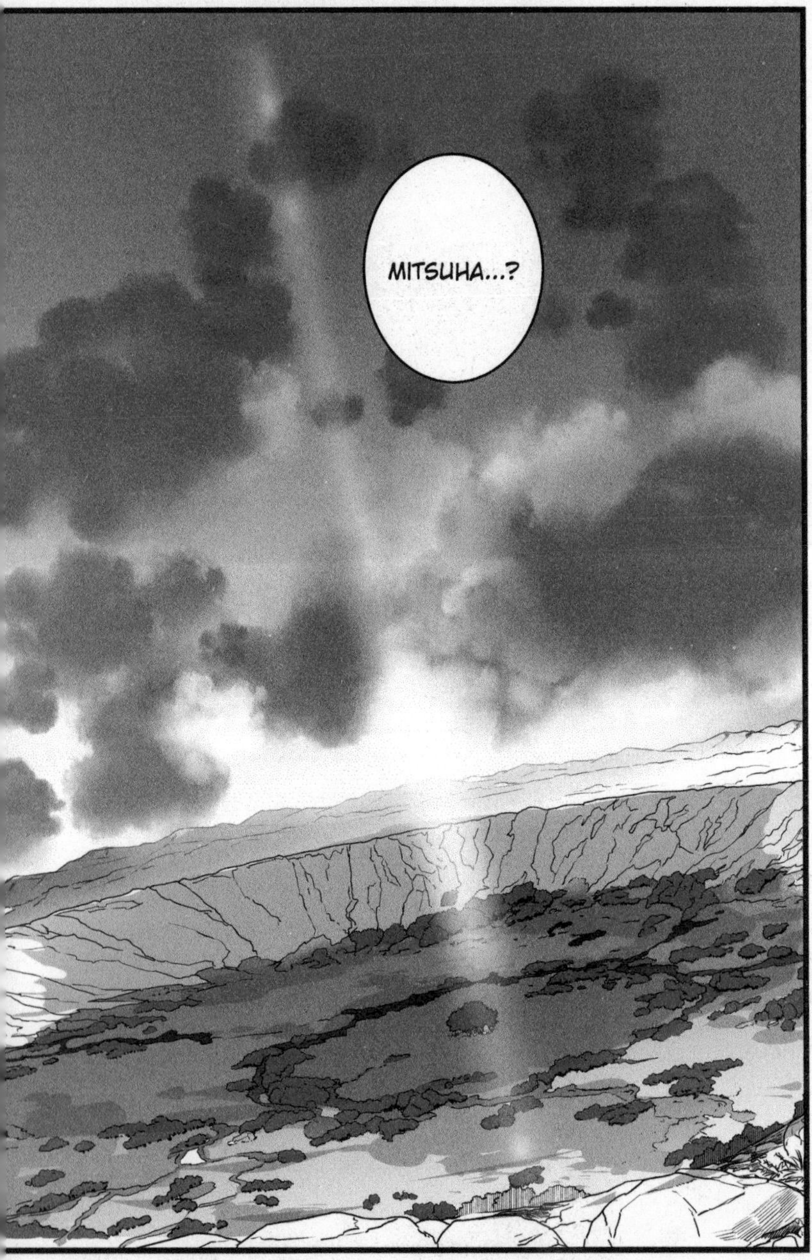
MITSUHA...?

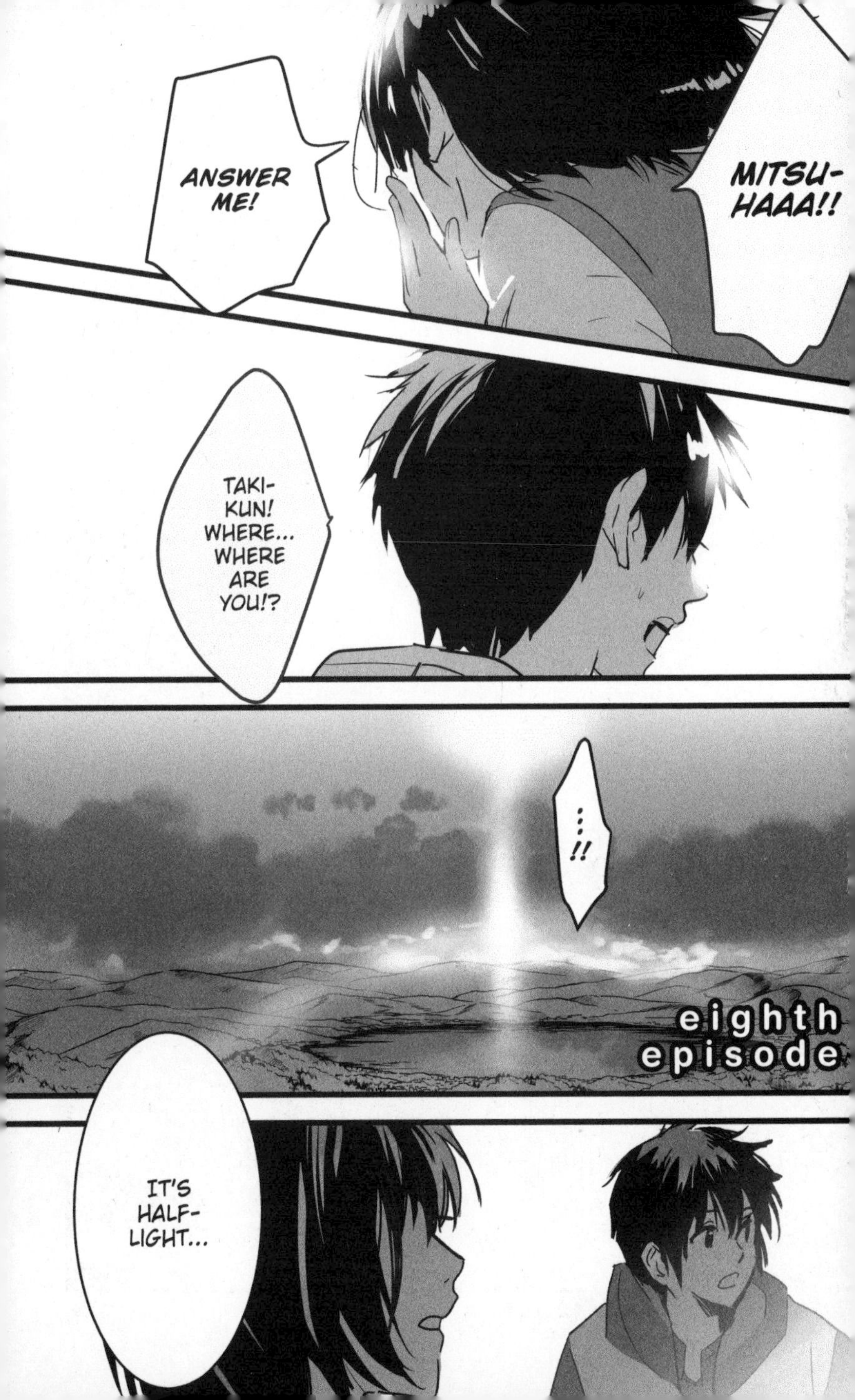
MITSU-HAAA!!
ANSWER ME!
TAKI-KUN! WHERE... WHERE ARE YOU!?
...!!
eighth episode
IT'S HALF-LIGHT...

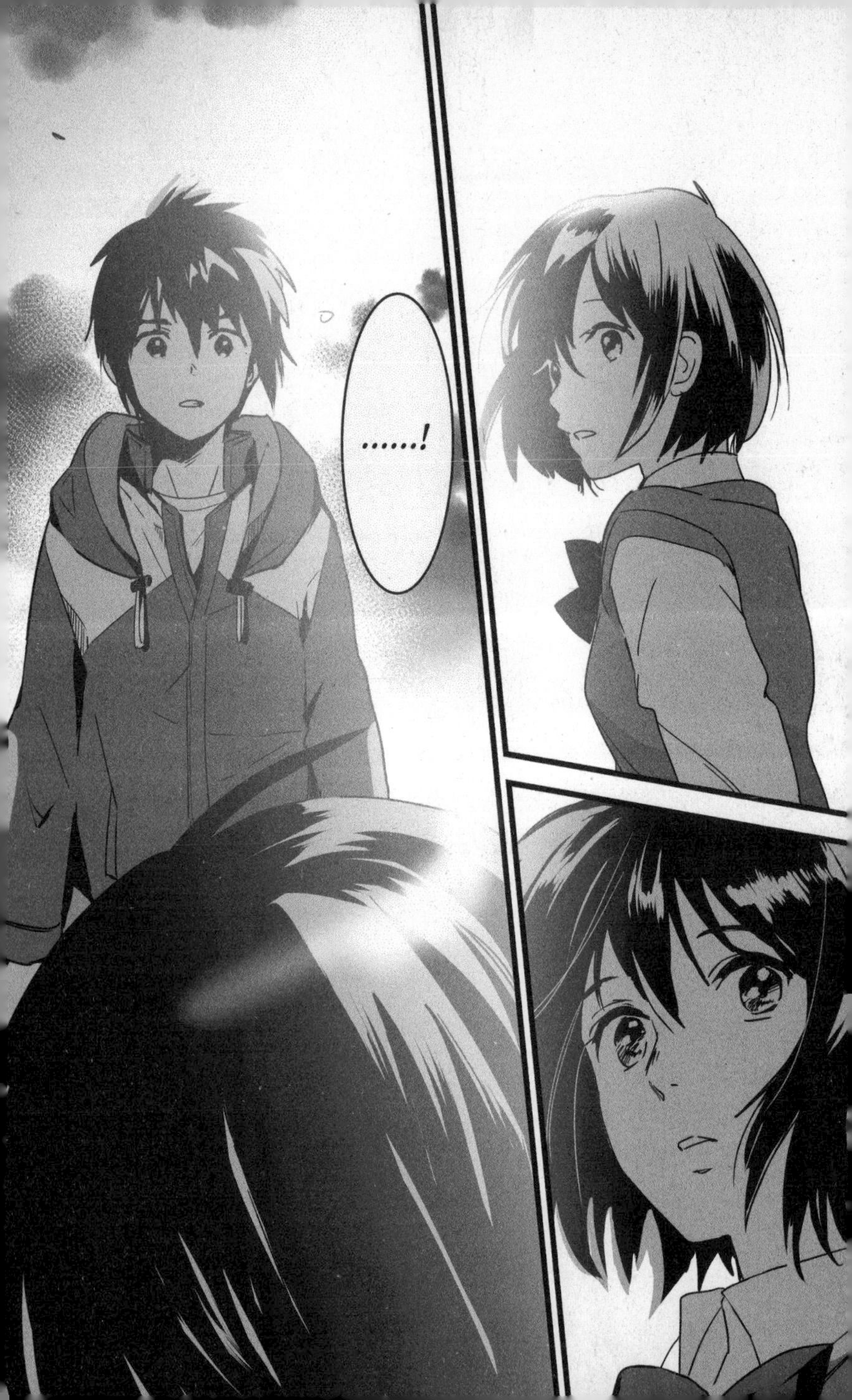
……!

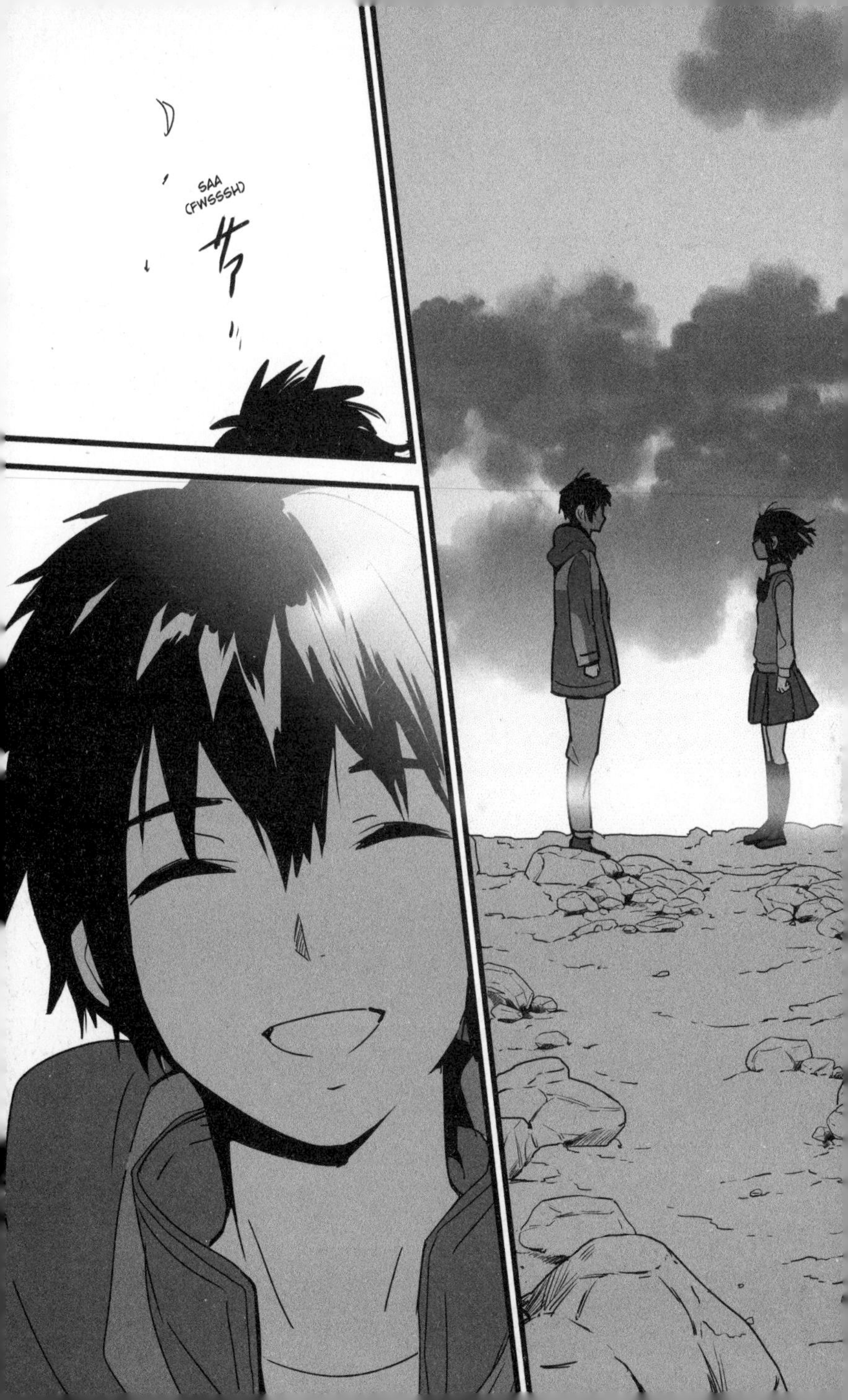
SAA
(FWSSSH)

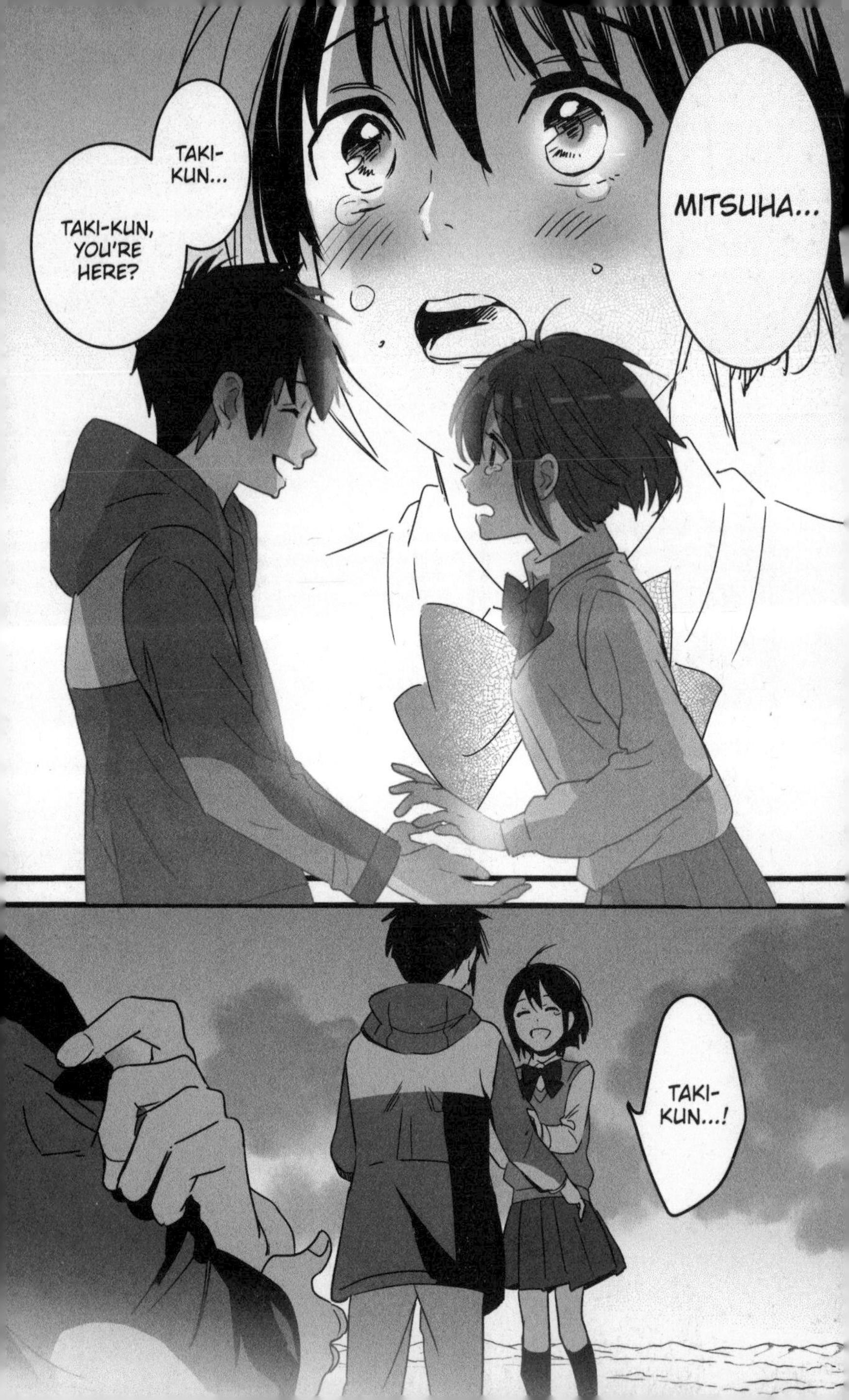
MITSUHA...
TAKI-KUN...
TAKI-KUN, YOU'RE HERE?
TAKI-KUN...!

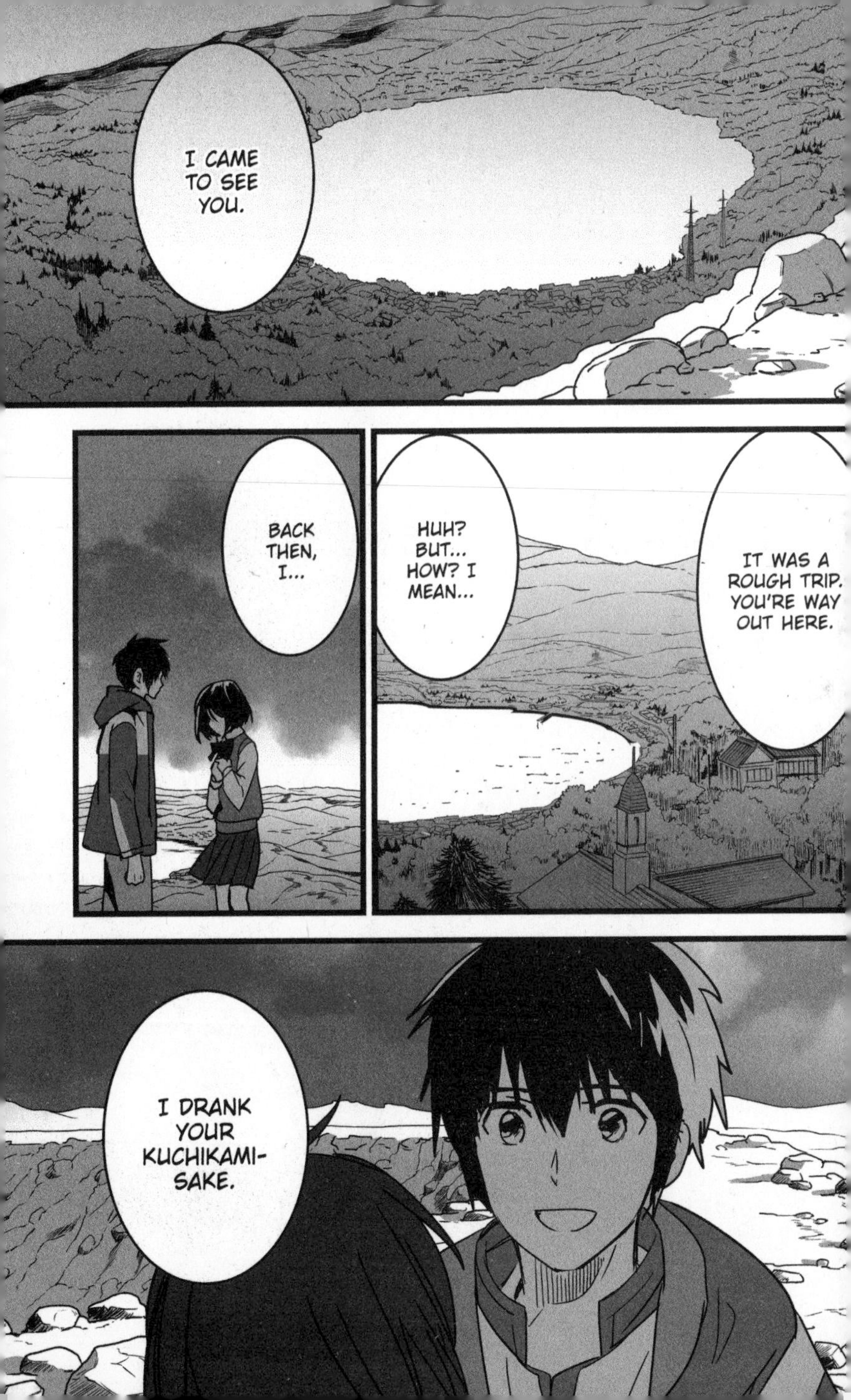
I CAME TO SEE YOU.
IT WAS A ROUGH TRIP. YOU'RE WAY OUT HERE.
HUH? BUT... HOW? I MEAN...
BACK THEN, I...
I DRANK YOUR KUCHIKAMI-SAKE.

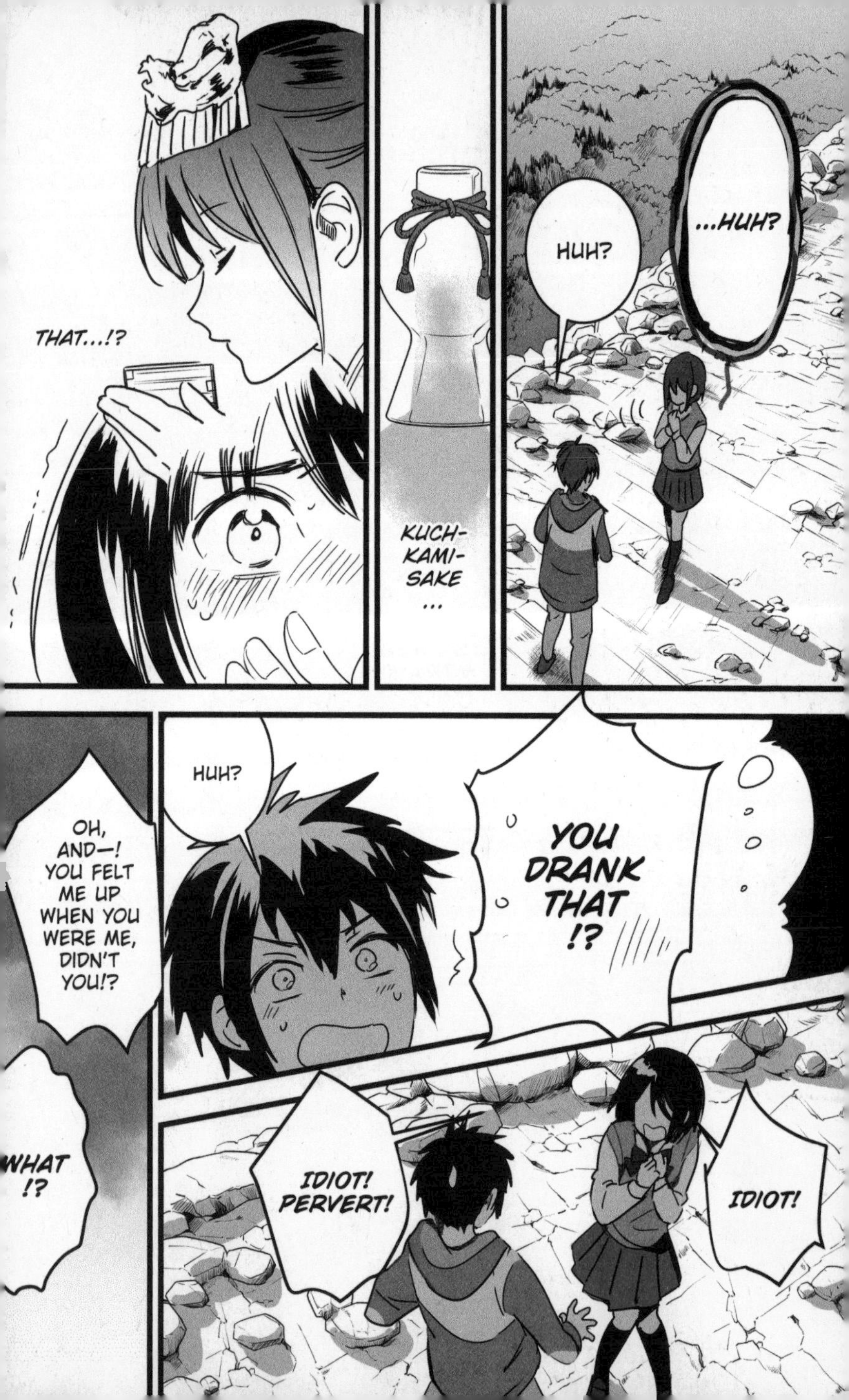
...HUH?
HUH?
KUCH-KAMI-SAKE ...
THAT...!?
YOU DRANK THAT !?
HUH?
OH, AND—! YOU FELT ME UP WHEN YOU WERE ME, DIDN'T YOU!?
WHAT !?
IDIOT!
IDIOT! PERVERT!

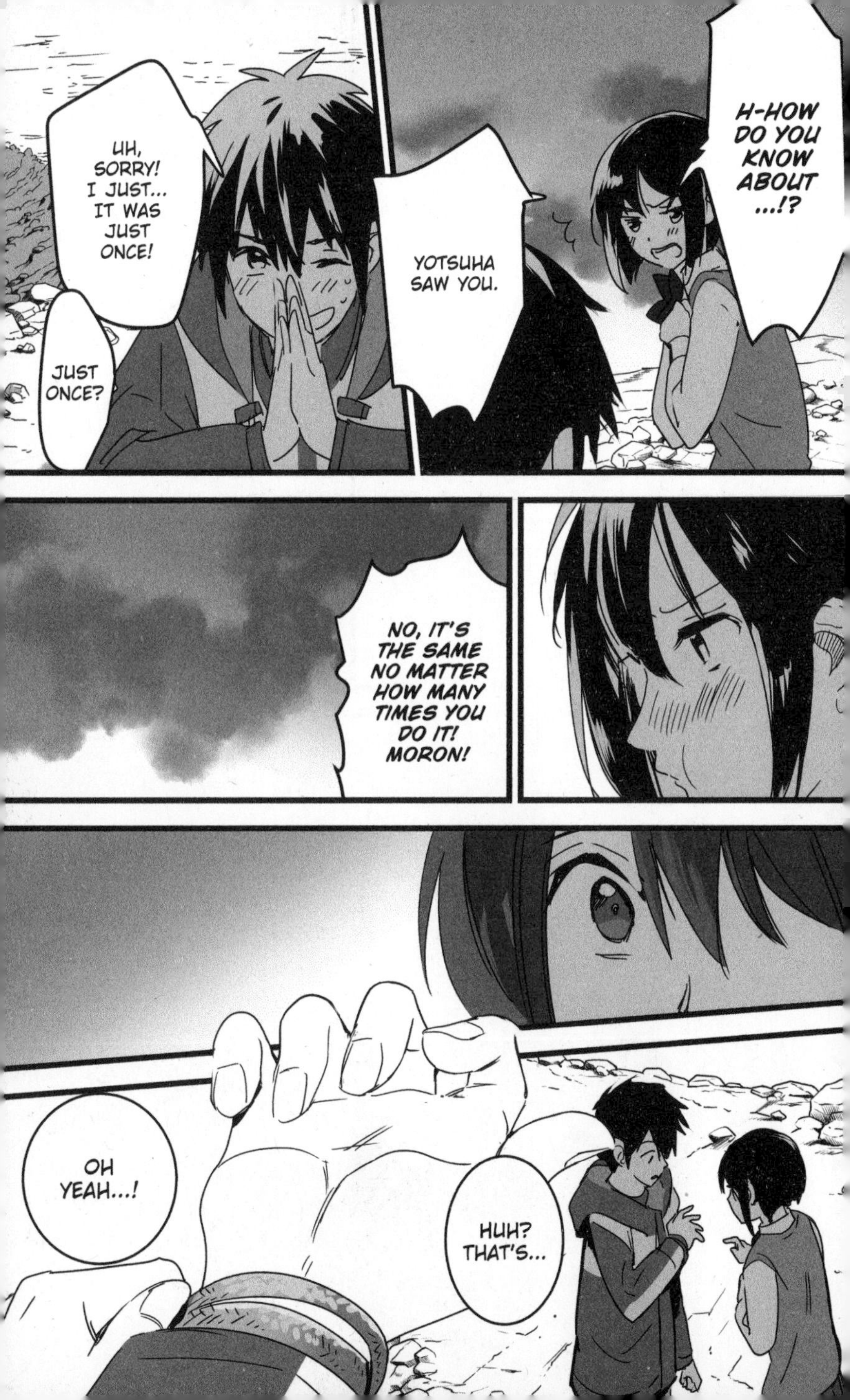
H-HOW DO YOU KNOW ABOUT ...!?
YOTSUHA SAW YOU.
UH, SORRY! I JUST... IT WAS JUST ONCE!
JUST ONCE?
NO, IT'S THE SAME NO MATTER HOW MANY TIMES YOU DO IT! MORON!
HUH? THAT'S...
OH YEAH...!

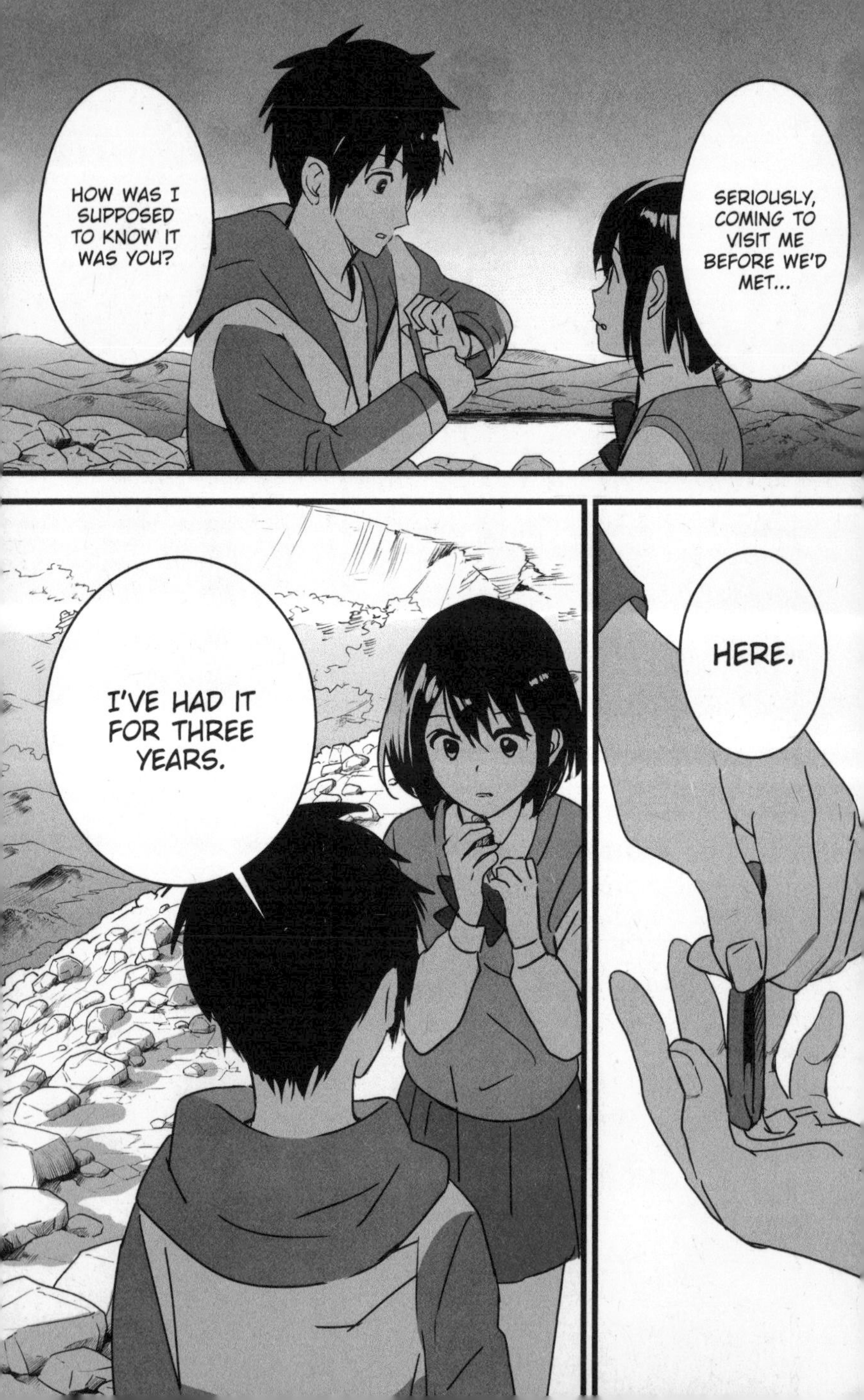
SERIOUSLY, COMING TO VISIT ME BEFORE WE'D MET...
HOW WAS I SUPPOSED TO KNOW IT WAS YOU?
HERE.
I'VE HAD IT FOR THREE YEARS.

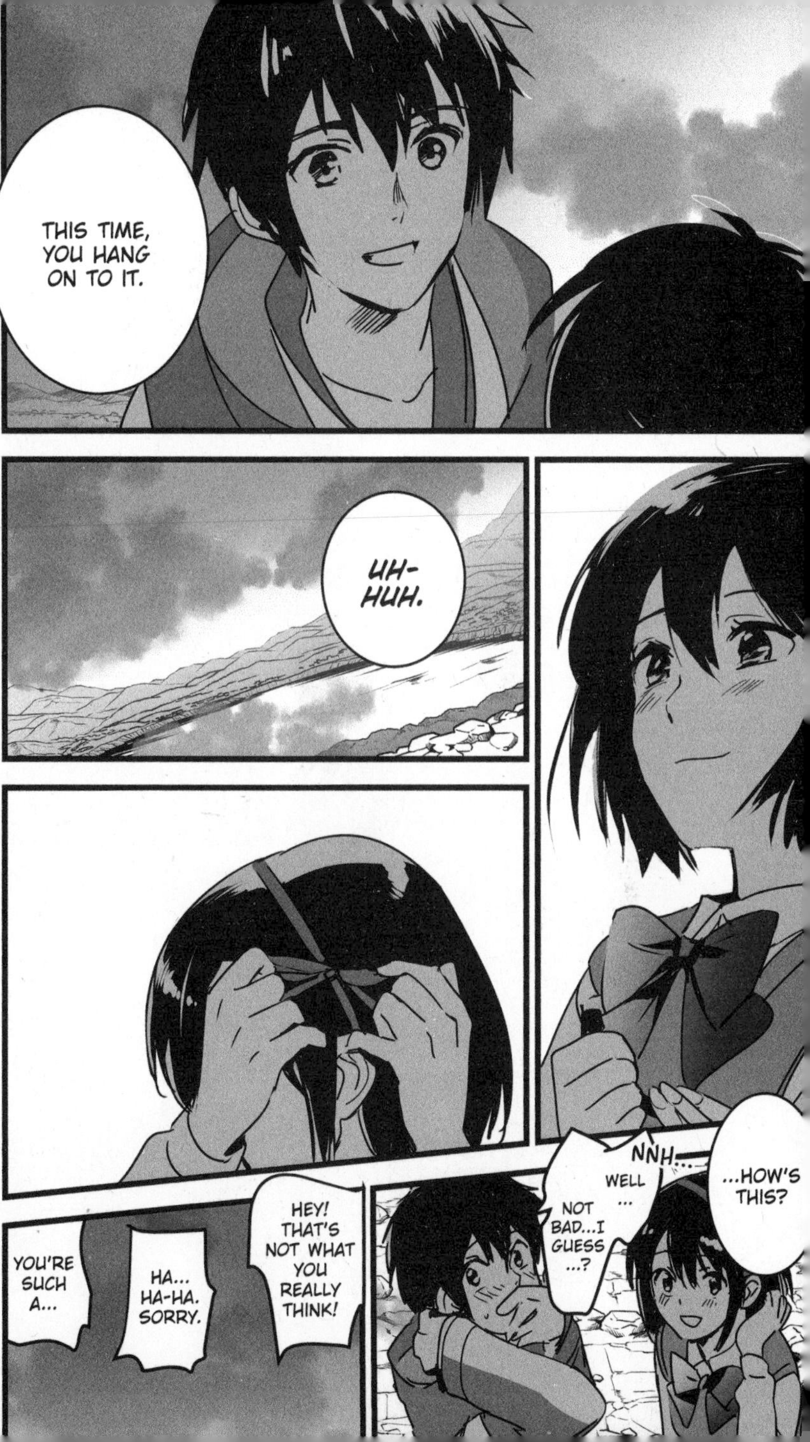
THIS TIME, YOU HANG ON TO IT.
UH-HUH.
...HOW'S THIS?
NNH...
WELL...
NOT BAD...I GUESS...?
HEY! THAT'S NOT WHAT YOU REALLY THINK!
HA... HA-HA. SORRY.
YOU'RE SUCH A...

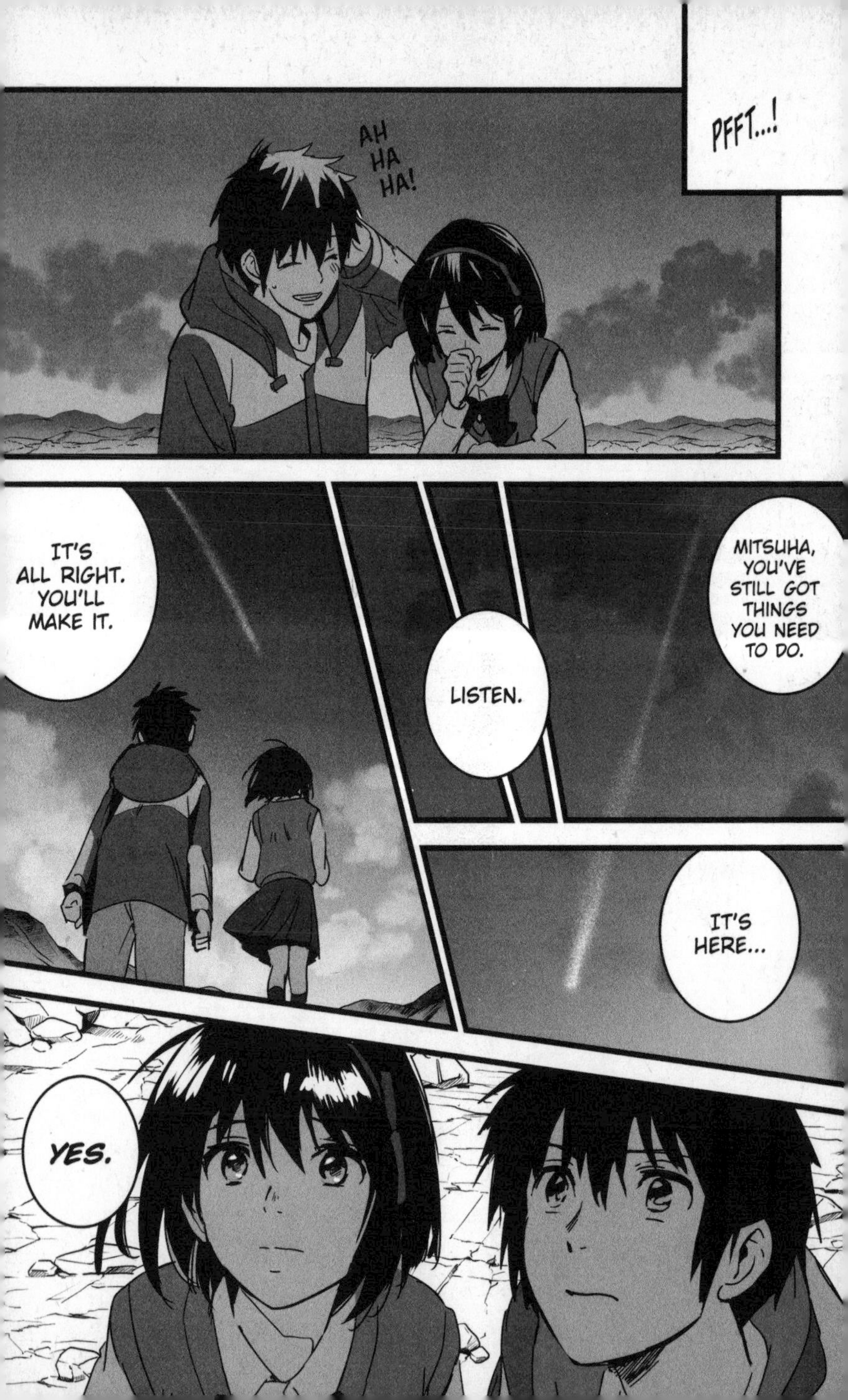
PFFT...!
AH HA HA!
MITSUHA, YOU'VE STILL GOT THINGS YOU NEED TO DO.
LISTEN.
IT'S HERE...
IT'S ALL RIGHT. YOU'LL MAKE IT.
YES.

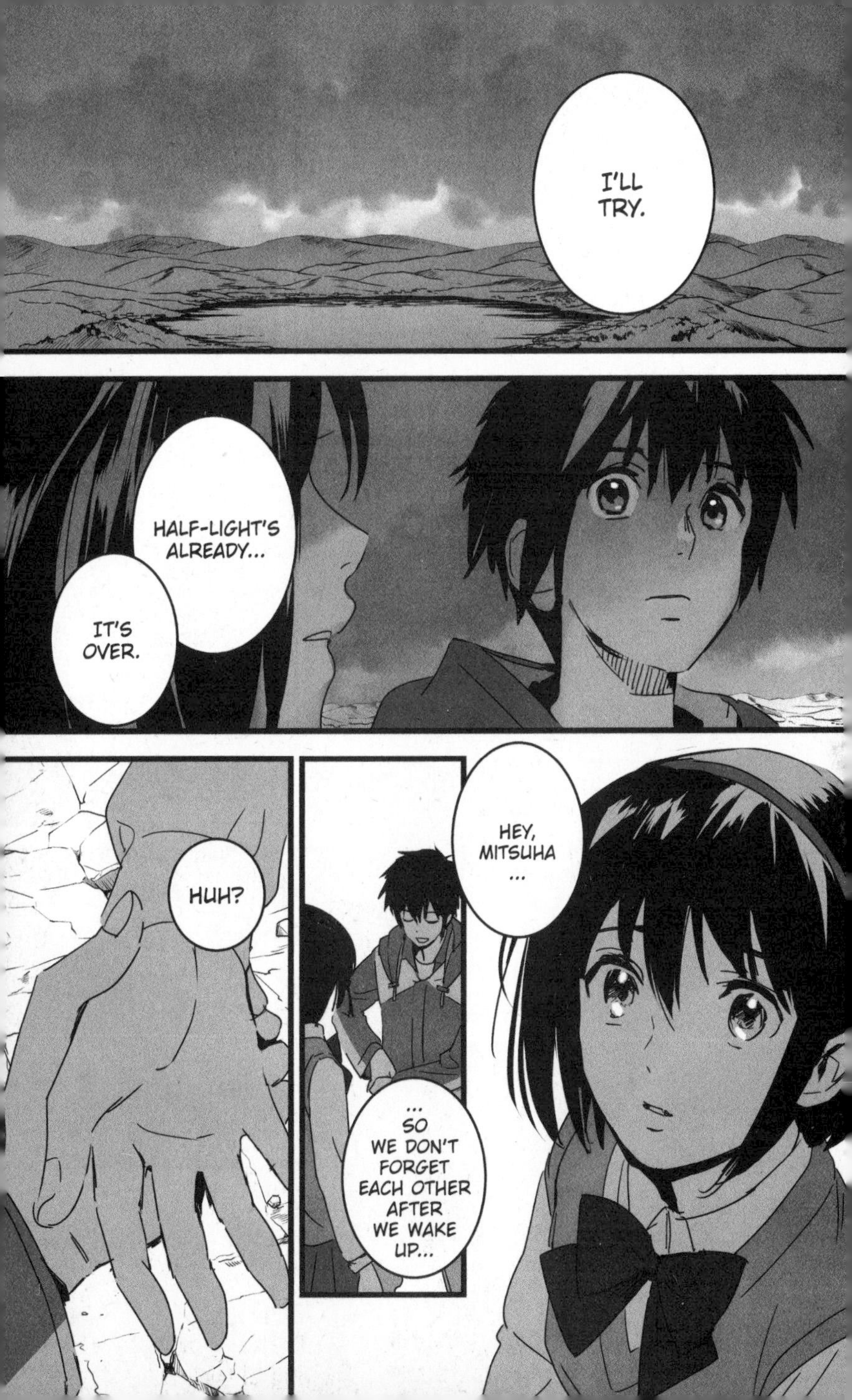
I'LL TRY.
HALF-LIGHT'S ALREADY...
IT'S OVER.
HEY, MITSUHA ...
... SO WE DON'T FORGET EACH OTHER AFTER WE WAKE UP...
HUH?

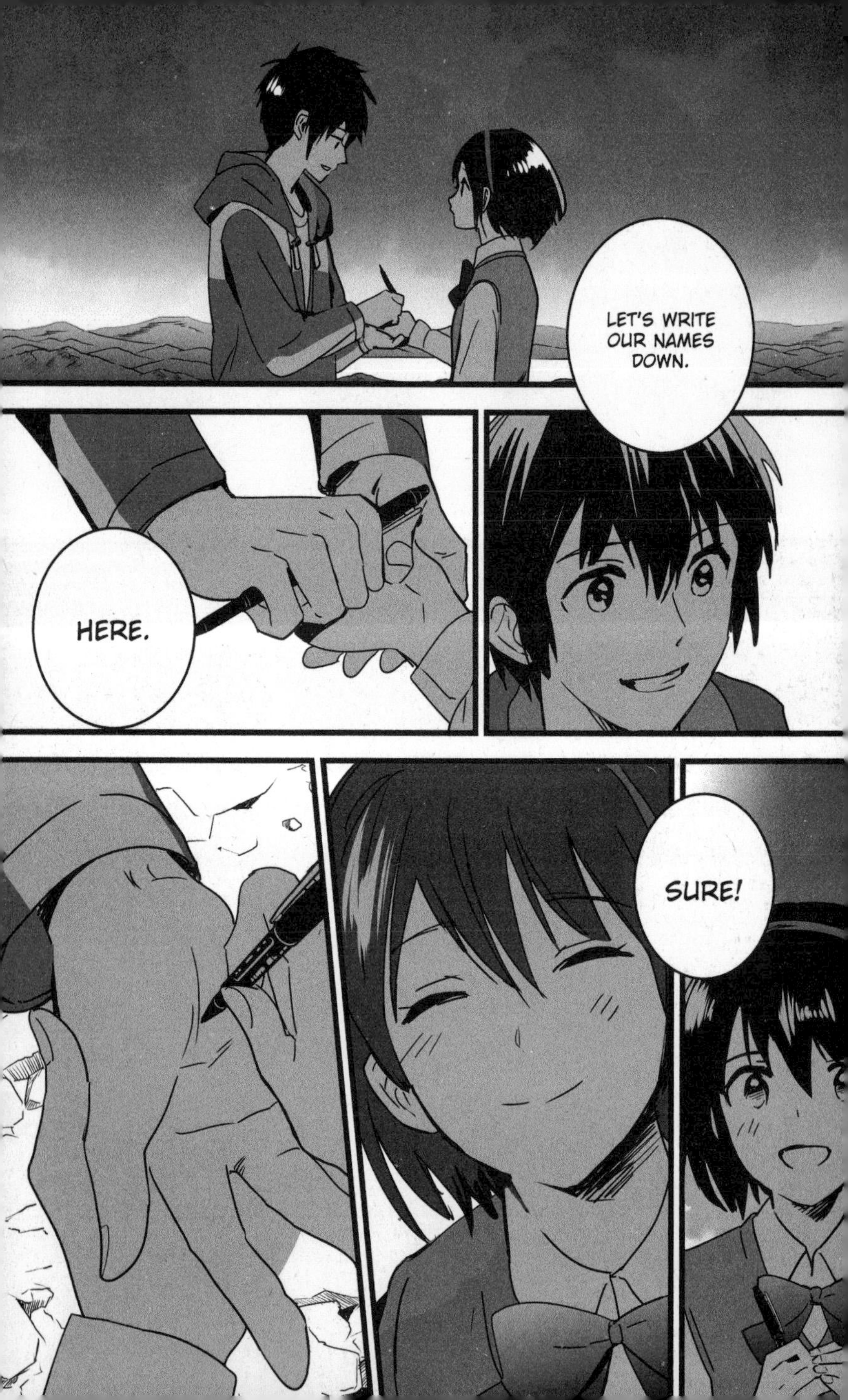
LET'S WRITE OUR NAMES DOWN.
HERE.
SURE!

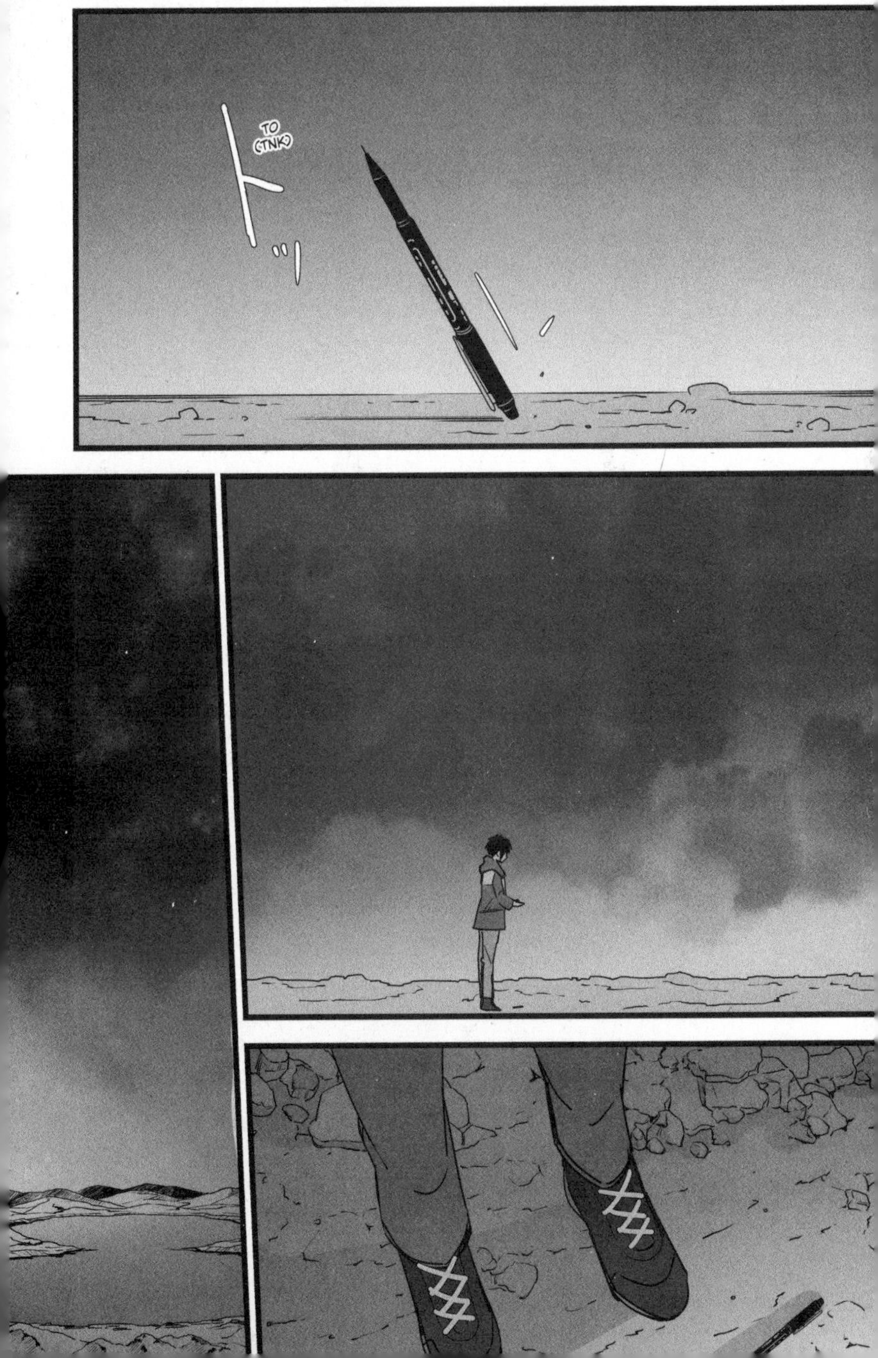
TO
(TNK)

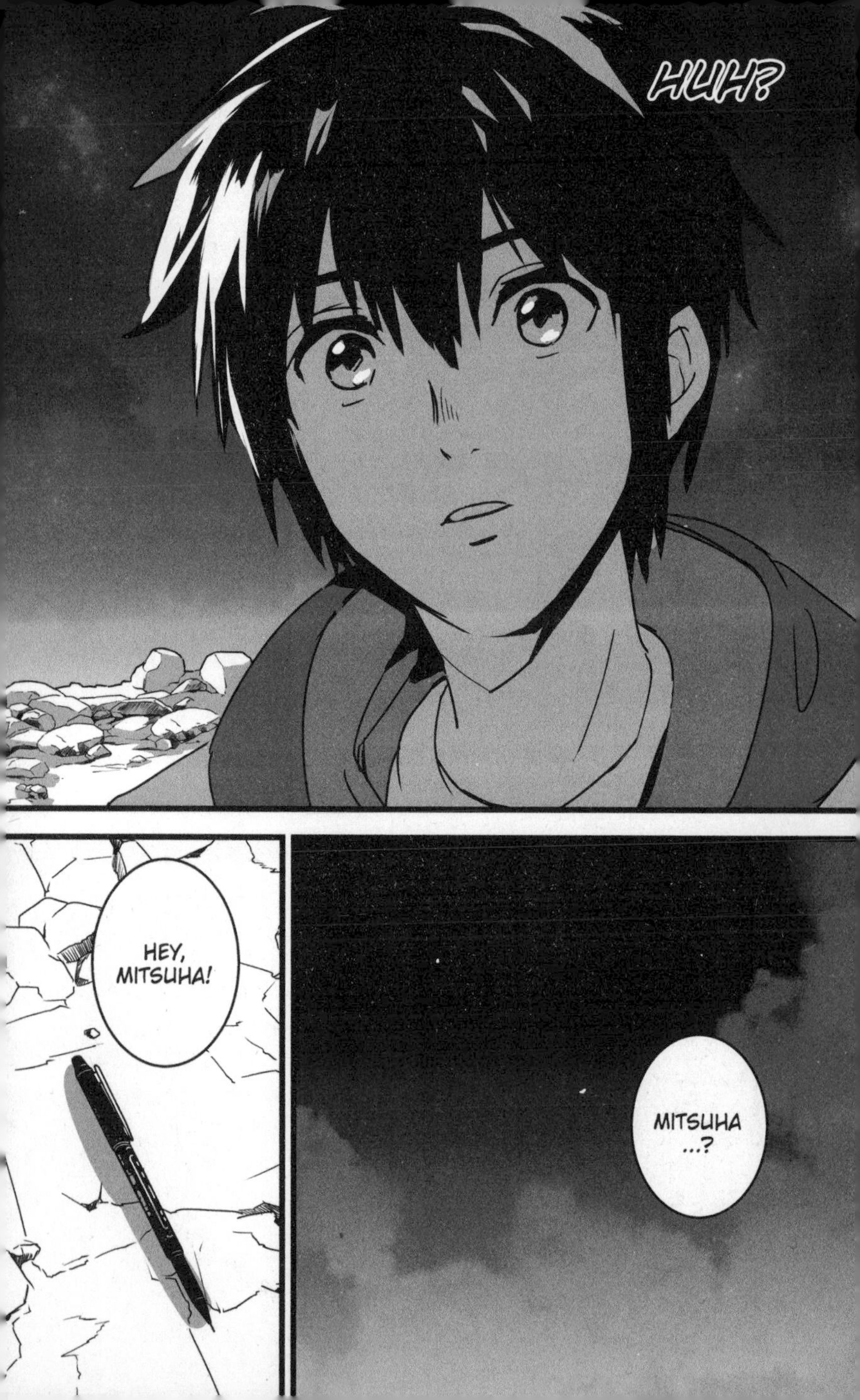
HUH?
MITSUHA ...?
HEY, MITSUHA!

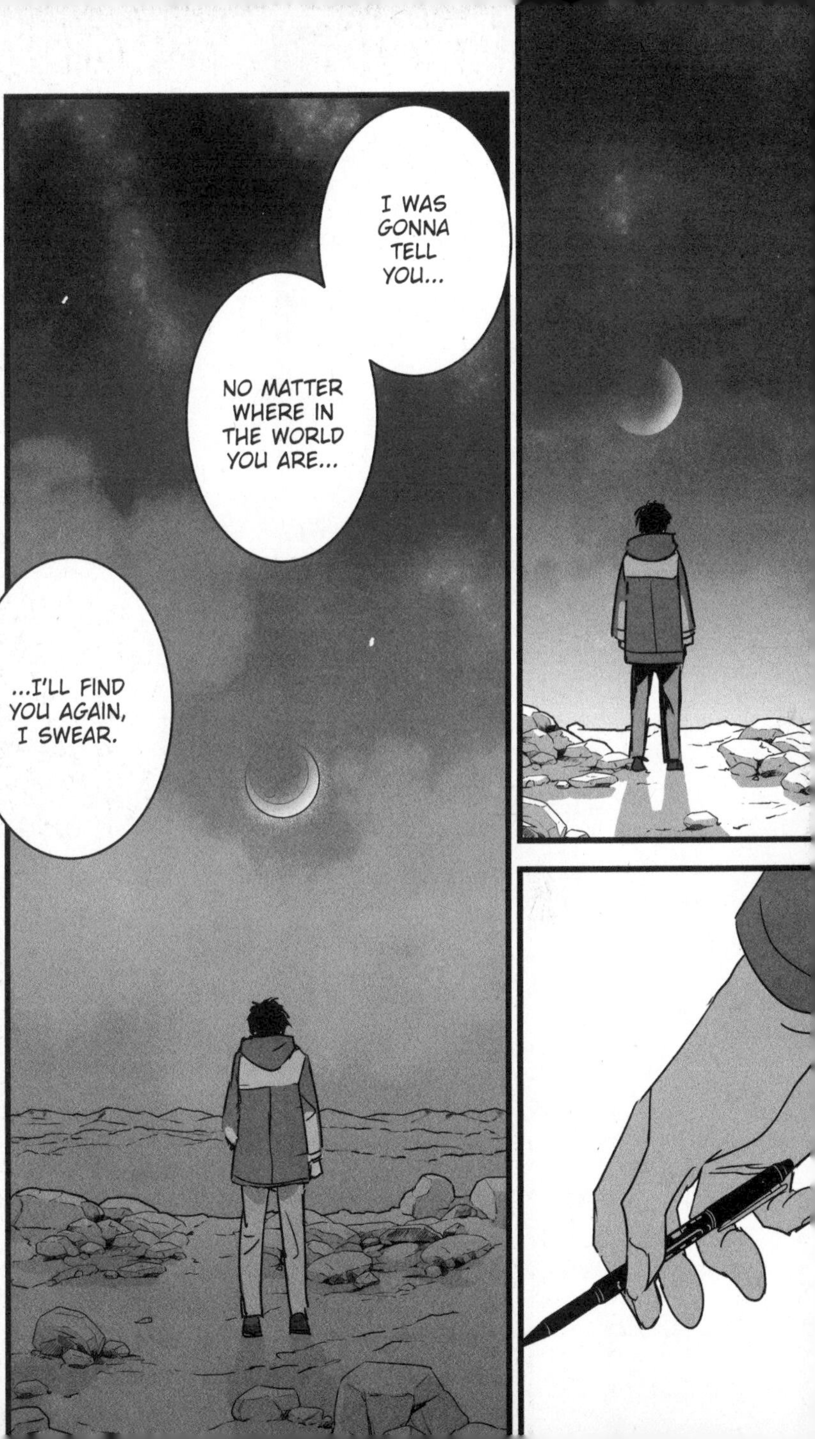
I WAS GONNA TELL YOU...
NO MATTER WHERE IN THE WORLD YOU ARE...
...I'LL FIND YOU AGAIN, I SWEAR.

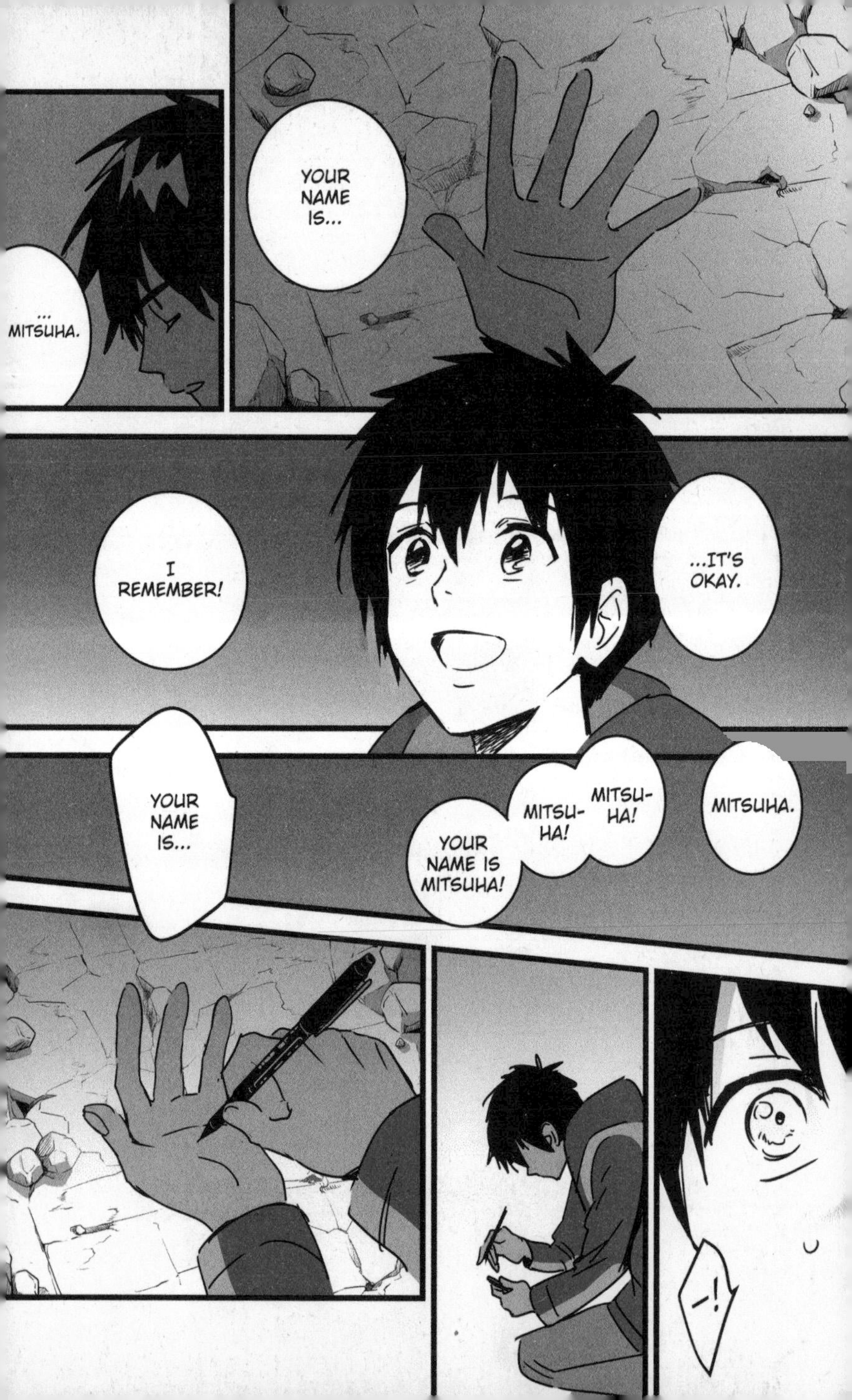
YOUR NAME IS...
... MITSUHA.
...IT'S OKAY.
I REMEMBER!
MITSUHA.
MITSU-HA!
MITSU-HA!
YOUR NAME IS MITSUHA!
YOUR NAME IS...
—!

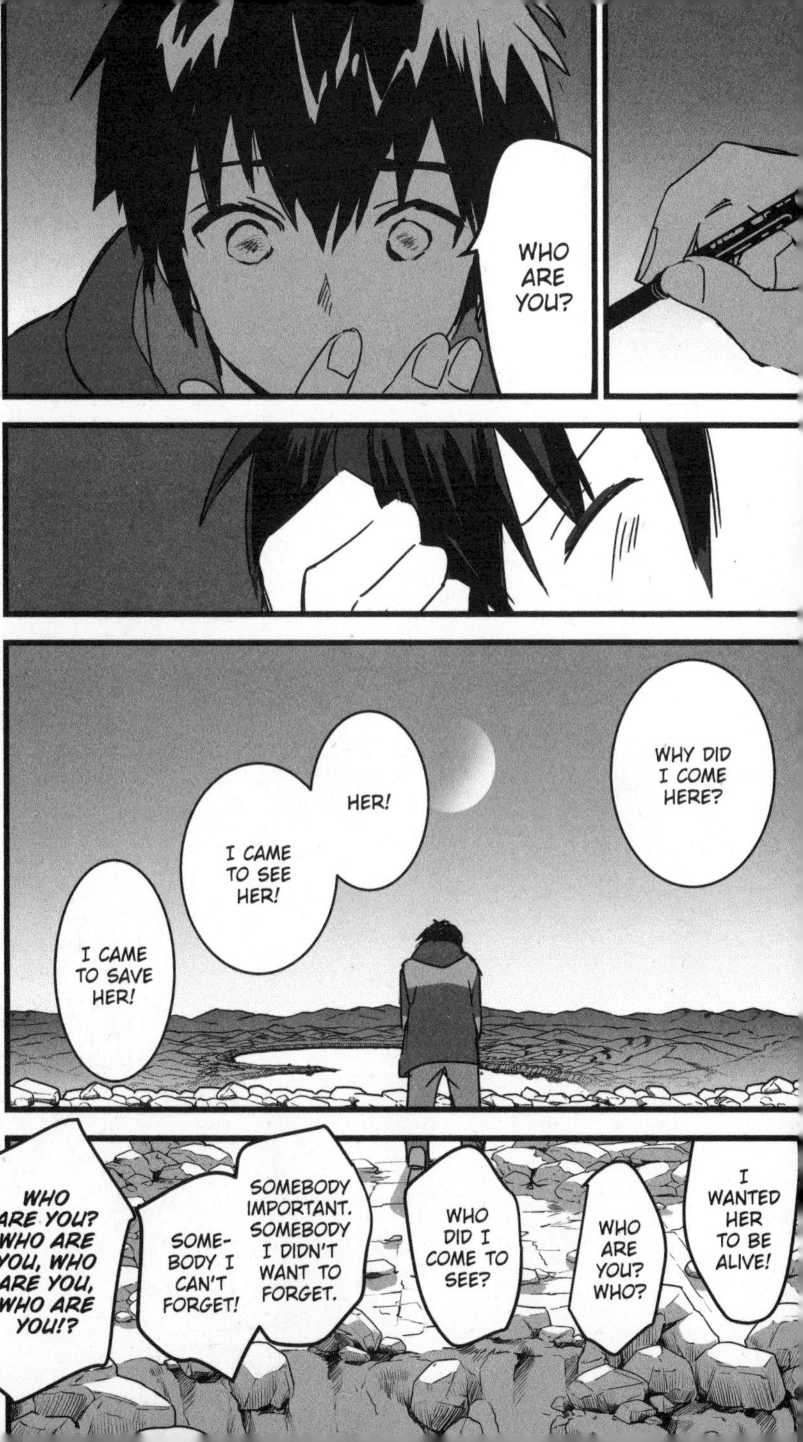
WHO ARE YOU?
WHY DID I COME HERE?
HER!
I CAME TO SEE HER!
I CAME TO SAVE HER!
I WANTED HER TO BE ALIVE!
WHO ARE YOU? WHO?
WHO DID I COME TO SEE?
SOMEBODY IMPORTANT. SOMEBODY I DIDN'T WANT TO FORGET.
SOME-BODY I CAN'T FORGET!
WHO ARE YOU? WHO ARE YOU, WHO ARE YOU, WHO ARE YOU!?

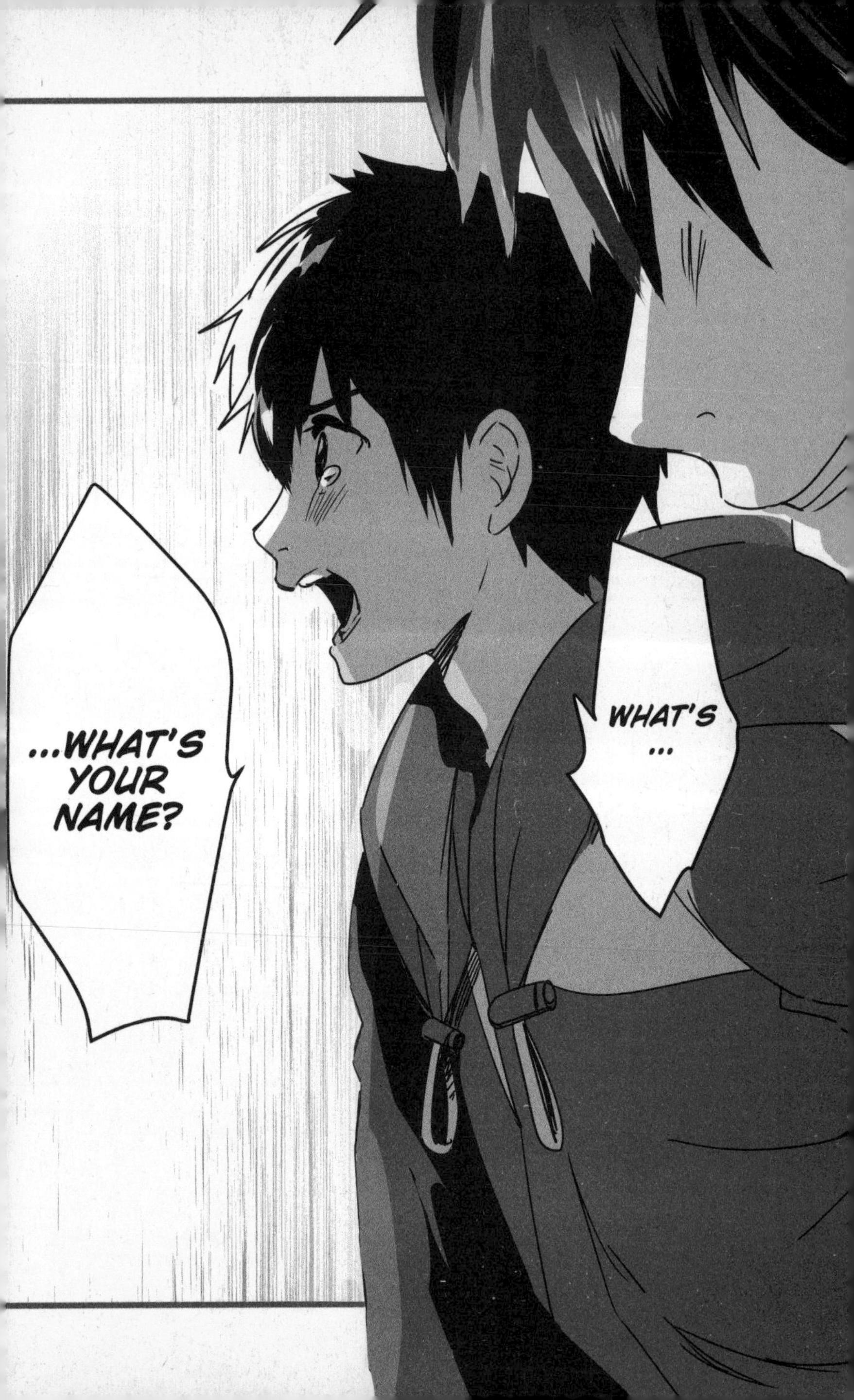
WHAT'S ...
...WHAT'S YOUR NAME?

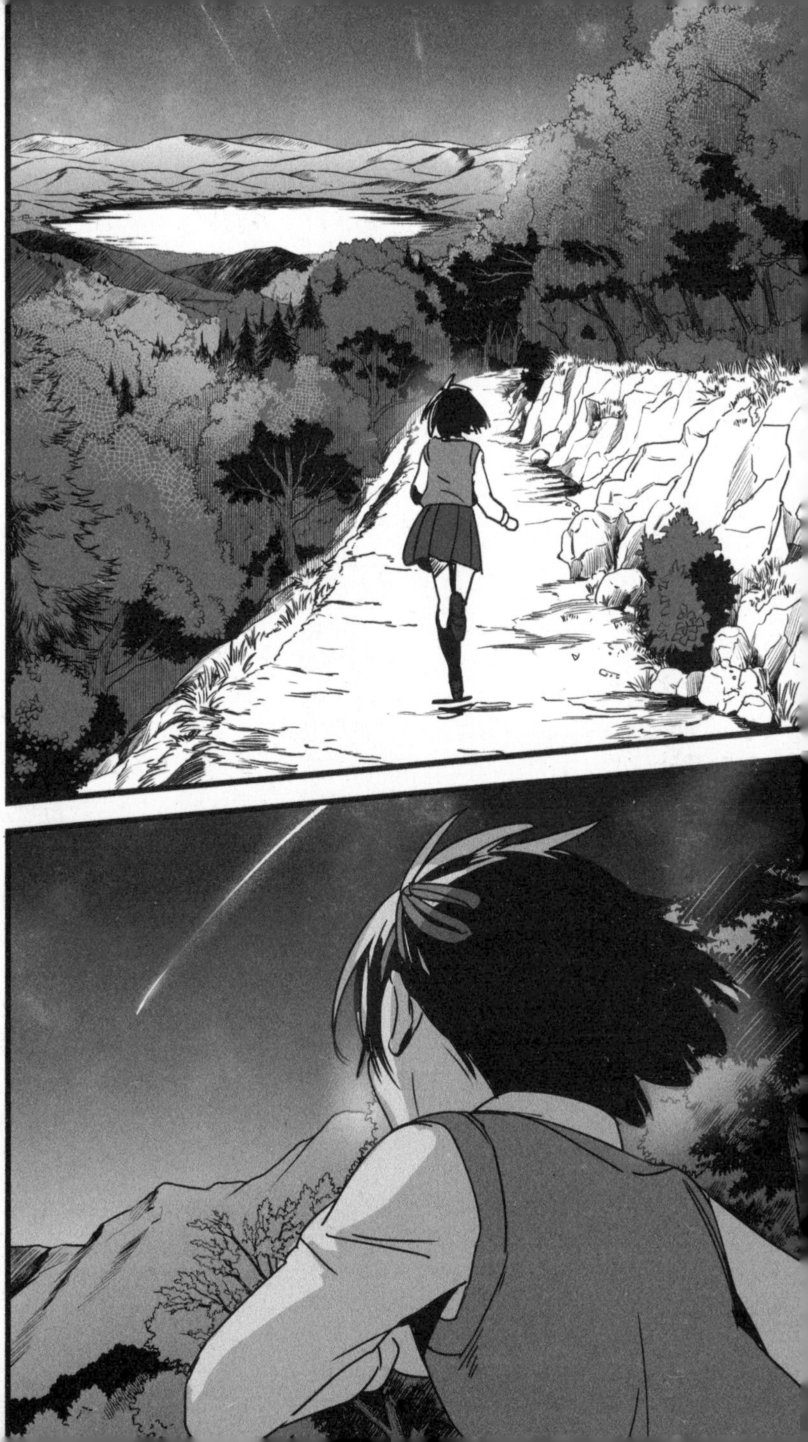

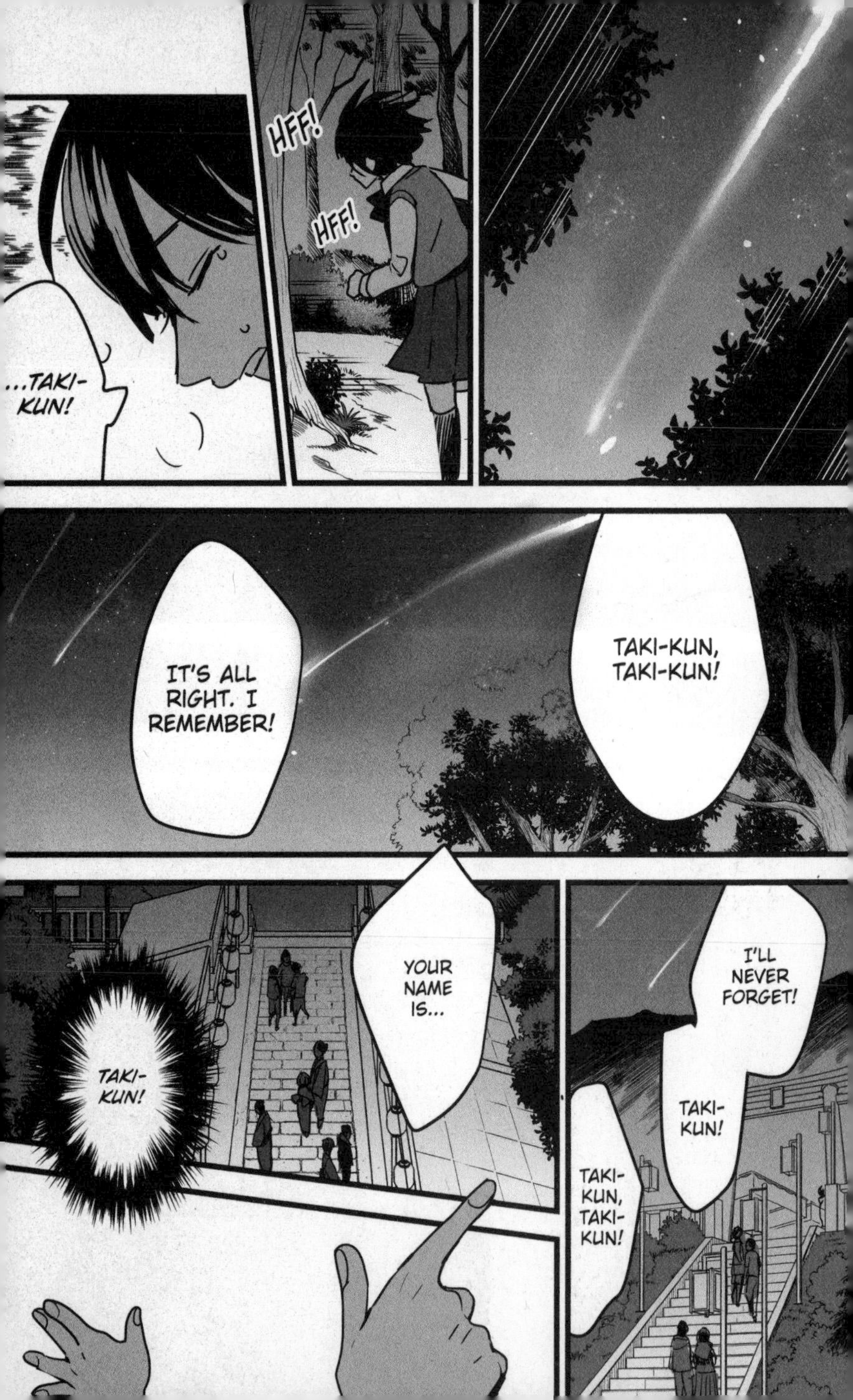
HFF!
HFF!
...TAKI-KUN!
TAKI-KUN, TAKI-KUN!
IT'S ALL RIGHT. I REMEMBER!
I'LL NEVER FORGET!
TAKI-KUN!
TAKI-KUN, TAKI-KUN!
YOUR NAME IS...
TAKI-KUN!

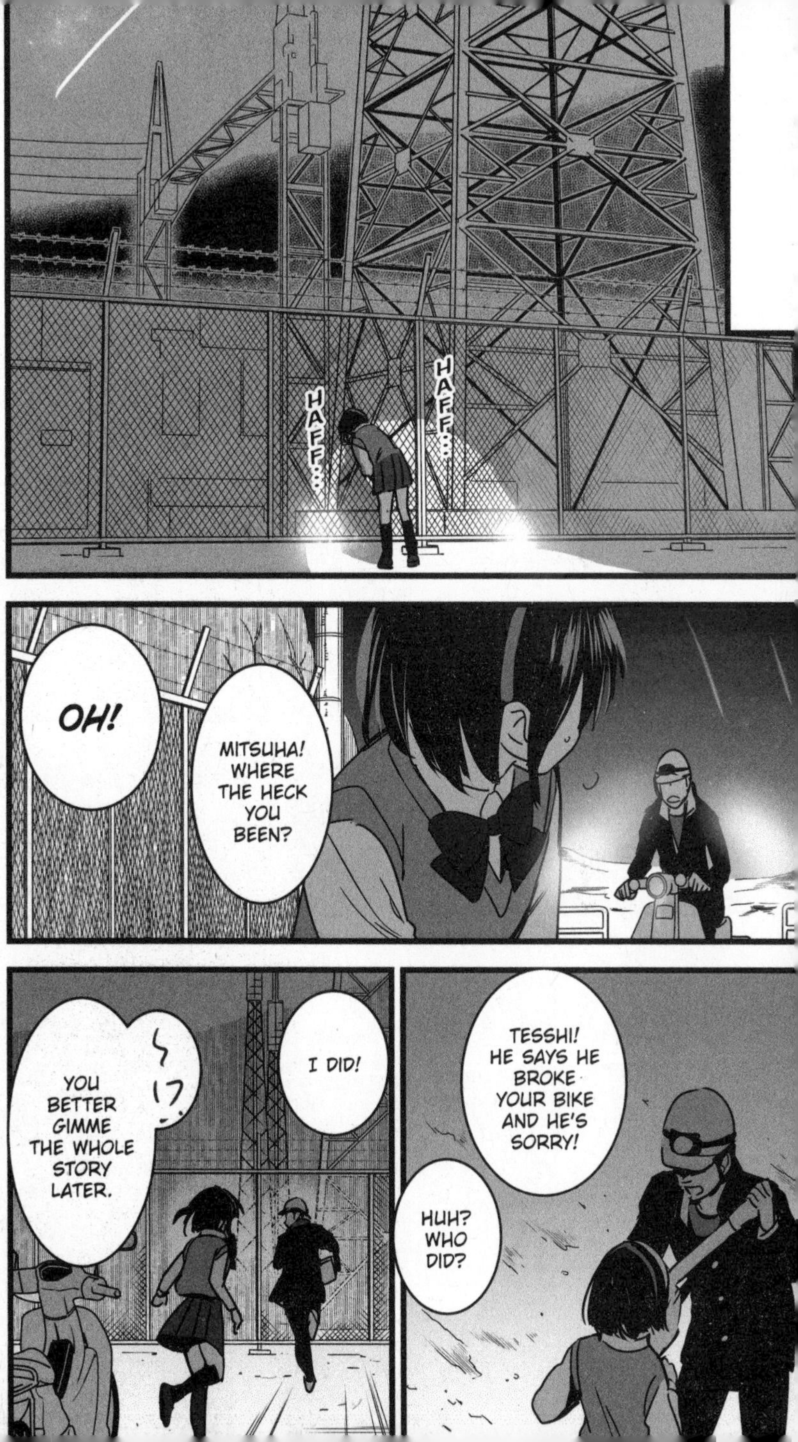
HAFF...
HAFF...
MITSUHA! WHERE THE HECK YOU BEEN?
OH!
TESSHI! HE SAYS HE BROKE YOUR BIKE AND HE'S SORRY!
HUH? WHO DID?
I DID!
YOU BETTER GIMME THE WHOLE STORY LATER.

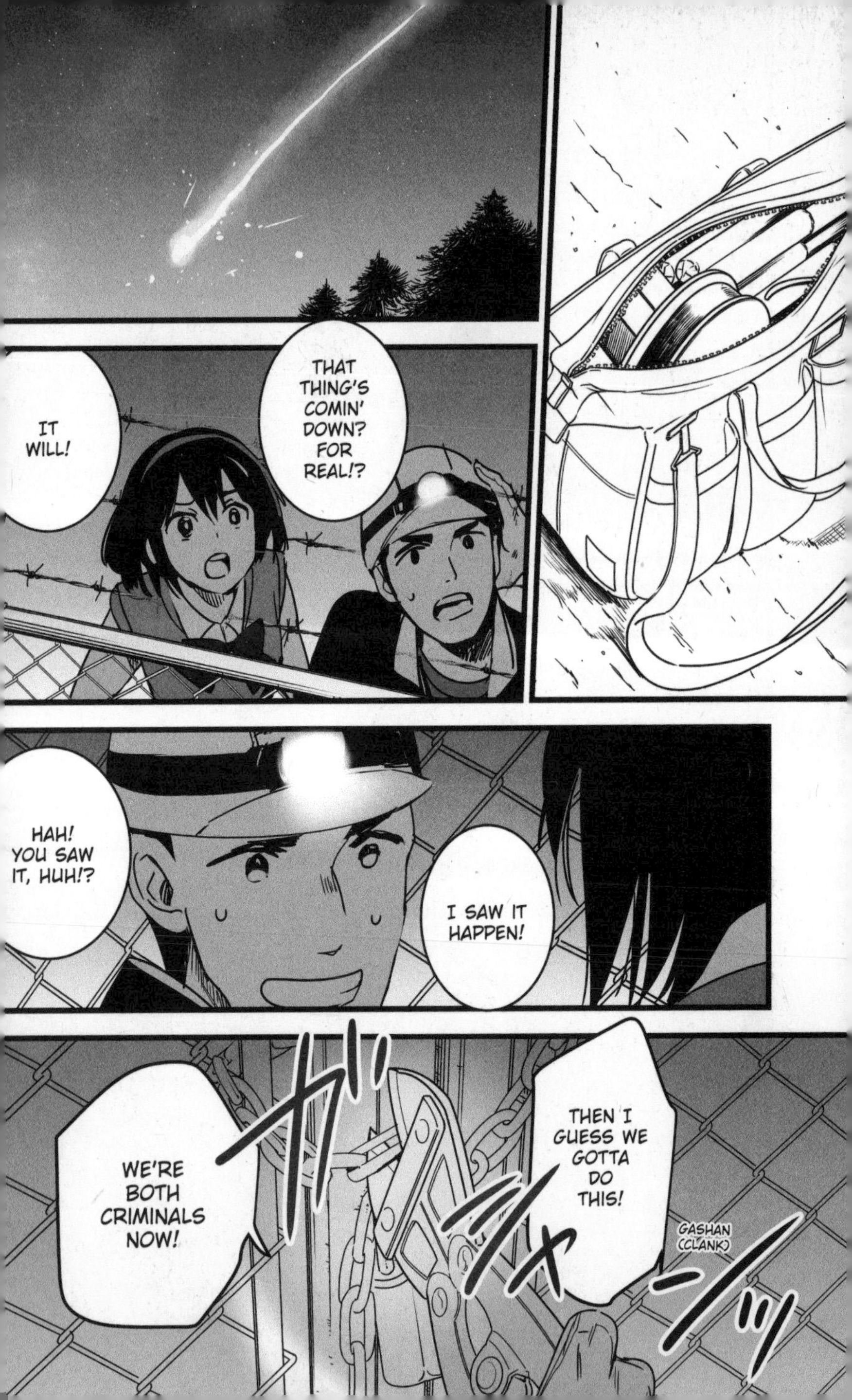
THAT THING'S COMIN' DOWN? FOR REAL!?
IT WILL!
I SAW IT HAPPEN!
HAH! YOU SAW IT, HUH!?
THEN I GUESS WE GOTTA DO THIS!
GASHAN (CLANK)
WE'RE BOTH CRIMINALS NOW!

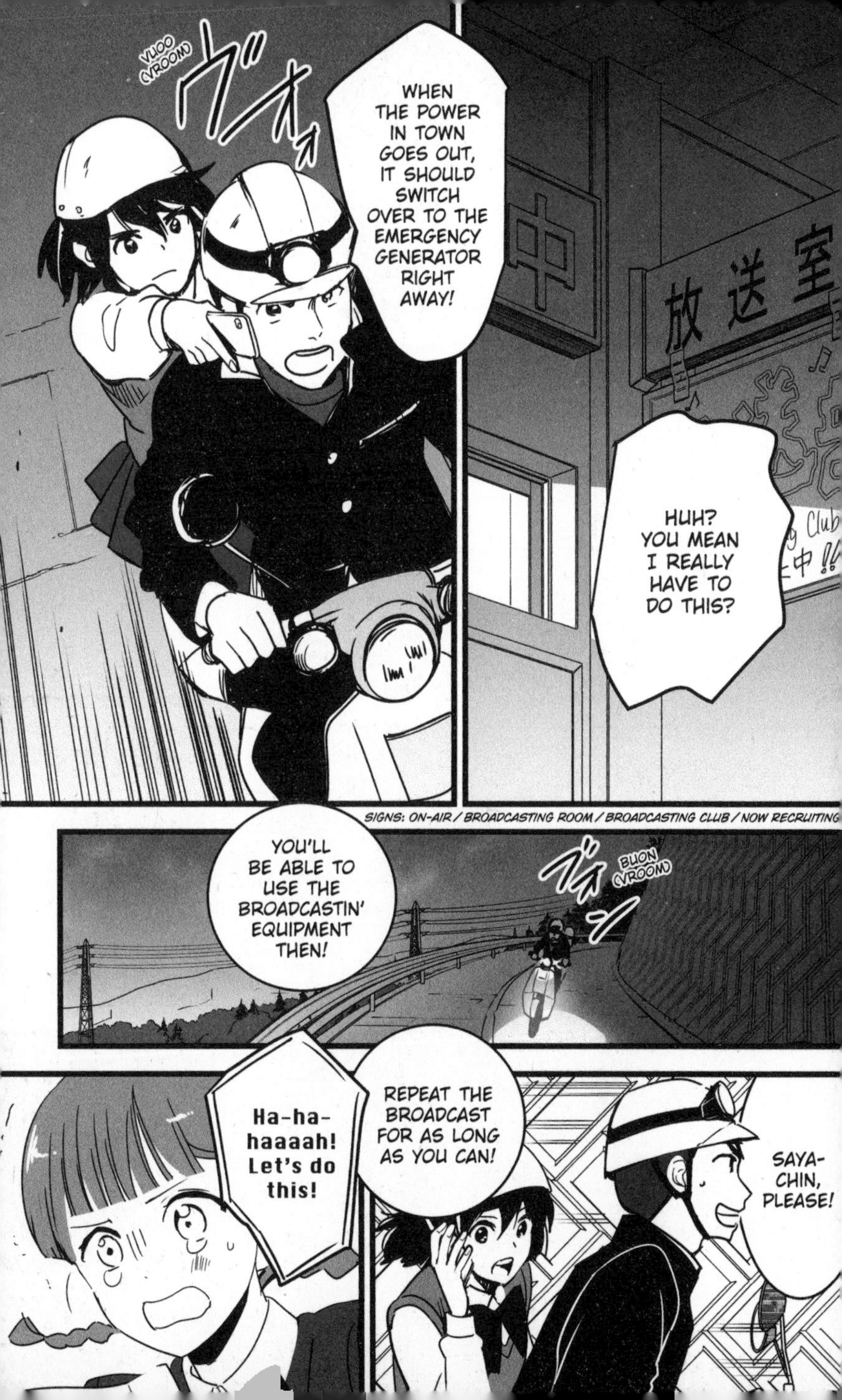
Club
HUH? YOU MEAN I REALLY HAVE TO DO THIS?
VUOO (VROOM)
WHEN THE POWER IN TOWN GOES OUT, IT SHOULD SWITCH OVER TO THE EMERGENCY GENERATOR RIGHT AWAY!
SIGNS: ON-AIR / BROADCASTING ROOM / BROADCASTING CLUB / NOW RECRUITING
BUON (VROOM)
YOU'LL BE ABLE TO USE THE BROADCASTIN' EQUIPMENT THEN!
SAYA-CHIN, PLEASE!
REPEAT THE BROADCAST FOR AS LONG AS YOU CAN!
Ha-ha-haaaah! Let's do this!

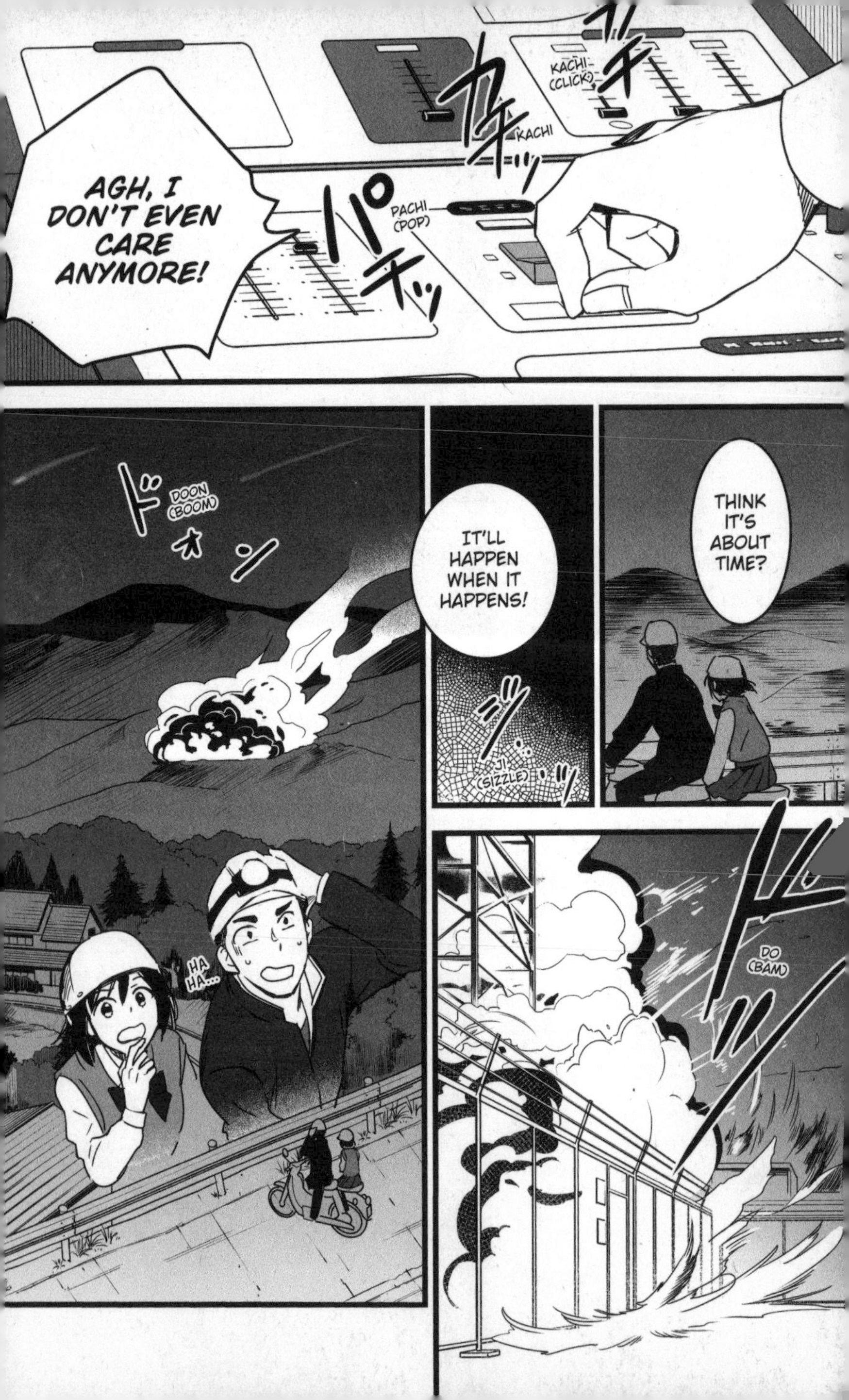
KACHI (CLICK)
KACHI
PACHI (POP)
AGH, I DON'T EVEN CARE ANYMORE!
THINK IT'S ABOUT TIME?
IT'LL HAPPEN WHEN IT HAPPENS!
JI (SIZZLE)
DOON (BOOM)
DO (BAM)
HA HA...

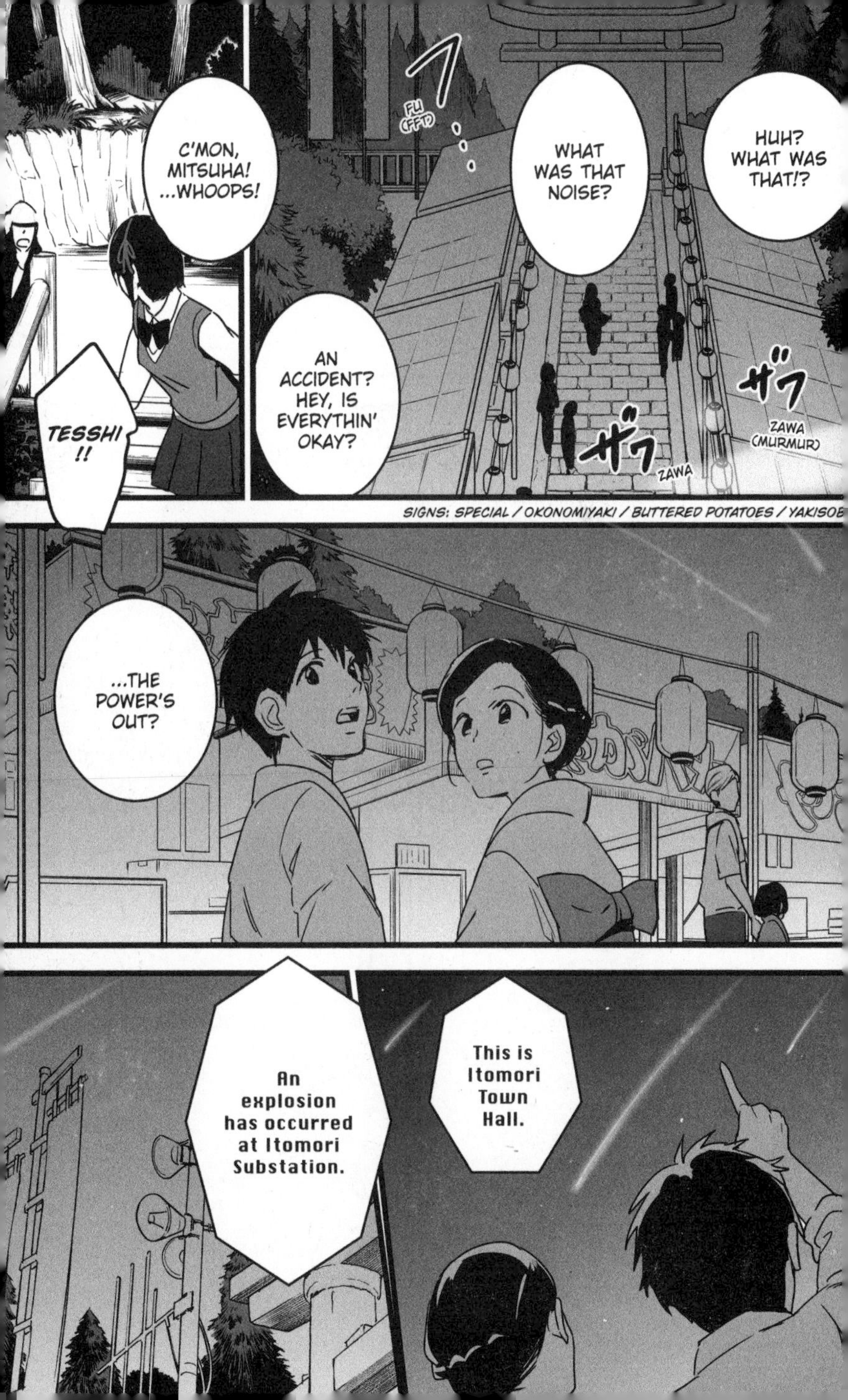
FU (FFT)
HUH? WHAT WAS THAT!?
WHAT WAS THAT NOISE?
ザワ
ZAWA (MURMUR)
ザワ
ZAWA
AN ACCIDENT? HEY, IS EVERYTHIN' OKAY?
C'MON, MITSUHA! ...WHOOPS!
TESSHI!!
SIGNS: SPECIAL / OKONOMIYAKI / BUTTERED POTATOES / YAKISOB
...THE POWER'S OUT?
This is Itomori Town Hall.
An explosion has occurred at Itomori Substation.

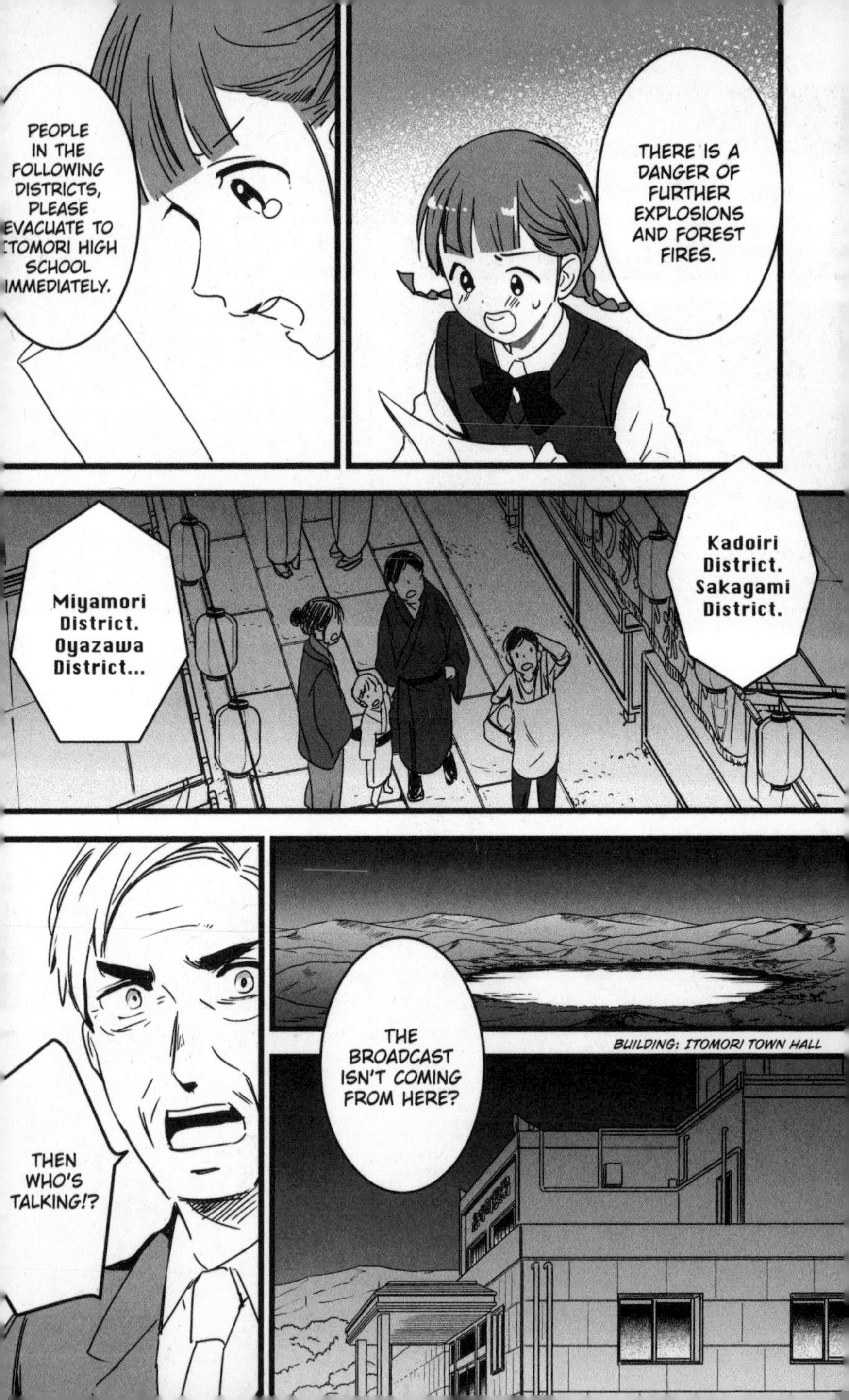
THERE IS A DANGER OF FURTHER EXPLOSIONS AND FOREST FIRES.
PEOPLE IN THE FOLLOWING DISTRICTS, PLEASE EVACUATE TO ITOMORI HIGH SCHOOL IMMEDIATELY.
Kadoiri District. Sakagami District.
Miyamori District. Oyazawa District...
BUILDING: ITOMORI TOWN HALL
THE BROADCAST ISN'T COMING FROM HERE?
THEN WHO'S TALKING!?

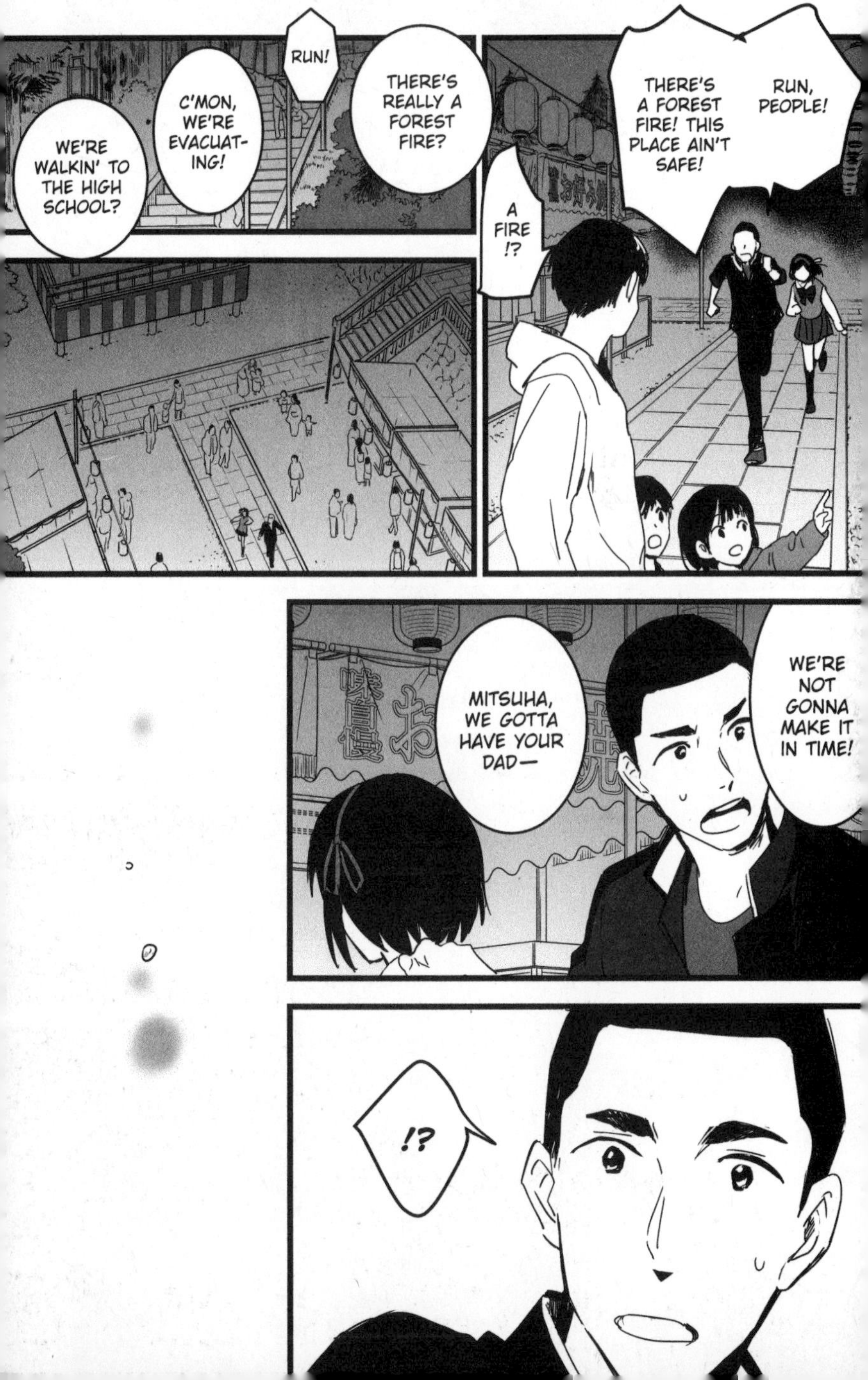
RUN, PEOPLE!
THERE'S A FOREST FIRE! THIS PLACE AIN'T SAFE!
A FIRE!?
THERE'S REALLY A FOREST FIRE?
RUN!
C'MON, WE'RE EVACUAT-ING!
WE'RE WALKIN' TO THE HIGH SCHOOL?
WE'RE NOT GONNA MAKE IT IN TIME!
MITSUHA, WE GOTTA HAVE YOUR DAD—
!?

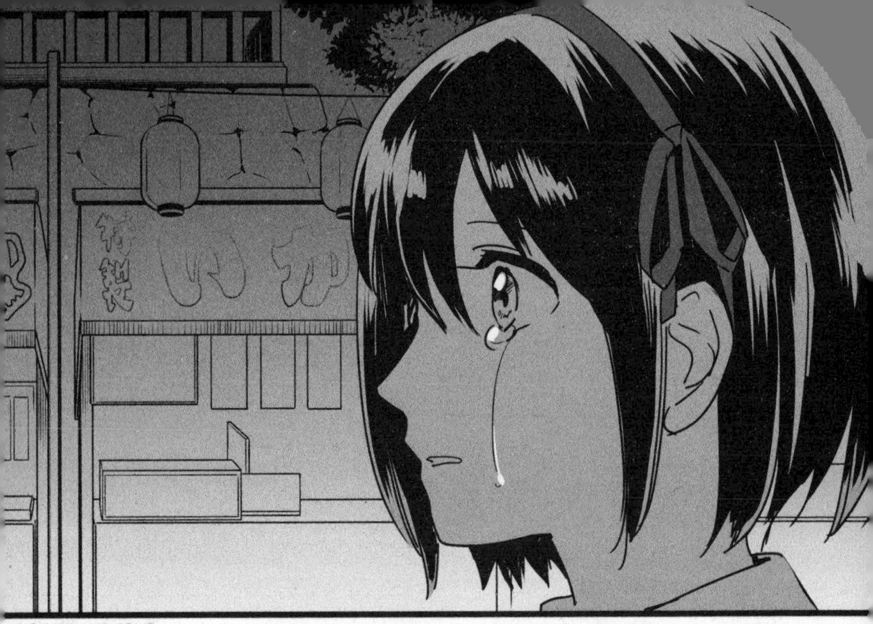

SIGN: DELUXE SQUID

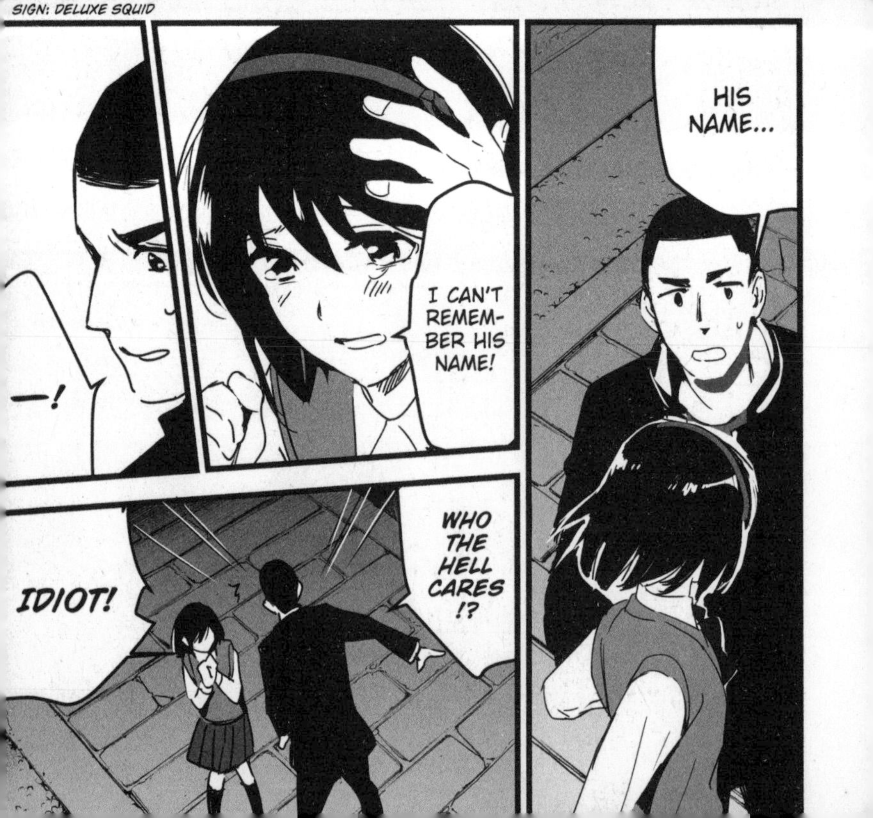
HIS NAME...
I CAN'T REMEMBER HIS NAME!
—!
WHO THE HELL CARES !?
IDIOT!

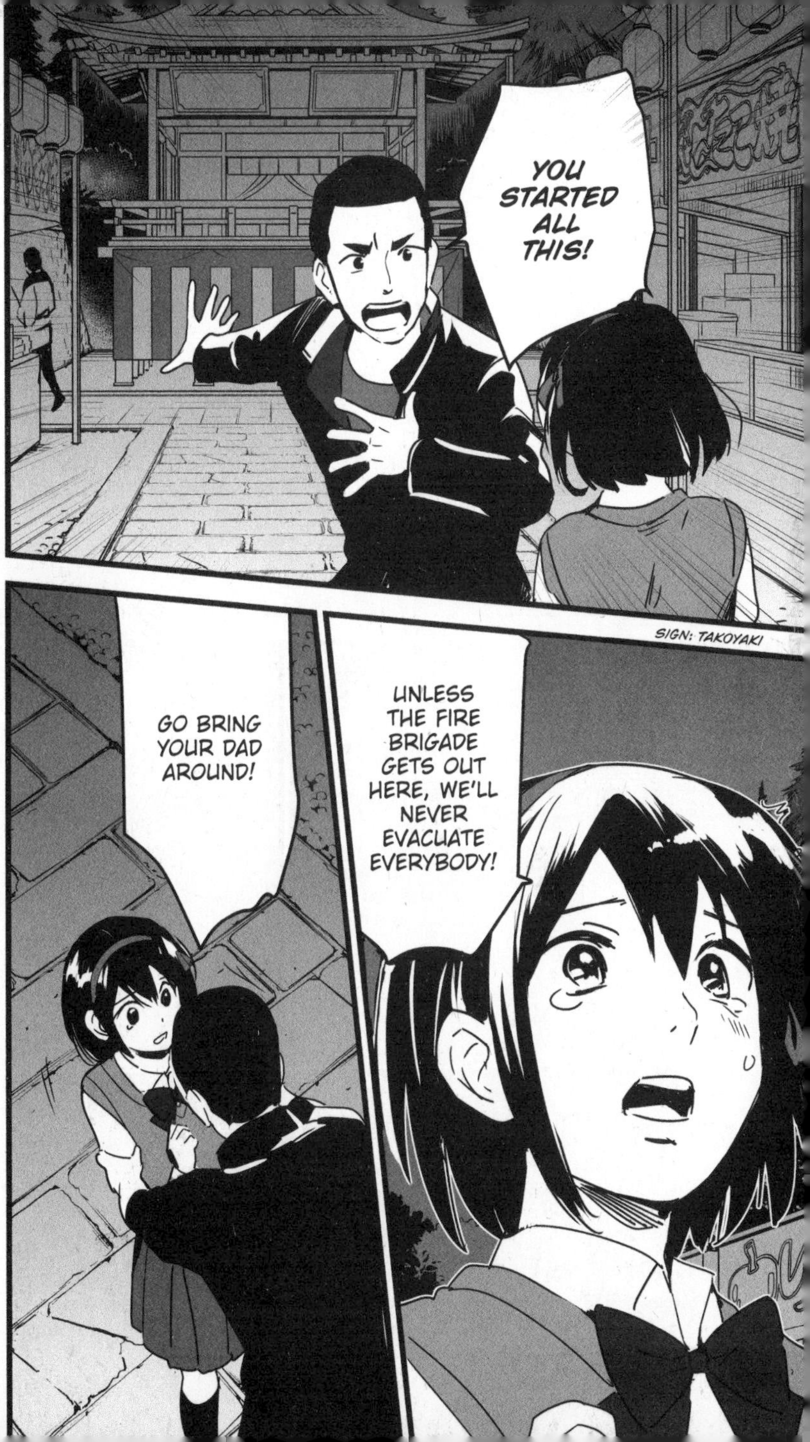
YOU STARTED ALL THIS!
SIGN: TAKOYAKI
UNLESS THE FIRE BRIGADE GETS OUT HERE, WE'LL NEVER EVACUATE EVERYBODY!
GO BRING YOUR DAD AROUND!

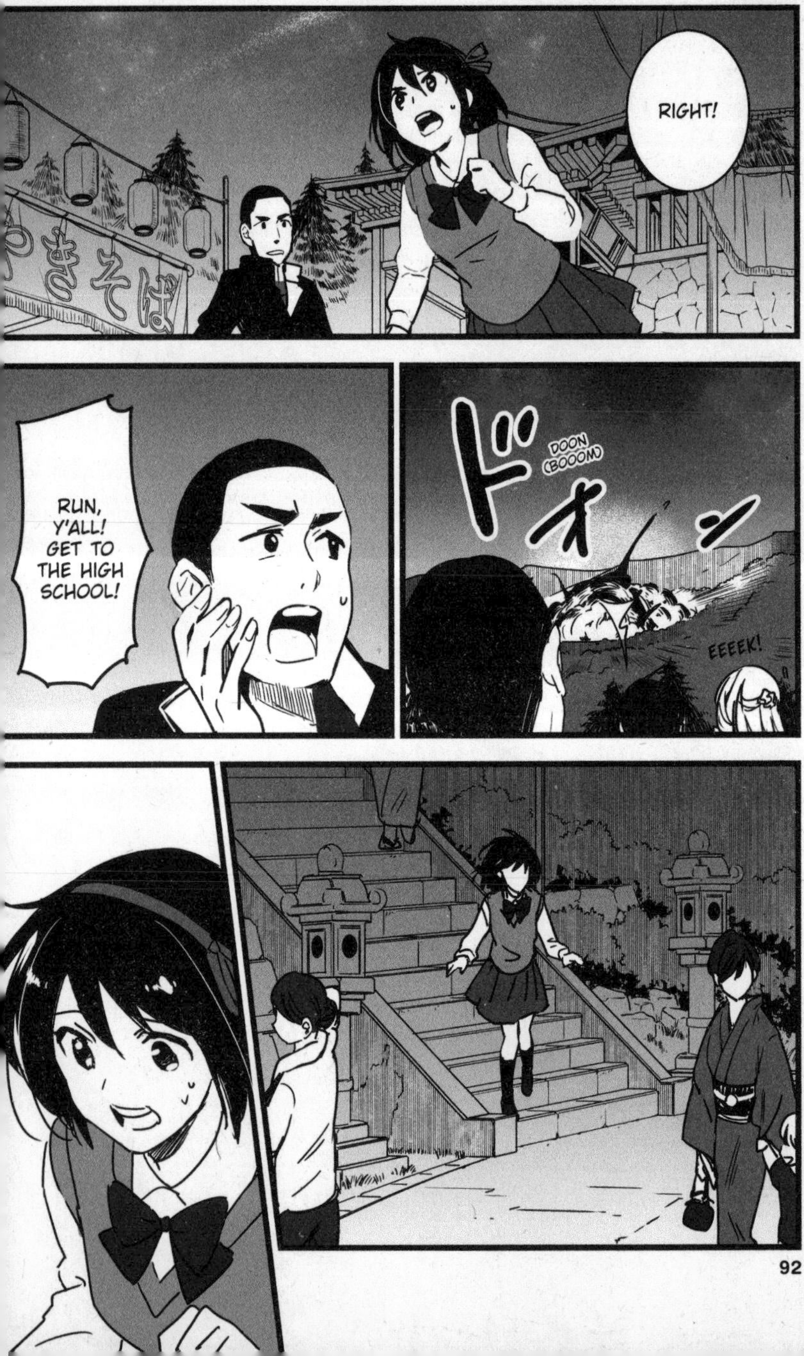
RIGHT!
やきそば
ドオン
DOON (BOOOM)
EEEEK!
RUN, Y'ALL! GET TO THE HIGH SCHOOL!

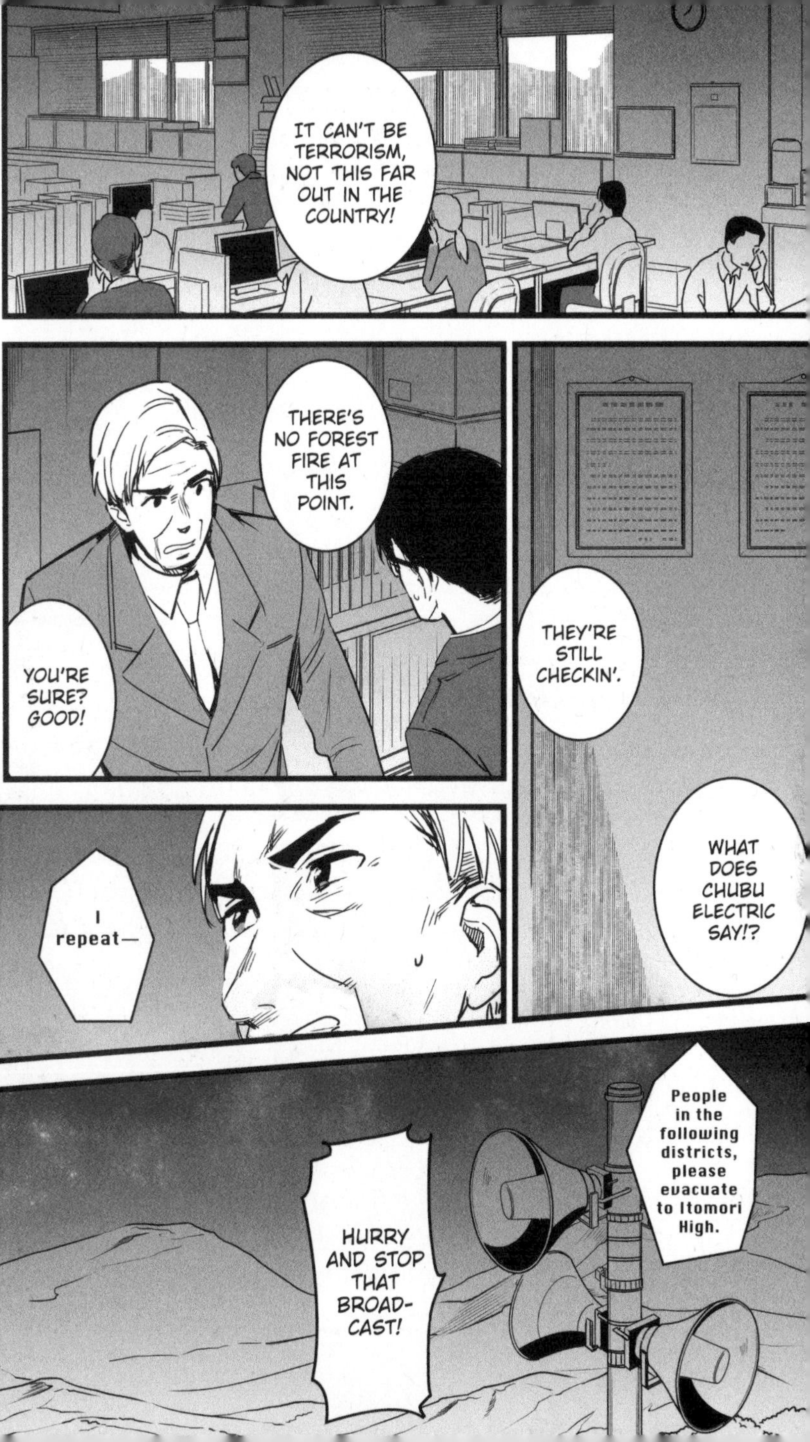
IT CAN'T BE TERRORISM, NOT THIS FAR OUT IN THE COUNTRY!
THEY'RE STILL CHECKIN'.
WHAT DOES CHUBU ELECTRIC SAY!?
THERE'S NO FOREST FIRE AT THIS POINT.
YOU'RE SURE? GOOD!
I repeat—
People in the following districts, please evacuate to Itomori High.
HURRY AND STOP THAT BROAD-CAST!

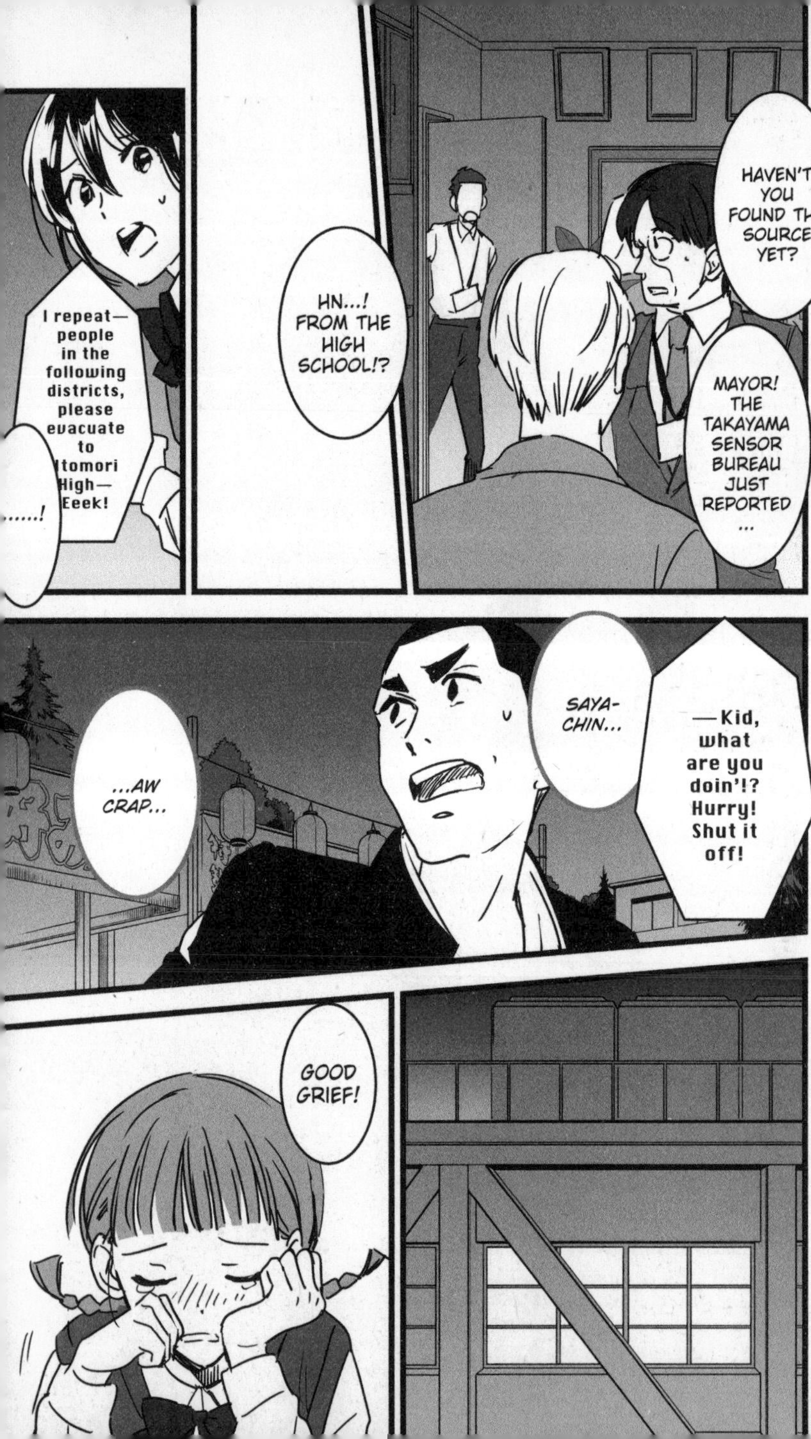
HAVEN'T YOU FOUND THE SOURCE YET?
MAYOR! THE TAKAYAMA SENSOR BUREAU JUST REPORTED ...
HN...! FROM THE HIGH SCHOOL!?
I repeat—people in the following districts, please evacuate to Itomori High—Eeek!
......!
—Kid, what are you doin'!? Hurry! Shut it off!
SAYA-CHIN...
...AW CRAP...
GOOD GRIEF!

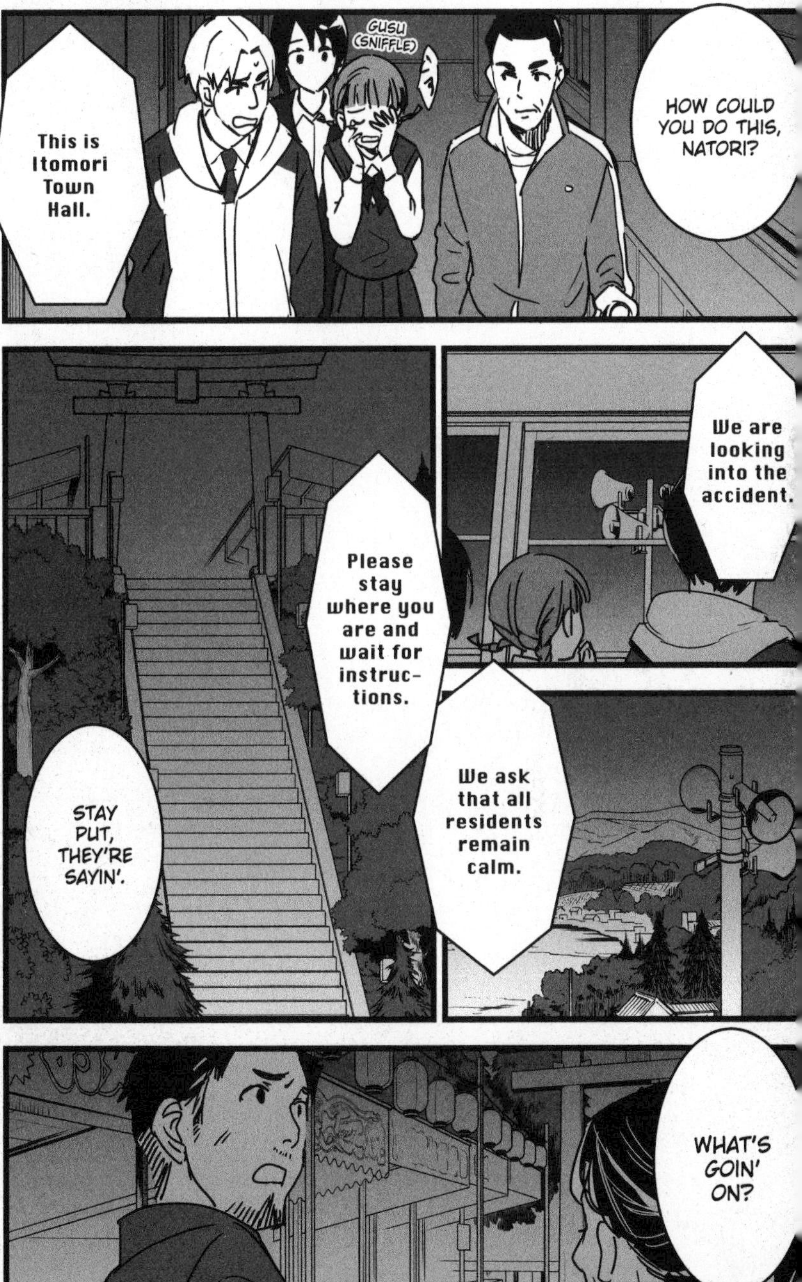
HOW COULD YOU DO THIS, NATORI?
GUSU (SNIFFLE)
This is Itomori Town Hall.
We are looking into the accident.
Please stay where you are and wait for instructions.
We ask that all residents remain calm.
STAY PUT, THEY'RE SAYIN'.
WHAT'S GOIN' ON?

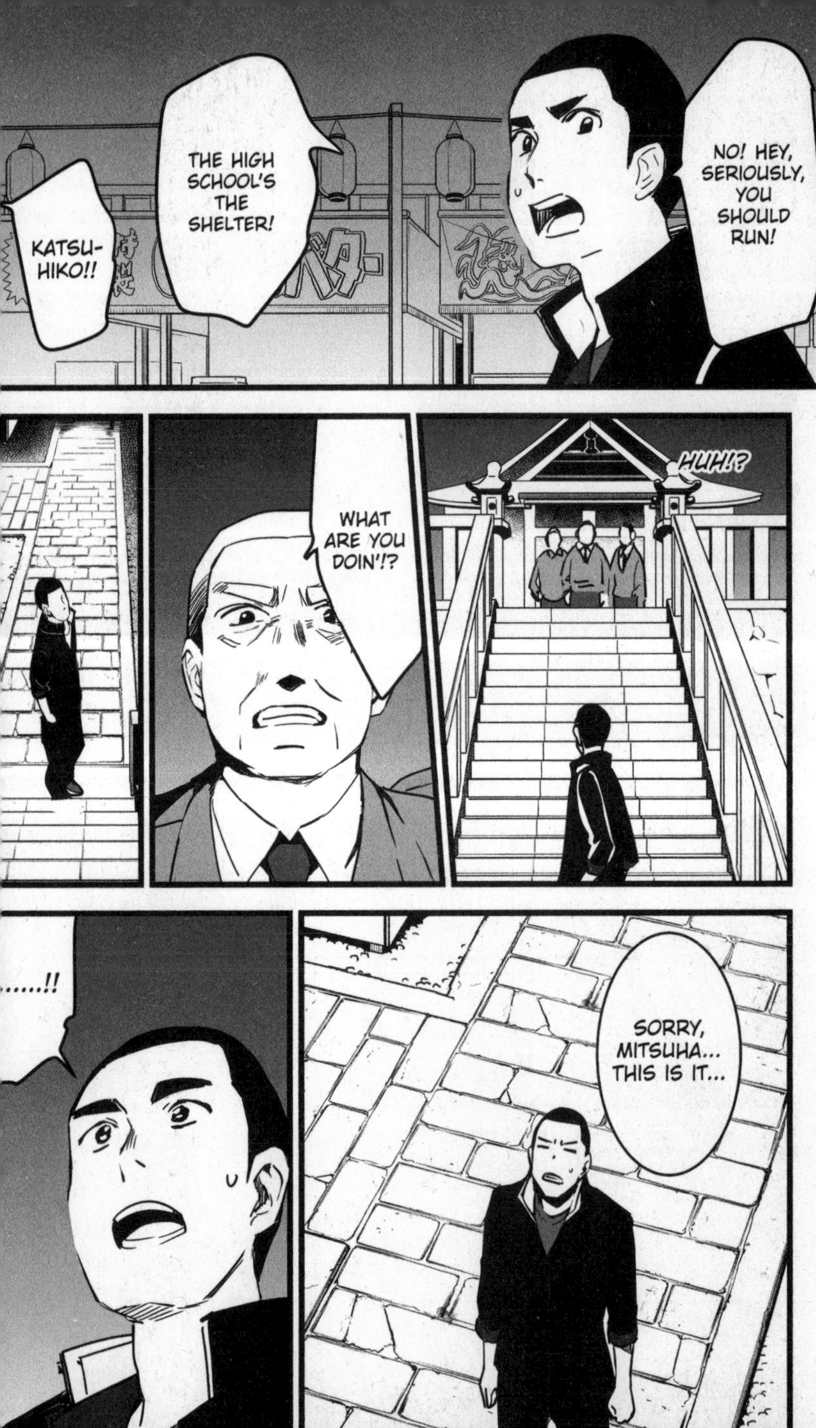
NO! HEY, SERIOUSLY, YOU SHOULD RUN!
THE HIGH SCHOOL'S THE SHELTER!
KATSU-HIKO!!
HUH!?
WHAT ARE YOU DOIN'!?
SORRY, MITSUHA... THIS IS IT...
......!!

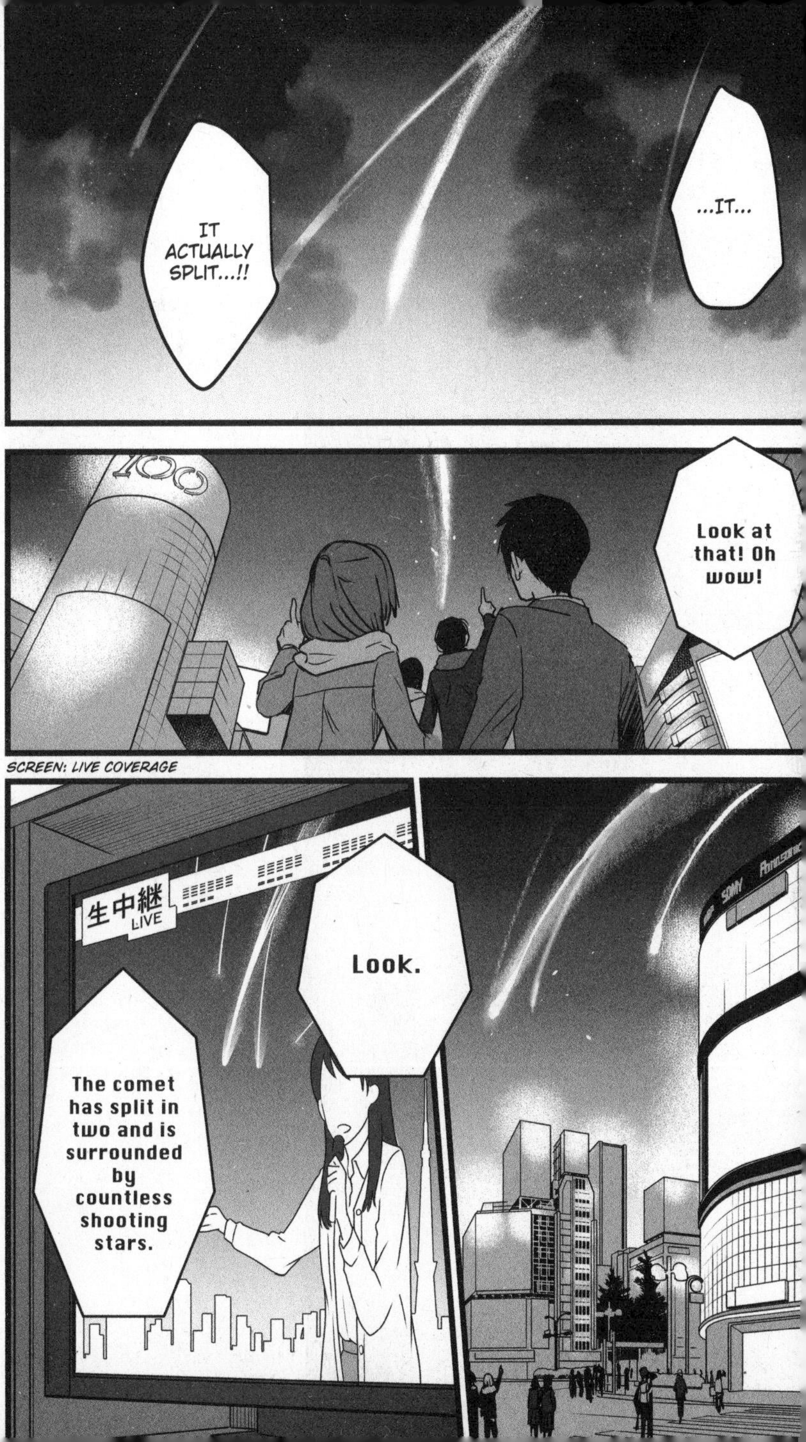

...IT...
IT ACTUALLY SPLIT...!!
Look at that! Oh wow!
SCREEN: LIVE COVERAGE
生中継
LIVE
Look.
The comet has split in two and is surrounded by countless shooting stars.

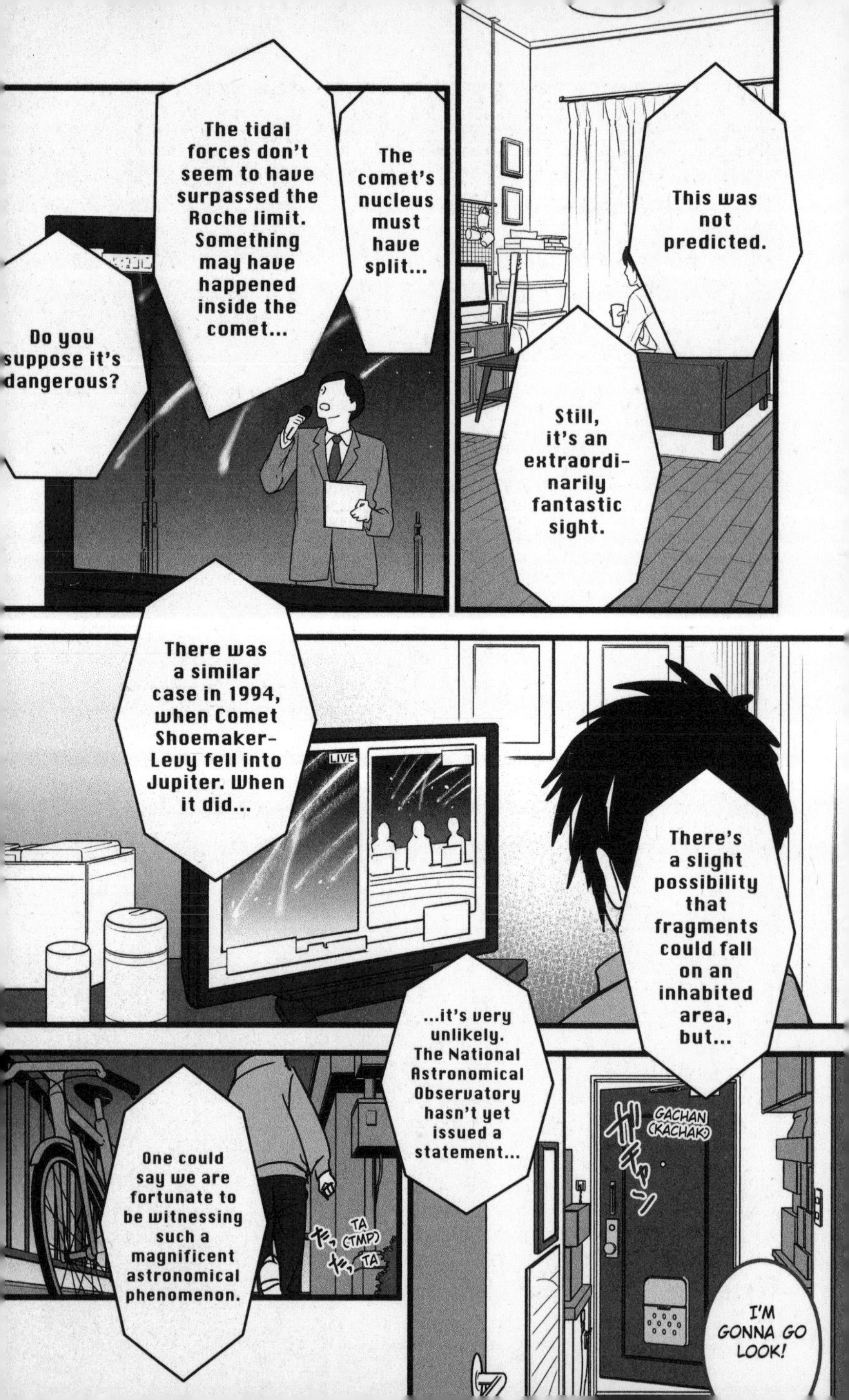
This was not predicted.
Still, it's an extraordinarily fantastic sight.
The comet's nucleus must have split...
The tidal forces don't seem to have surpassed the Roche limit. Something may have happened inside the comet...
Do you suppose it's dangerous?
There was a similar case in 1994, when Comet Shoemaker-Levy fell into Jupiter. When it did...
LIVE
There's a slight possibility that fragments could fall on an inhabited area, but...
...it's very unlikely. The National Astronomical Observatory hasn't yet issued a statement...
GACHAN (KACHAK)
I'M GONNA GO LOOK!
One could say we are fortunate to be witnessing such a magnificent astronomical phenomenon.
TA (TMP) TA

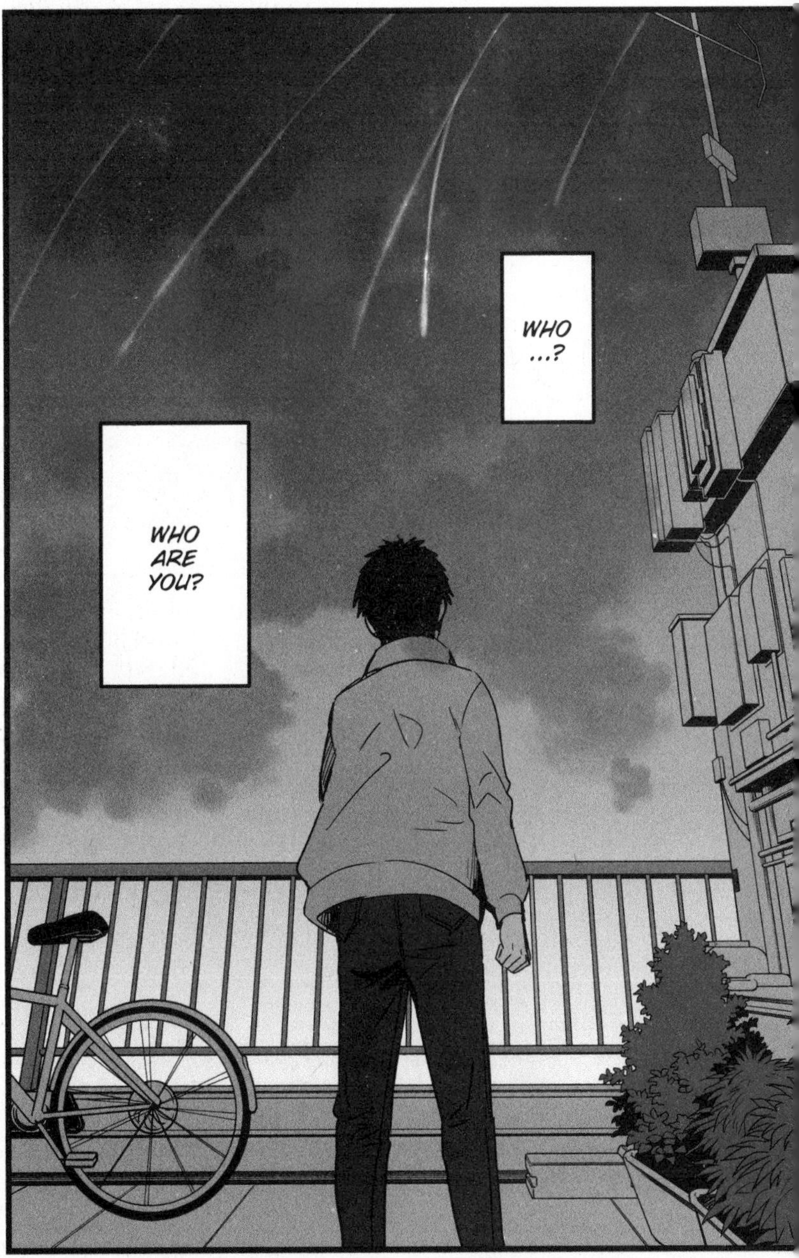
WHO ...?
WHO ARE YOU?

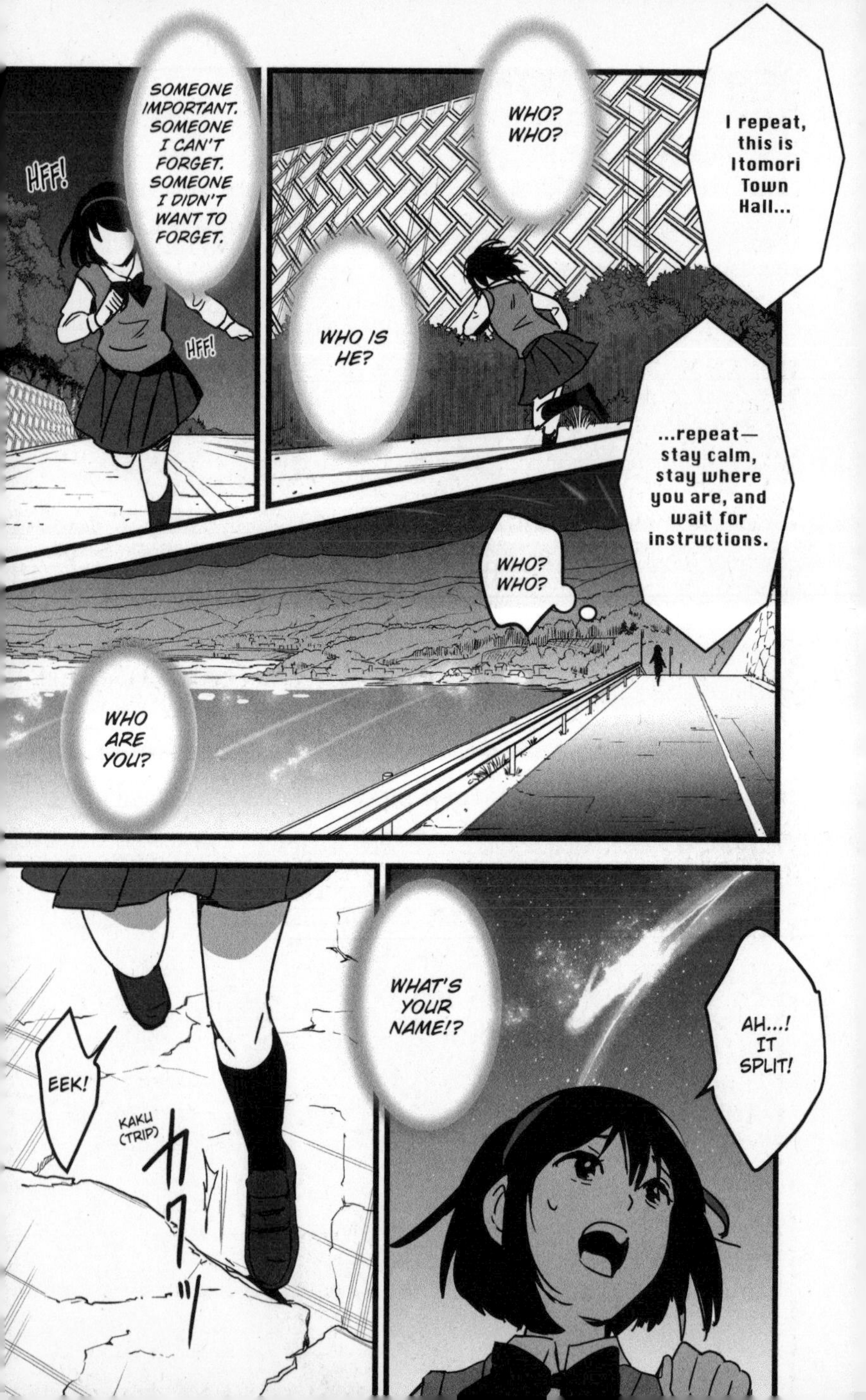
I repeat, this is Itomori Town Hall...
WHO? WHO?
WHO IS HE?
SOMEONE IMPORTANT. SOMEONE I CAN'T FORGET. SOMEONE I DIDN'T WANT TO FORGET.
HFF!
HFF!
...repeat—stay calm, stay where you are, and wait for instructions.
WHO? WHO?
WHO ARE YOU?
AH...! IT SPLIT!
WHAT'S YOUR NAME!?
EEK!
KAKU (TRIP)
カクッ

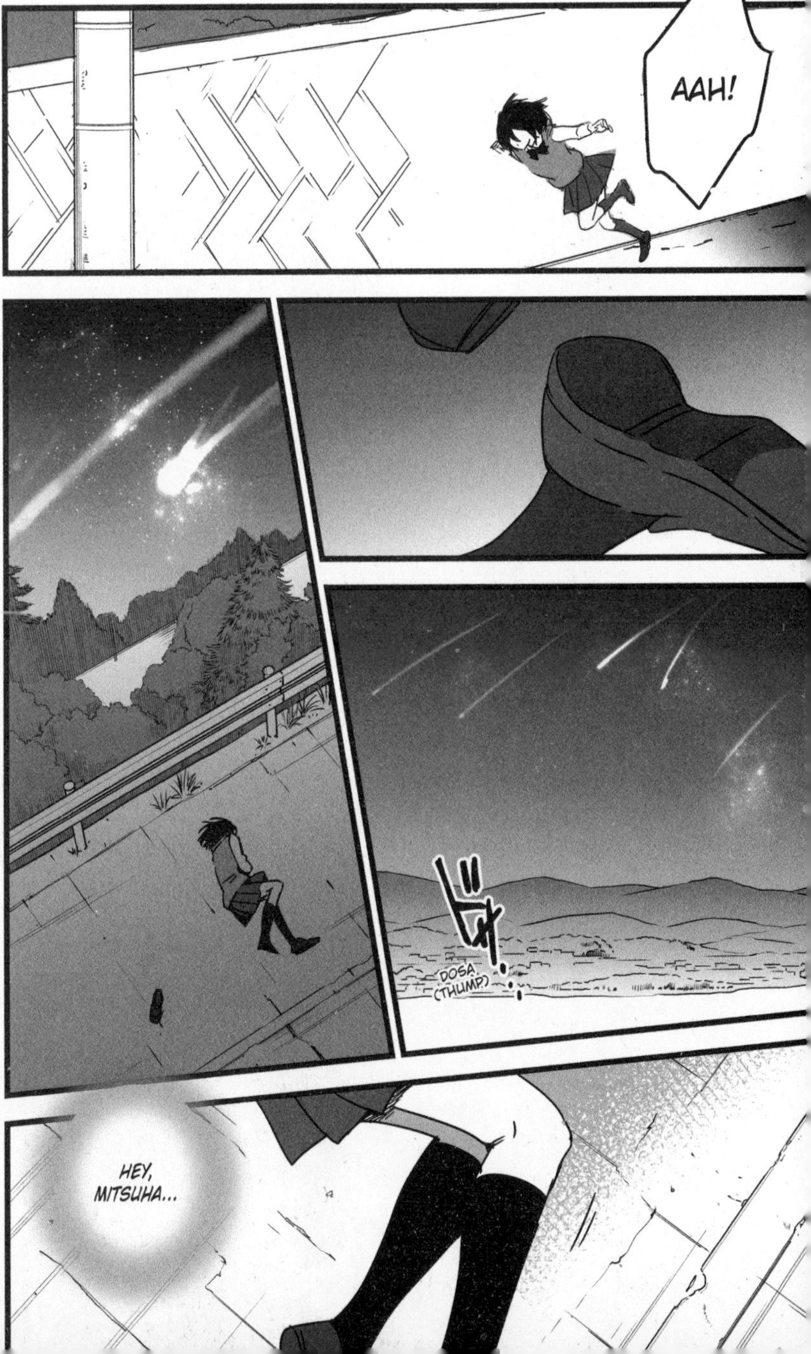
AAH!
DOSA (THUMP)
HEY, MITSUHA...

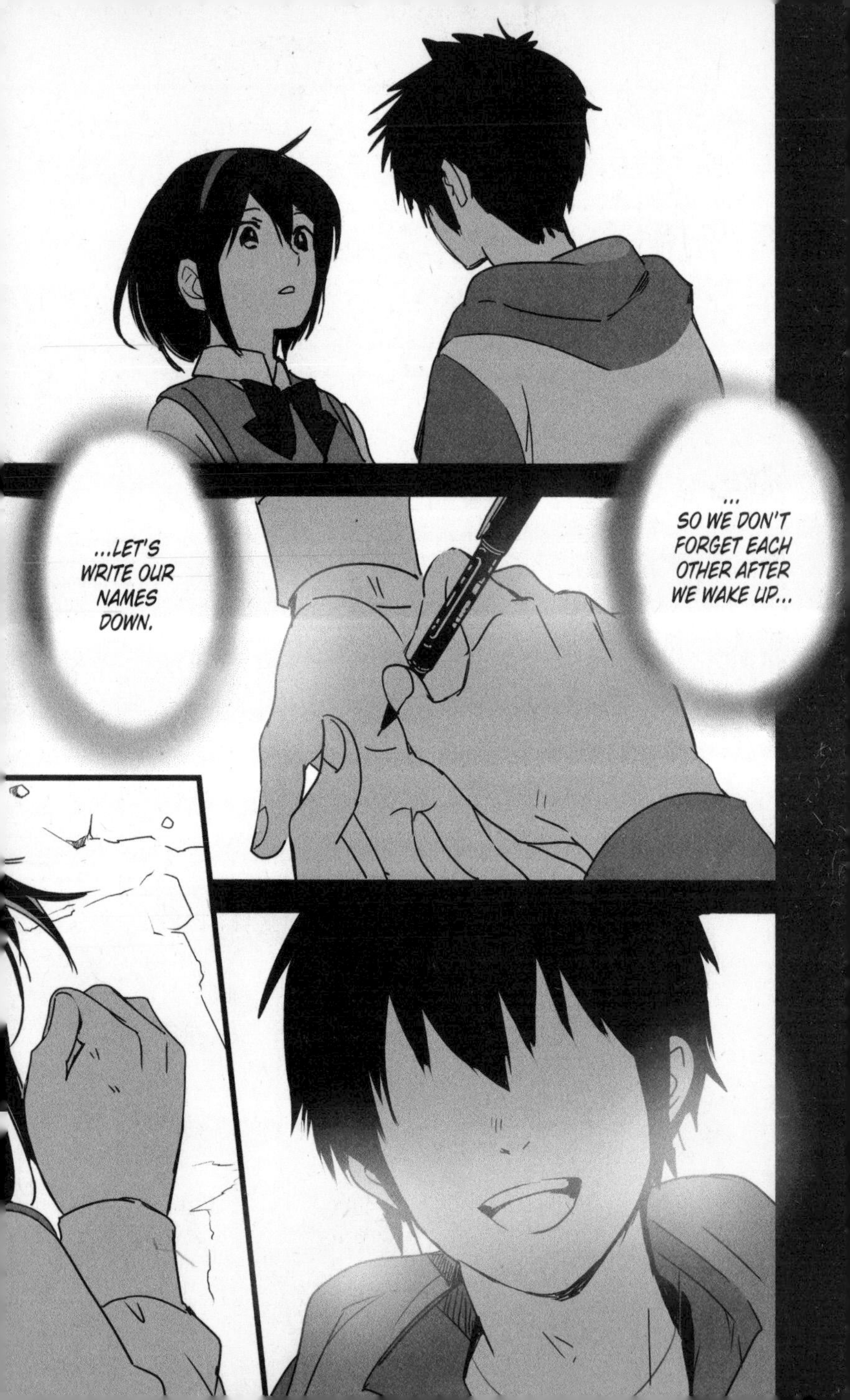
... SO WE DON'T FORGET EACH OTHER AFTER WE WAKE UP...
...LET'S WRITE OUR NAMES DOWN.

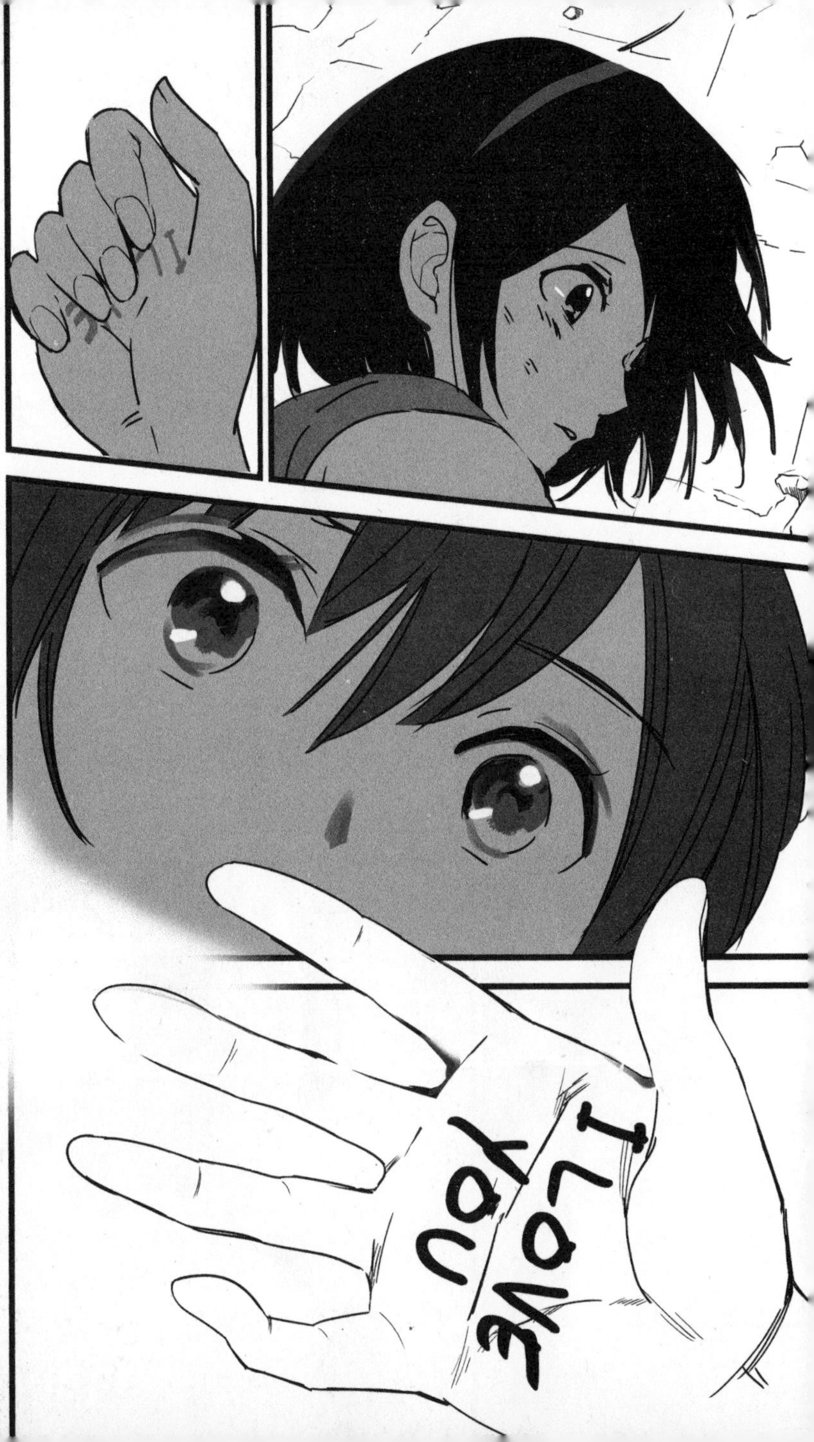
I LOVE YOU

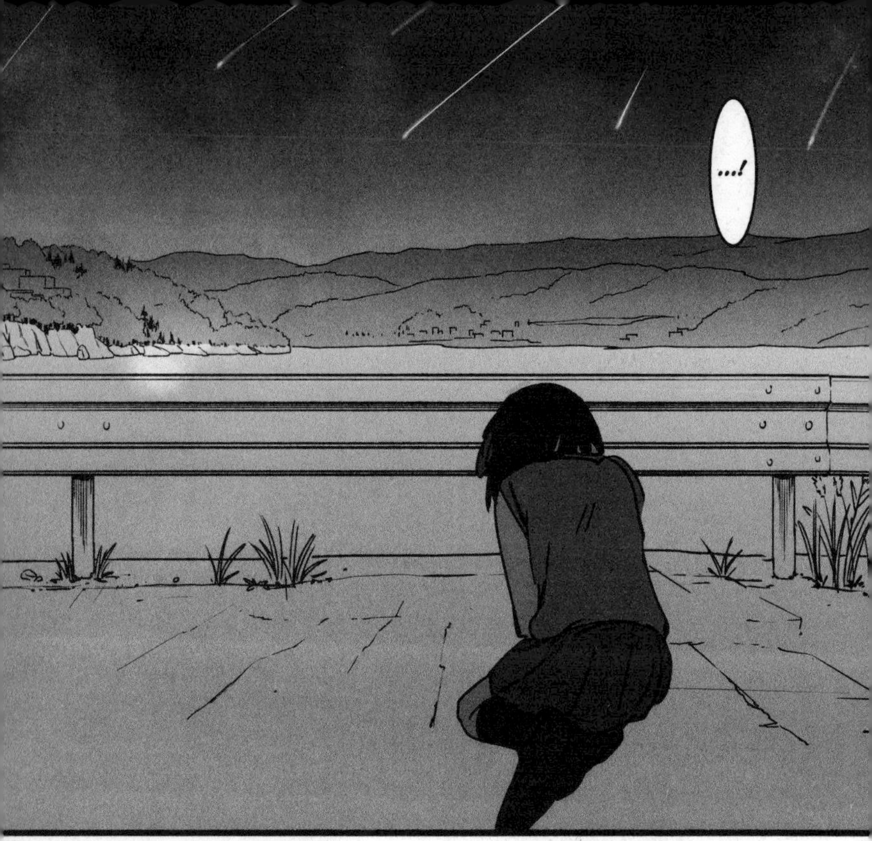
...!

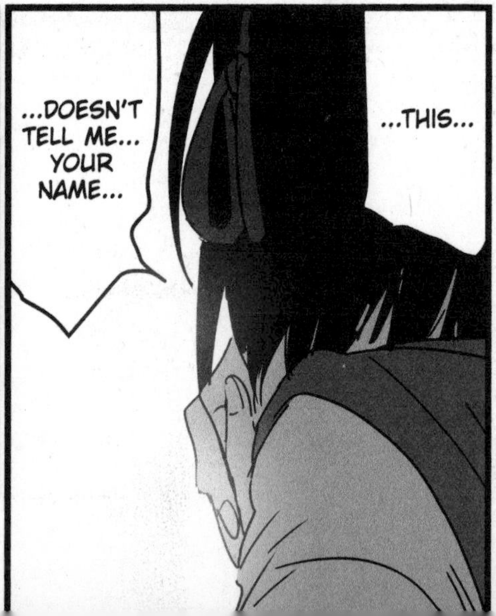
...THIS...
...DOESN'T TELL ME... YOUR NAME...

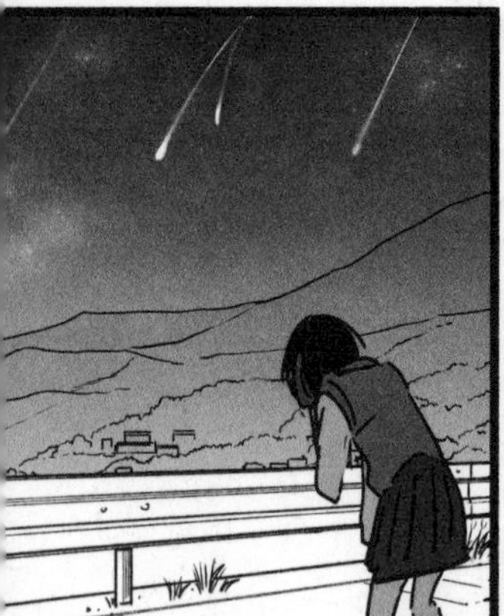

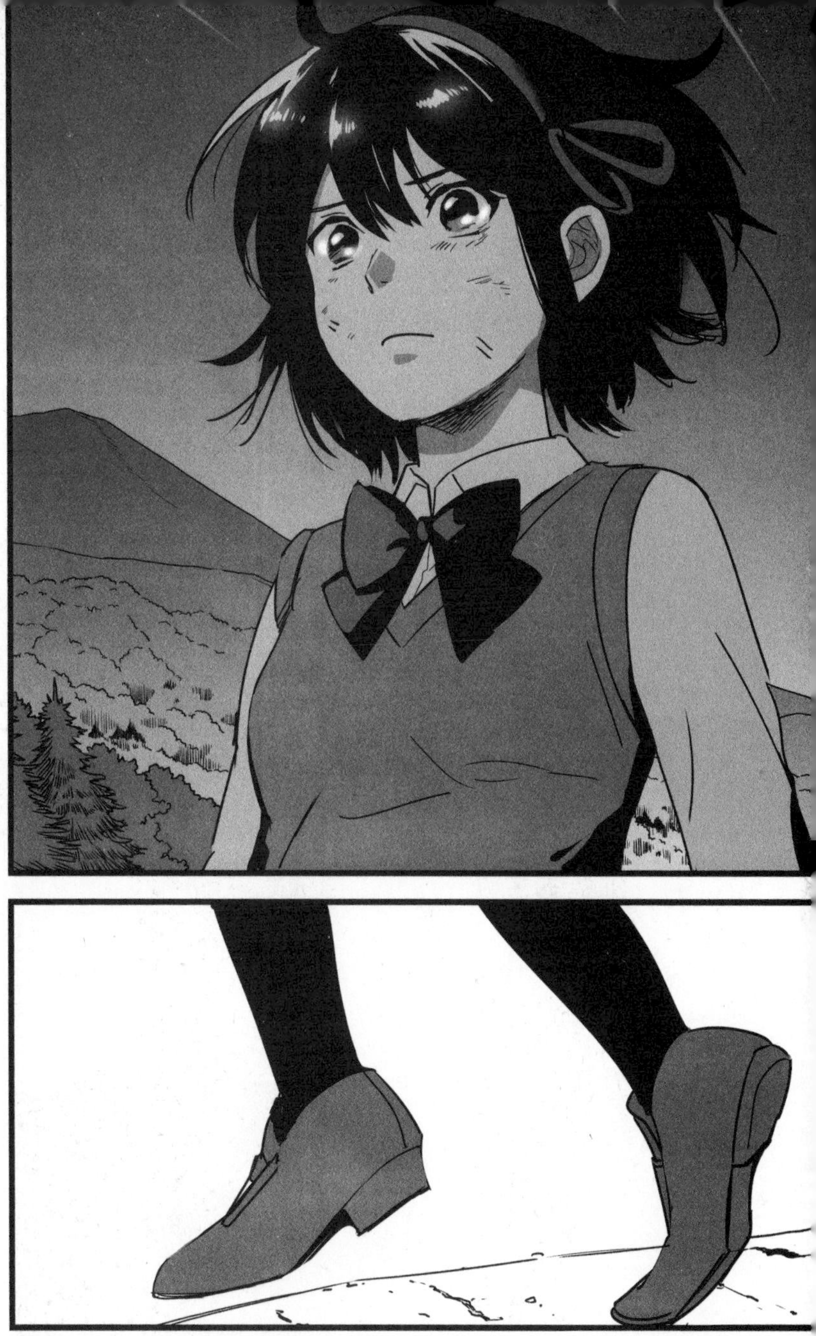

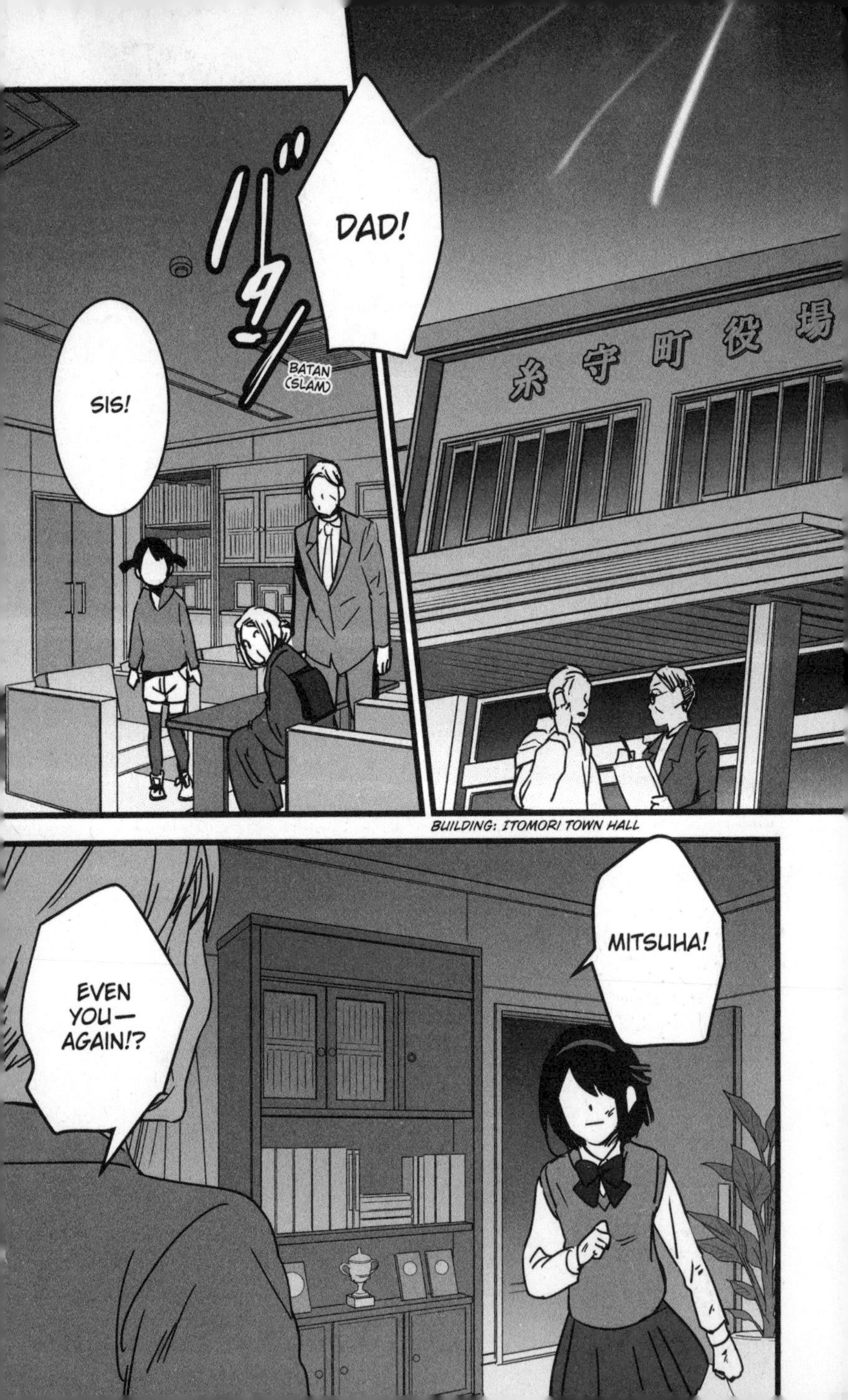
糸守町役場
BUILDING: ITOMORI TOWN HALL
DAD!
バタン
BATAN (SLAM)
SIS!
MITSUHA!
EVEN YOU—AGAIN!?

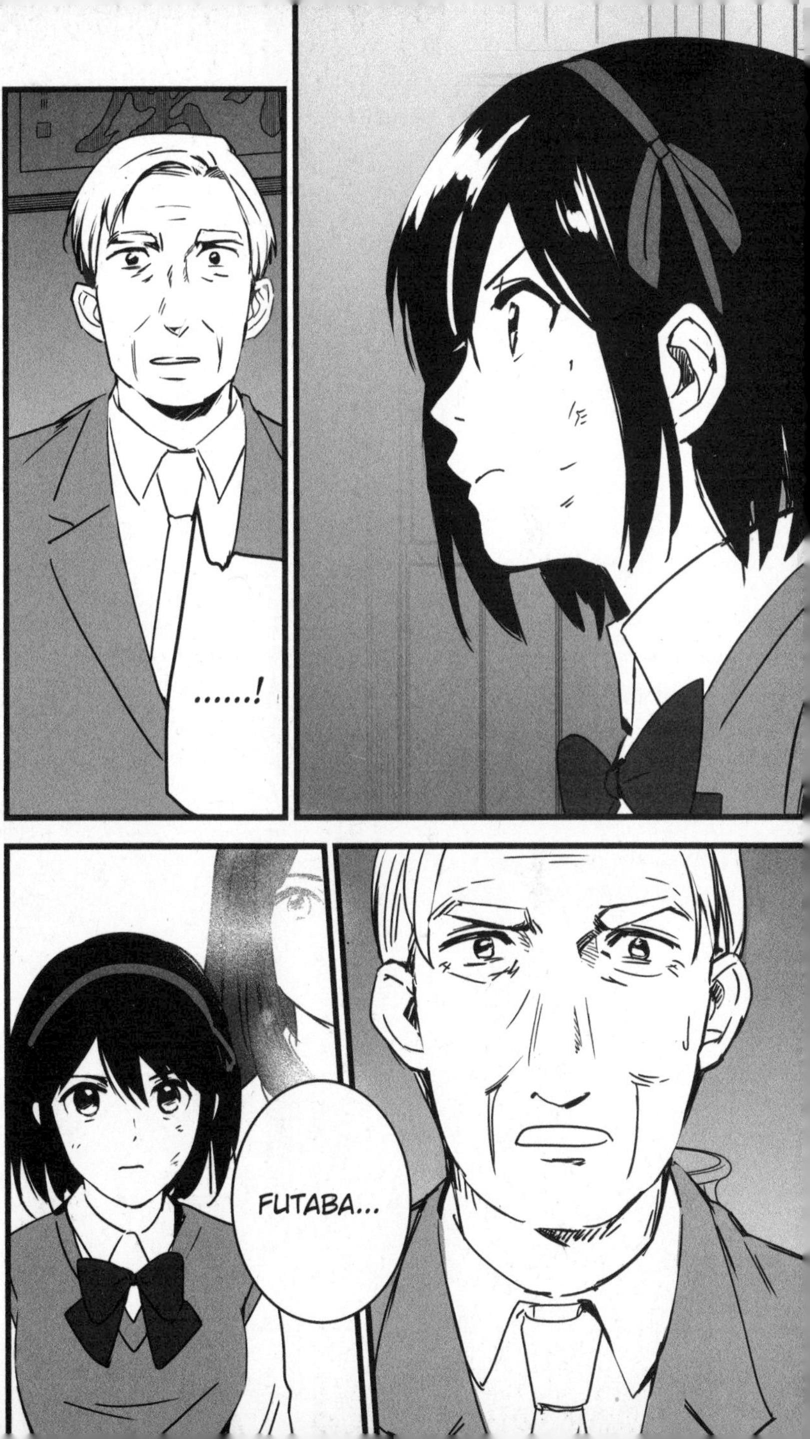
......!
FUTABA...

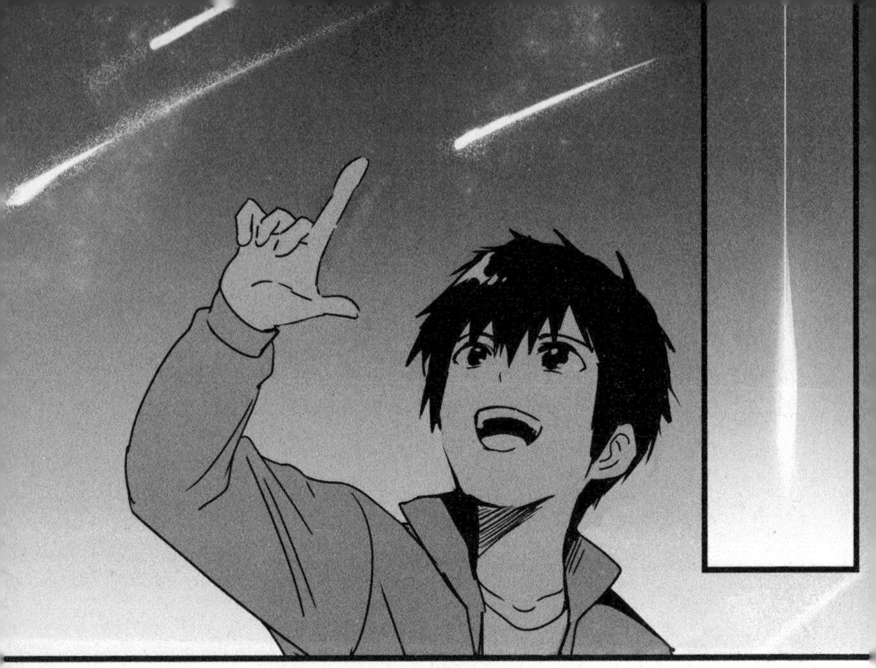
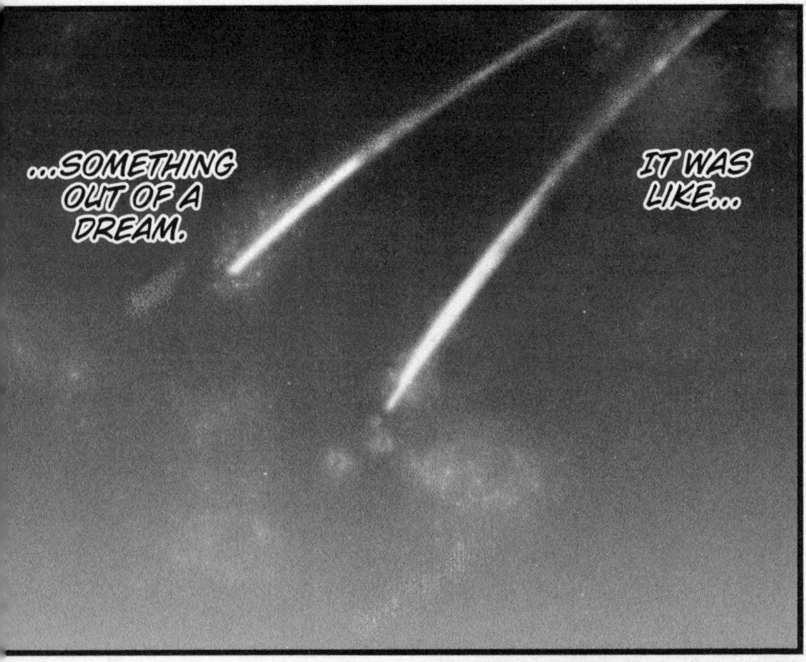
IT WAS LIKE...
...SOMETHING OUT OF A DREAM.

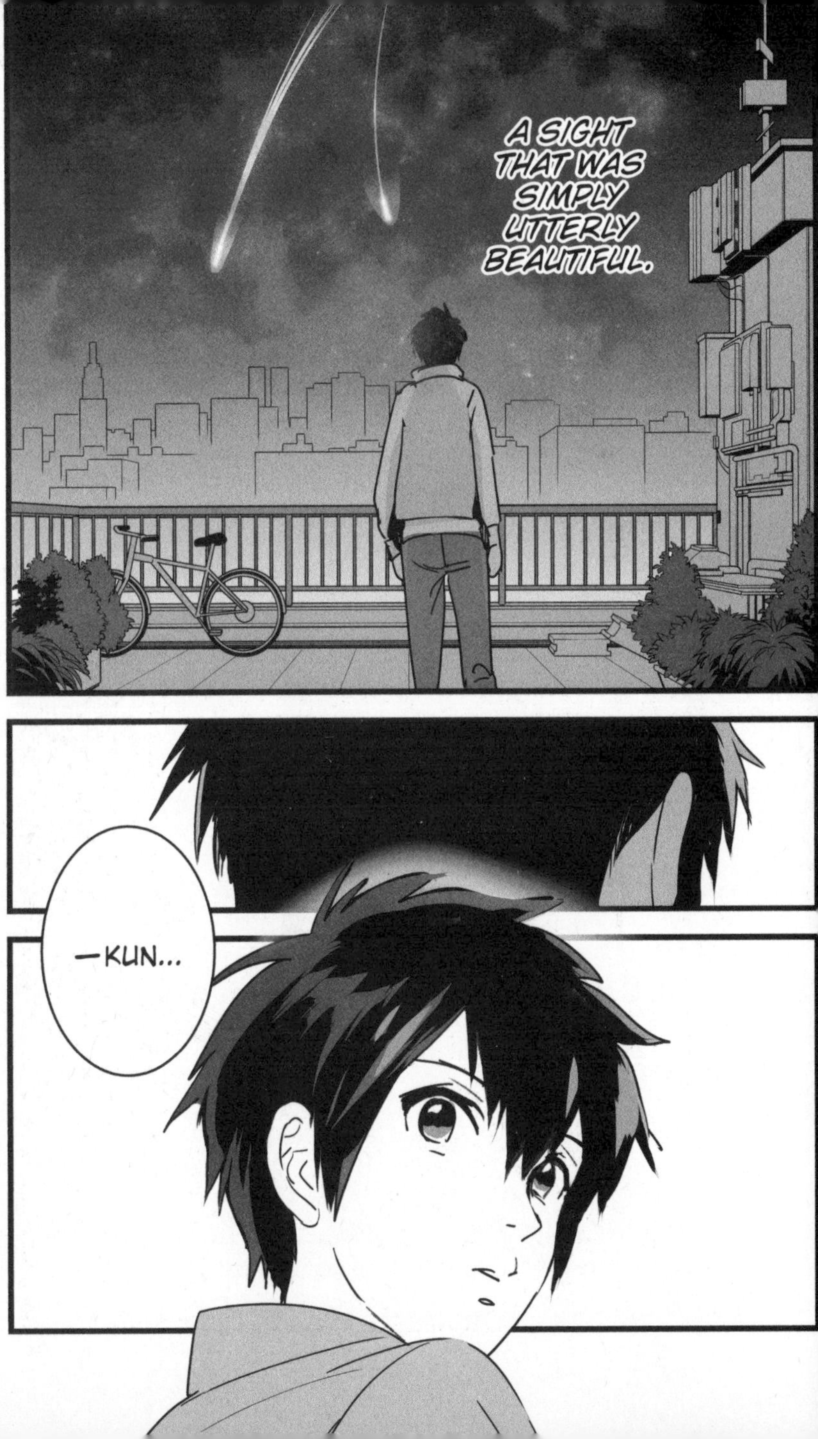
A SIGHT THAT WAS SIMPLY UTTERLY BEAUTIFUL.
—KUN...

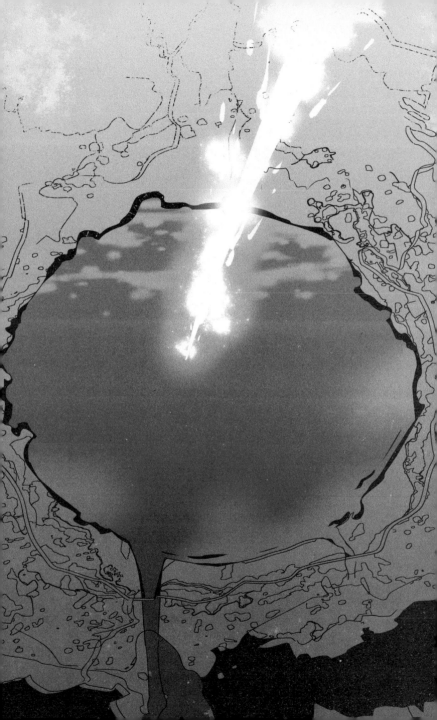

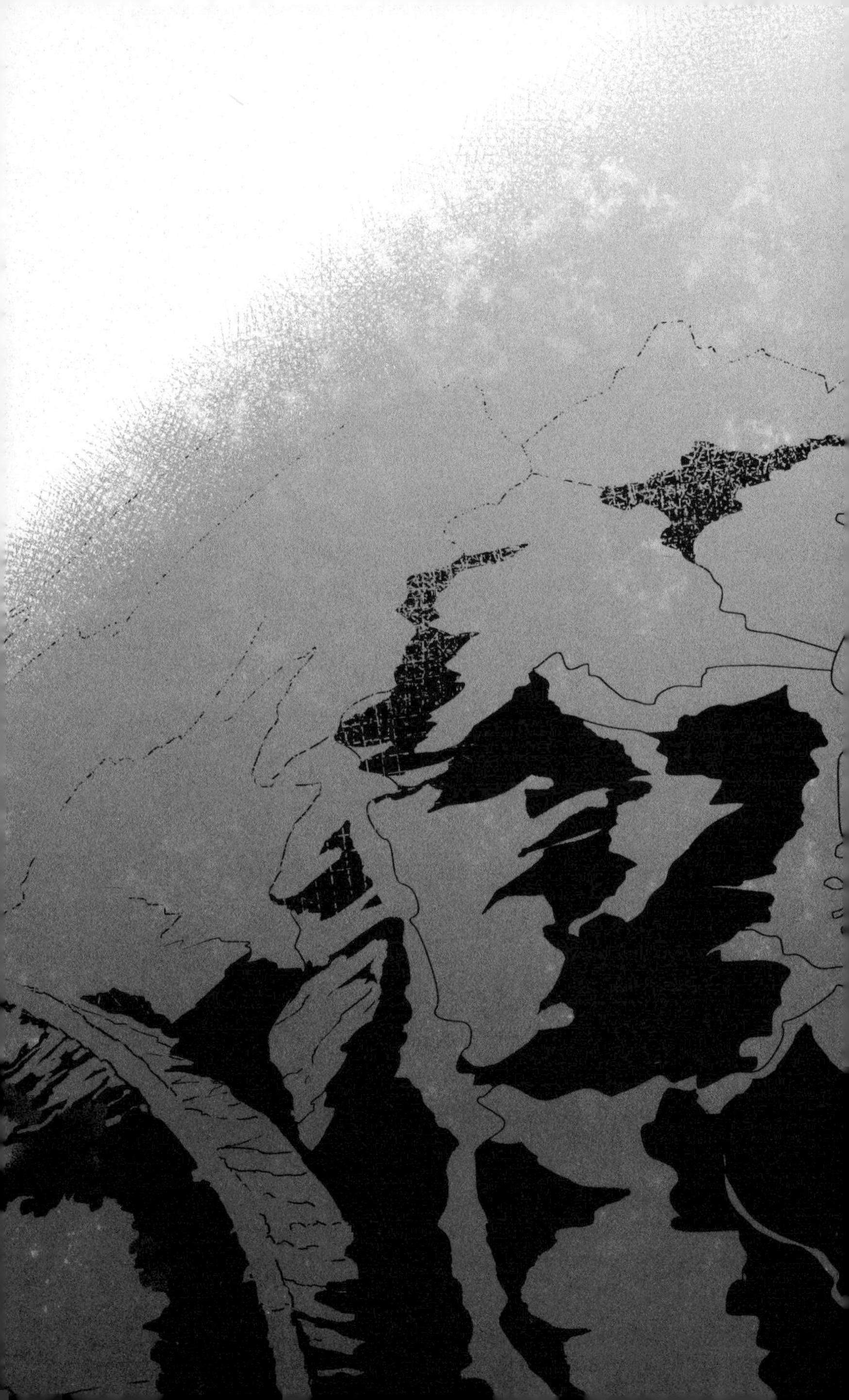

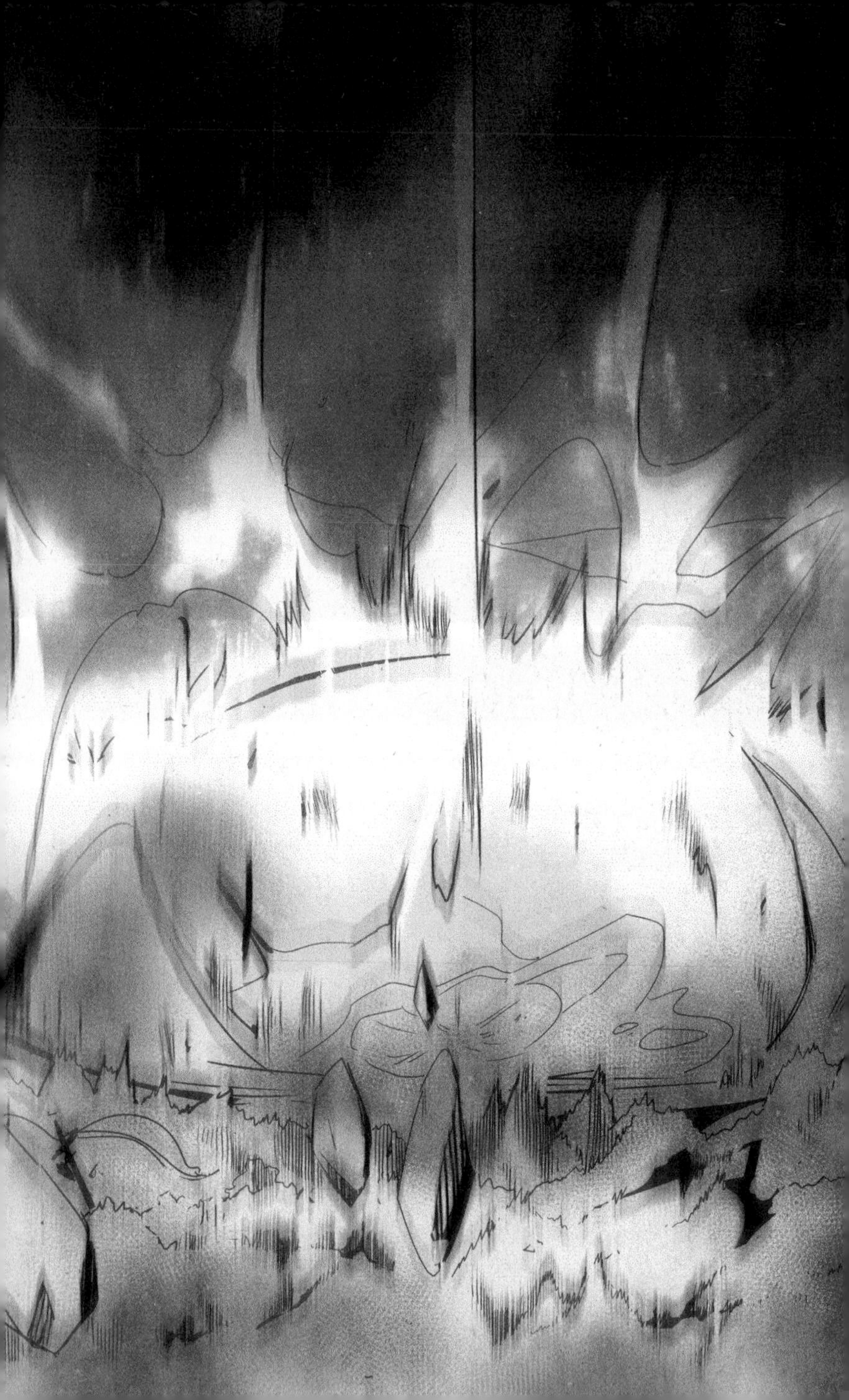

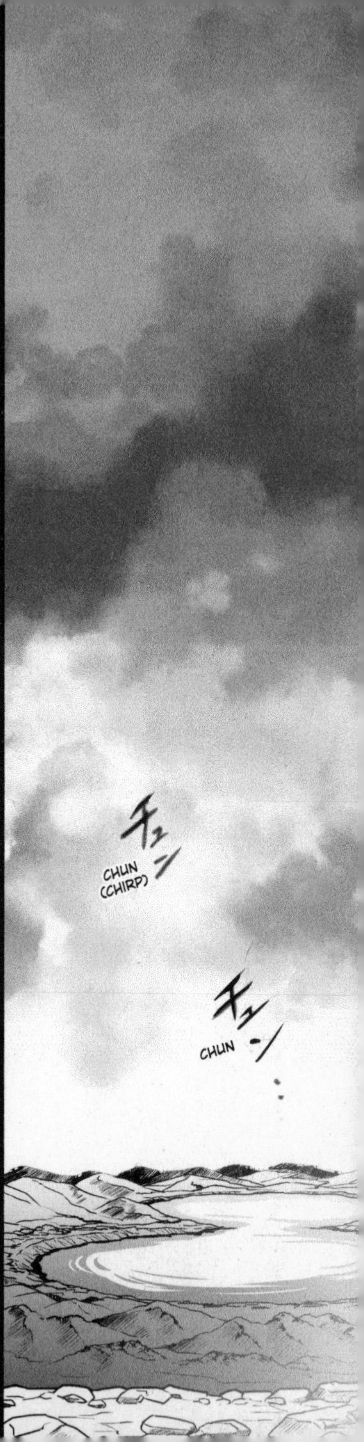
チュン
CHUN (CHIRP)
チュン
CHUN
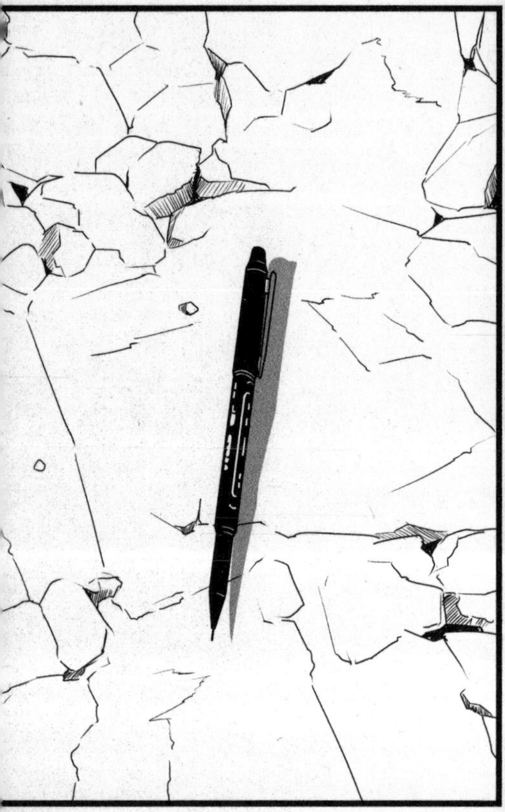
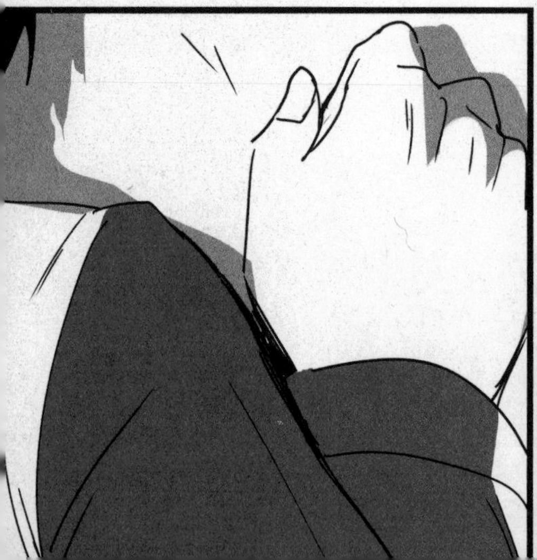

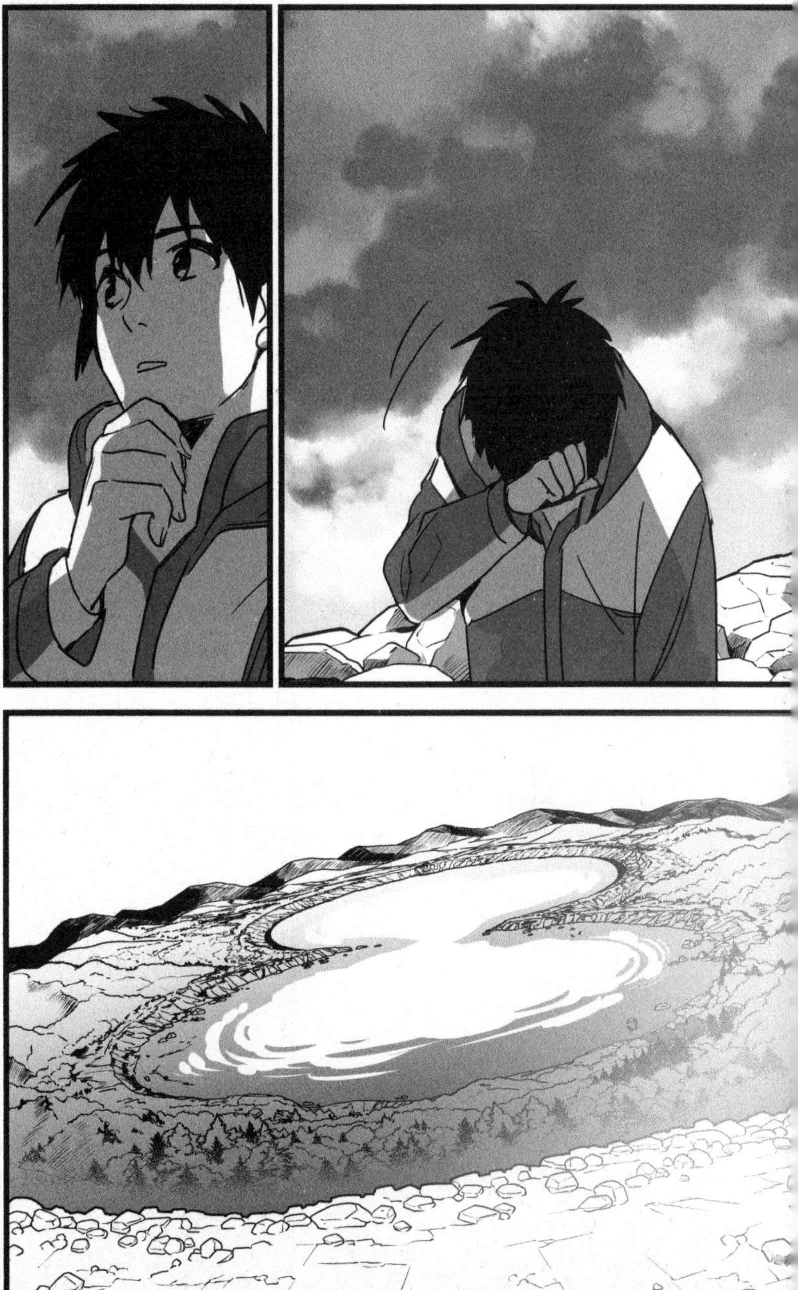

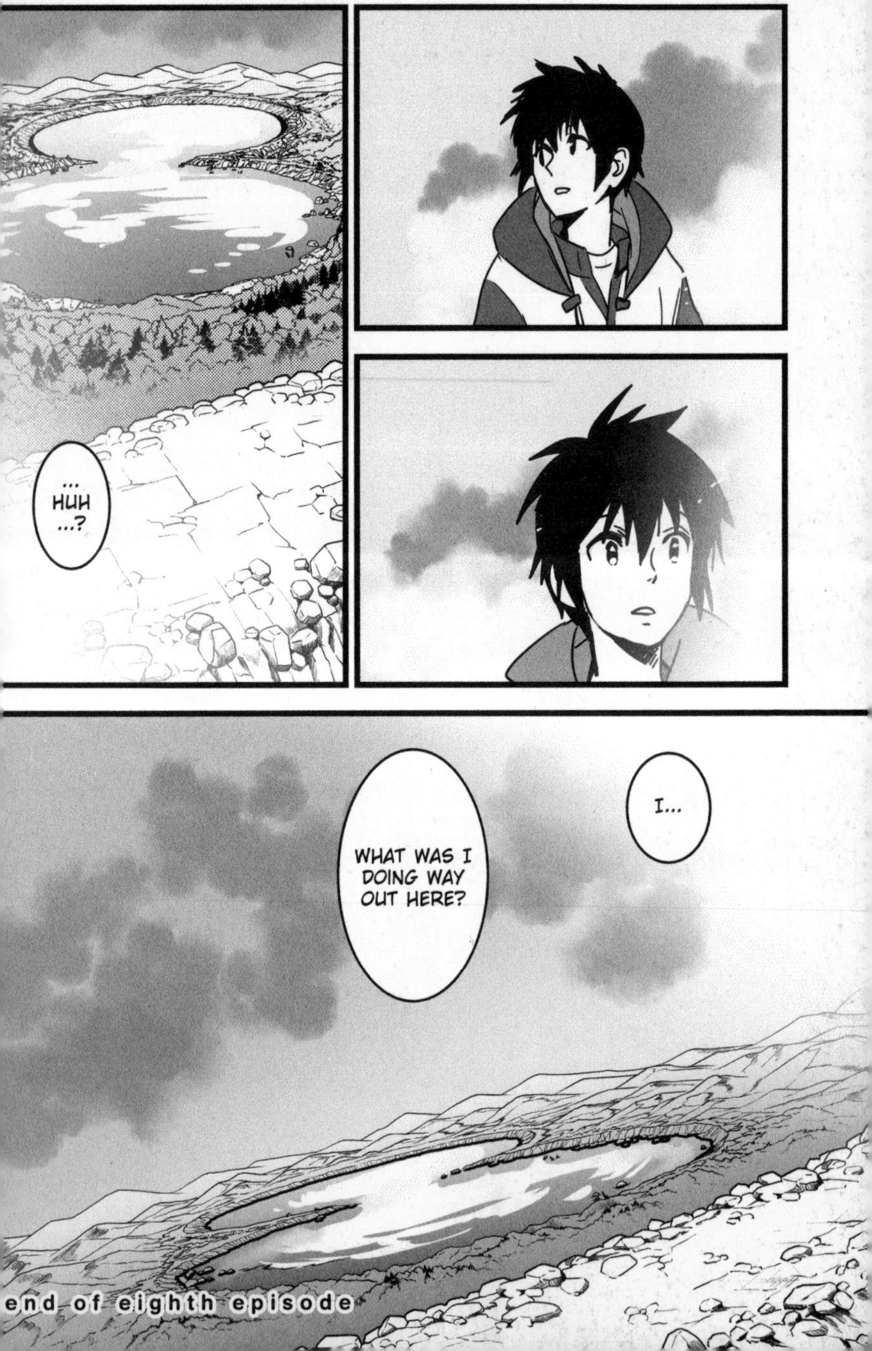
...HUH...?
I...
WHAT WAS I DOING WAY OUT HERE?
end of eighth episode

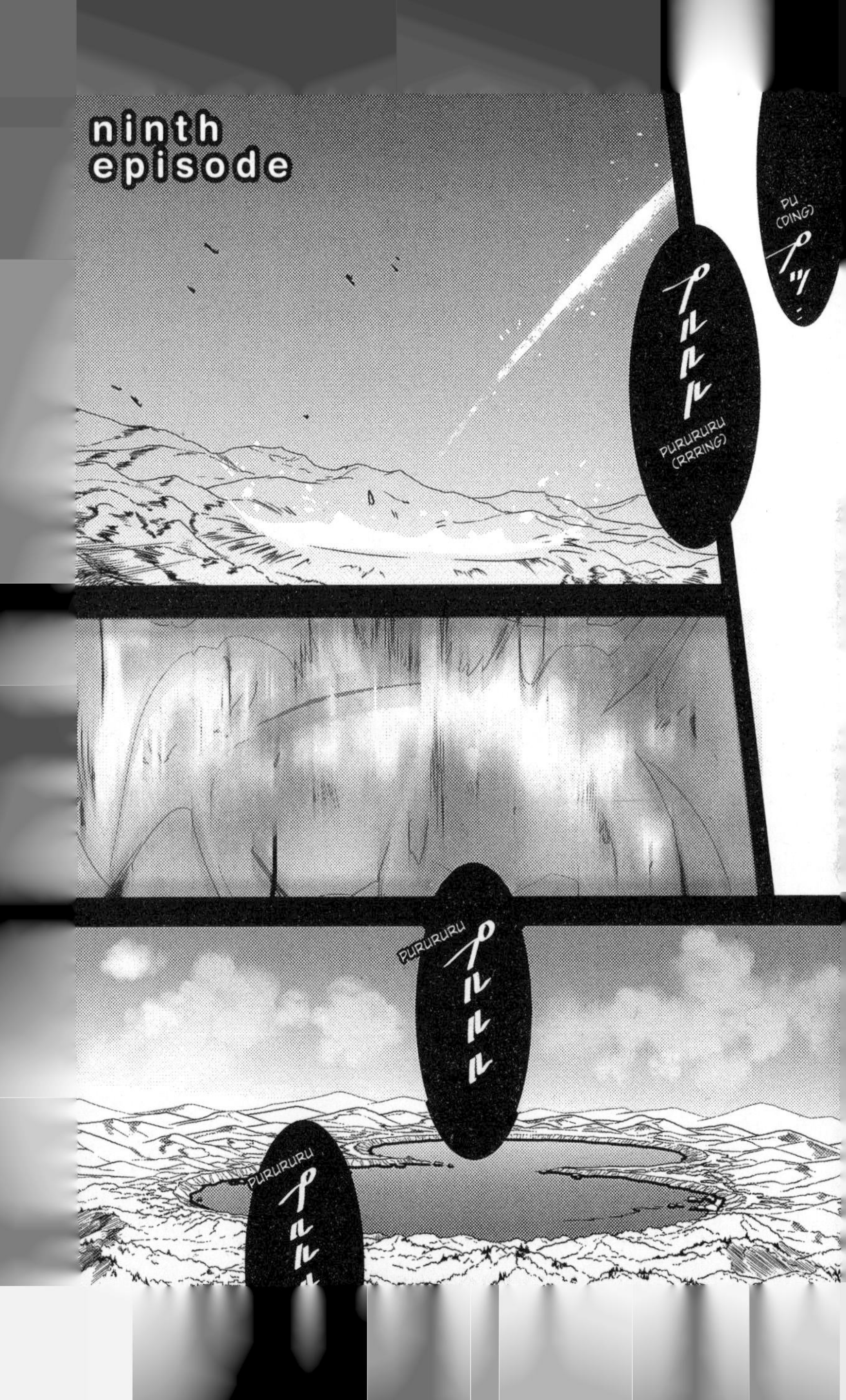
ninth episode
パッ
PU (DING)
プルルル
PURURURU (RRRING)
プルルル
PURURURU
プルルル
PURURURU

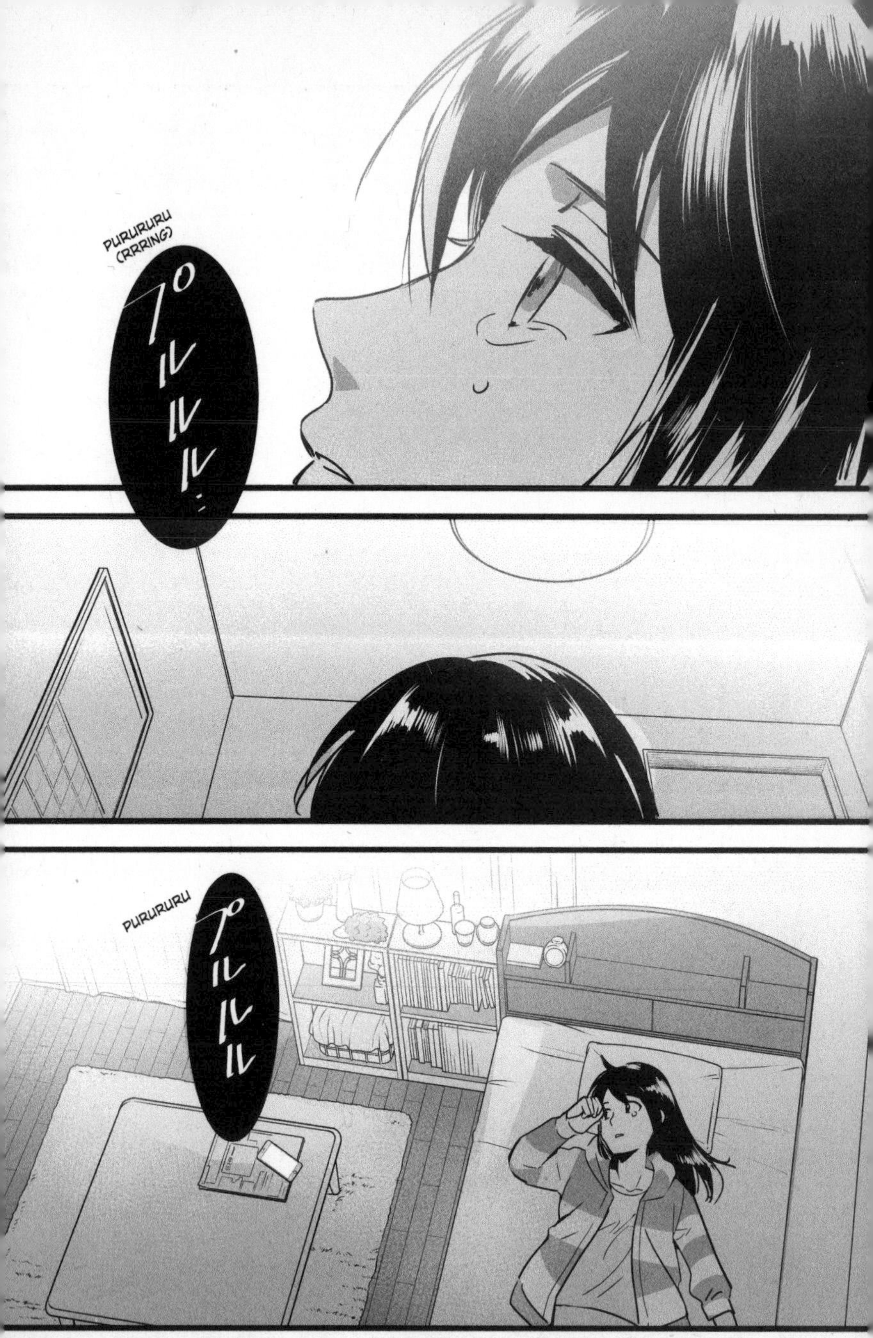
PURURURU (RRRING)
プルルル…
PURURURU
プルルル

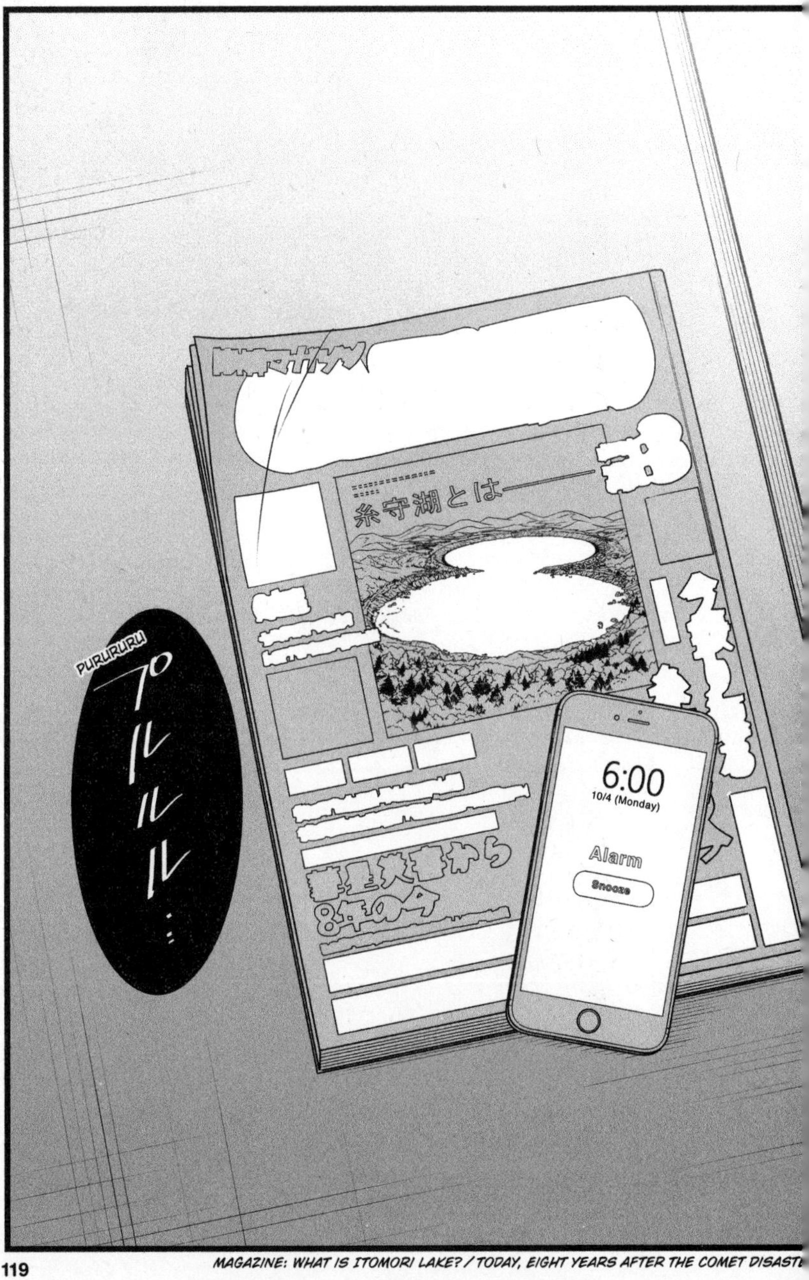
糸守湖とは——
彗星災害から
8年の今
6:00
10/4 (Monday)
Alarm
Snooze
PURURURU
プルルル…

MAGAZINE: WHAT IS ITOMORI LAKE? / TODAY, EIGHT YEARS AFTER THE COMET DISASTE

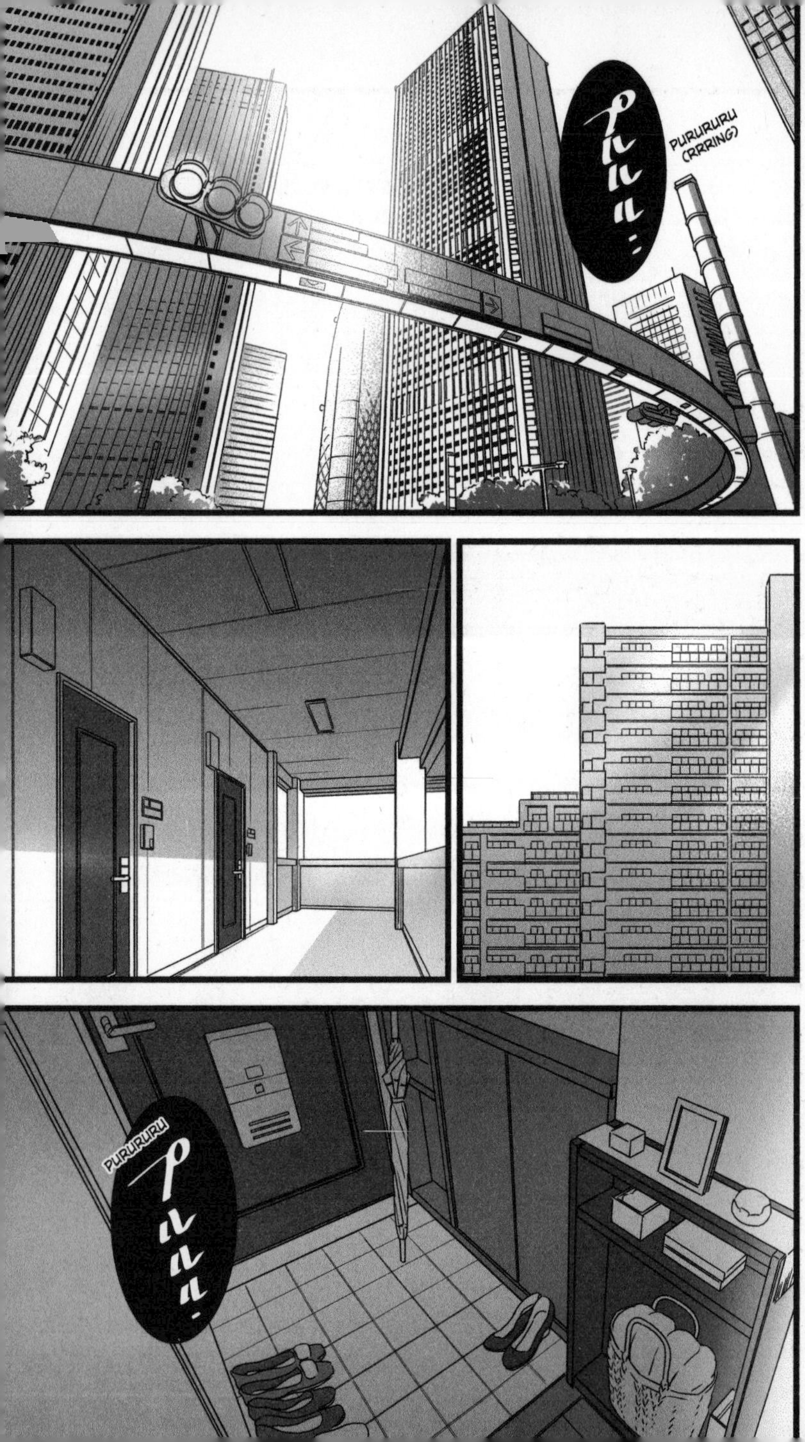
プルルル…
PURURURU (RRRING)
PURURURU
プルルル…

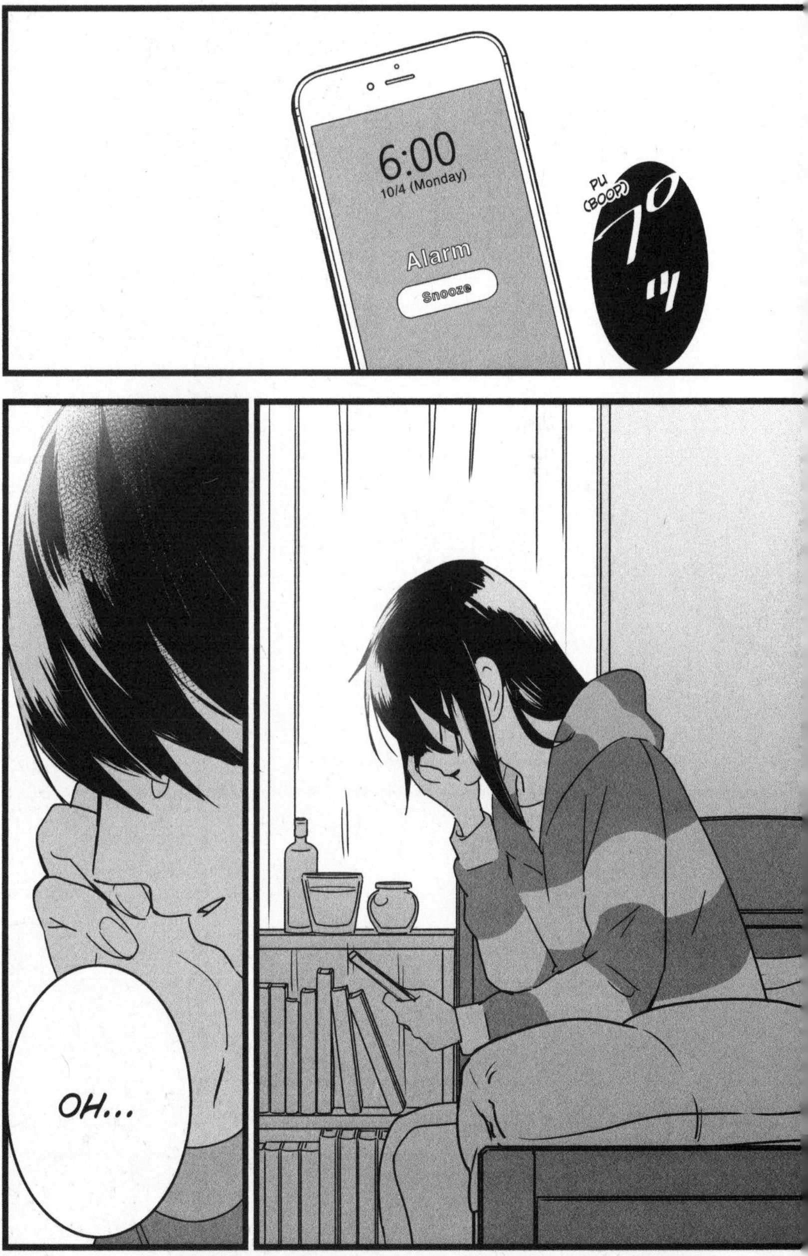
6:00
10/4 (Monday)
Alarm
Snooze
PU (BOOP)
プッ
OH...

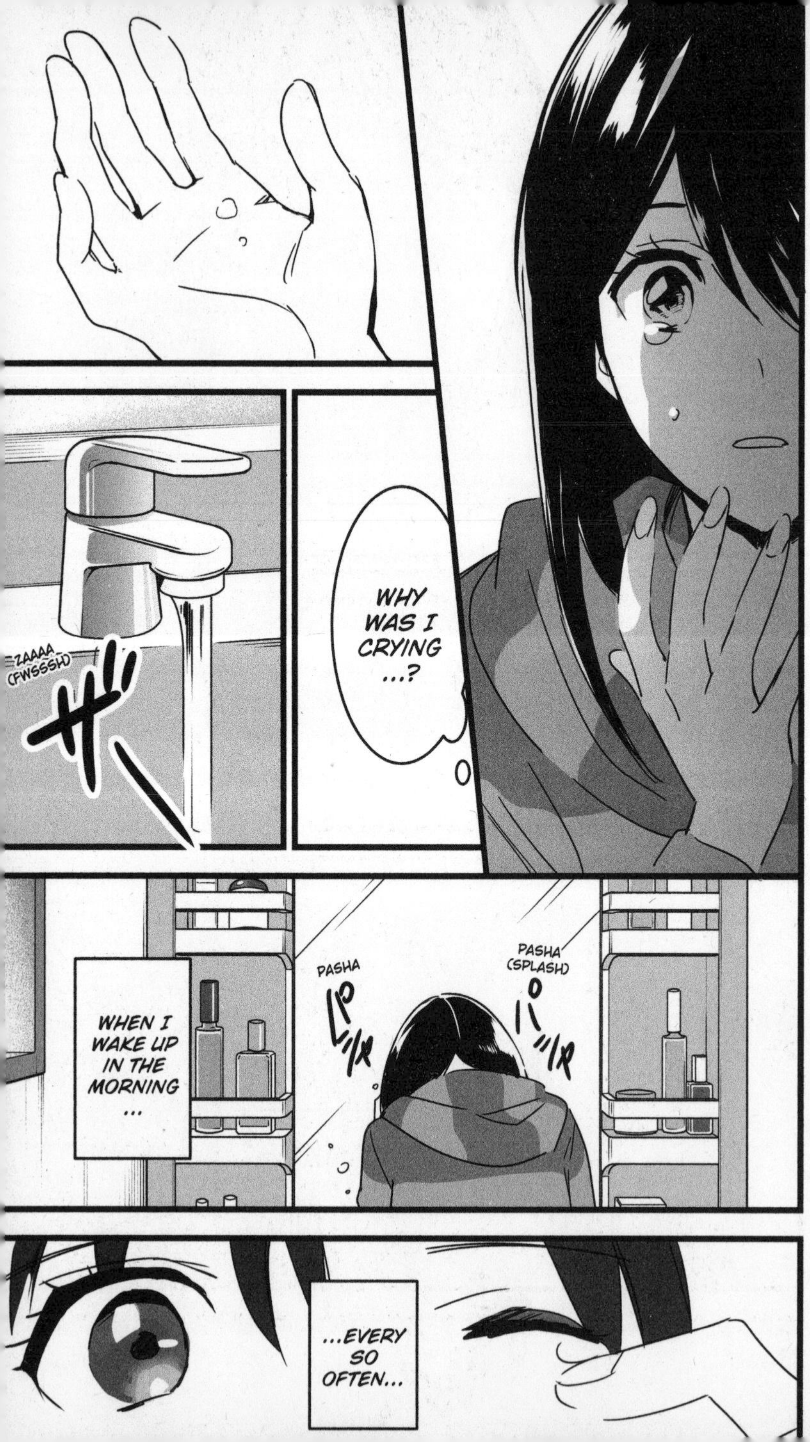
WHY WAS I CRYING ...?
ZAAAA (FWSSSH)
PASHA (SPLASH)
PASHA
WHEN I WAKE UP IN THE MORNING ...
...EVERY SO OFTEN...

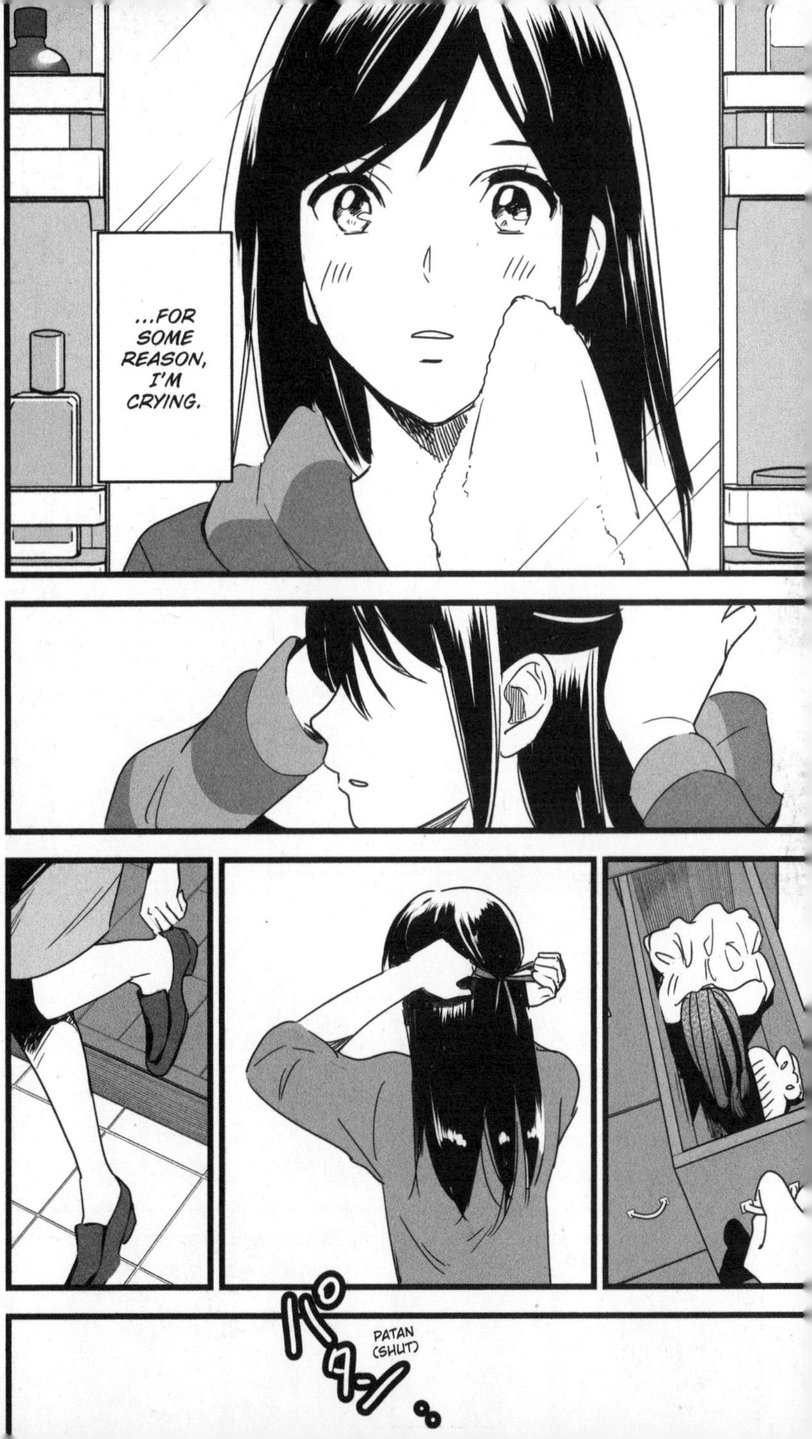
...FOR SOME REASON, I'M CRYING.
PATAN (SHUT)

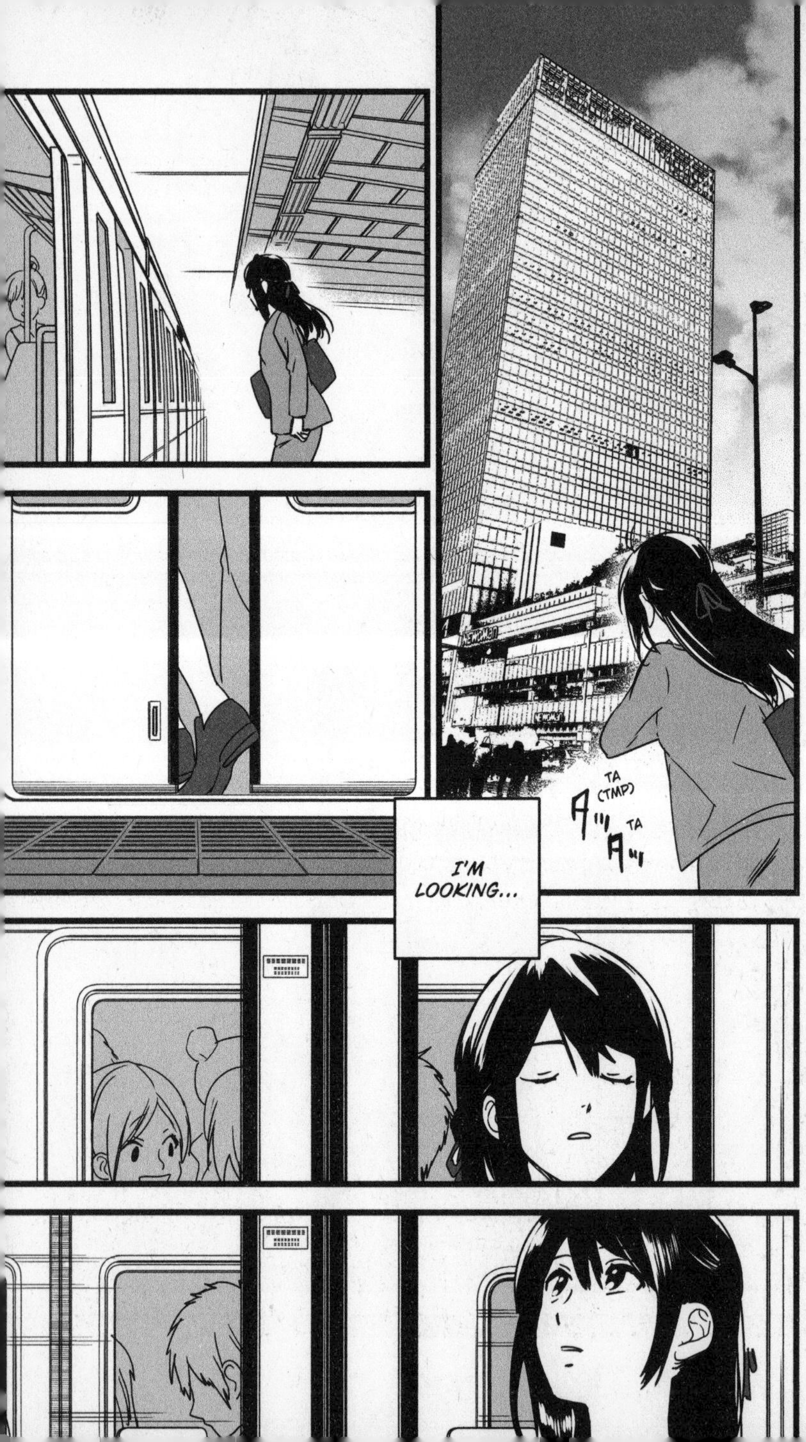
TA (TMP)
TA
I'M LOOKING...

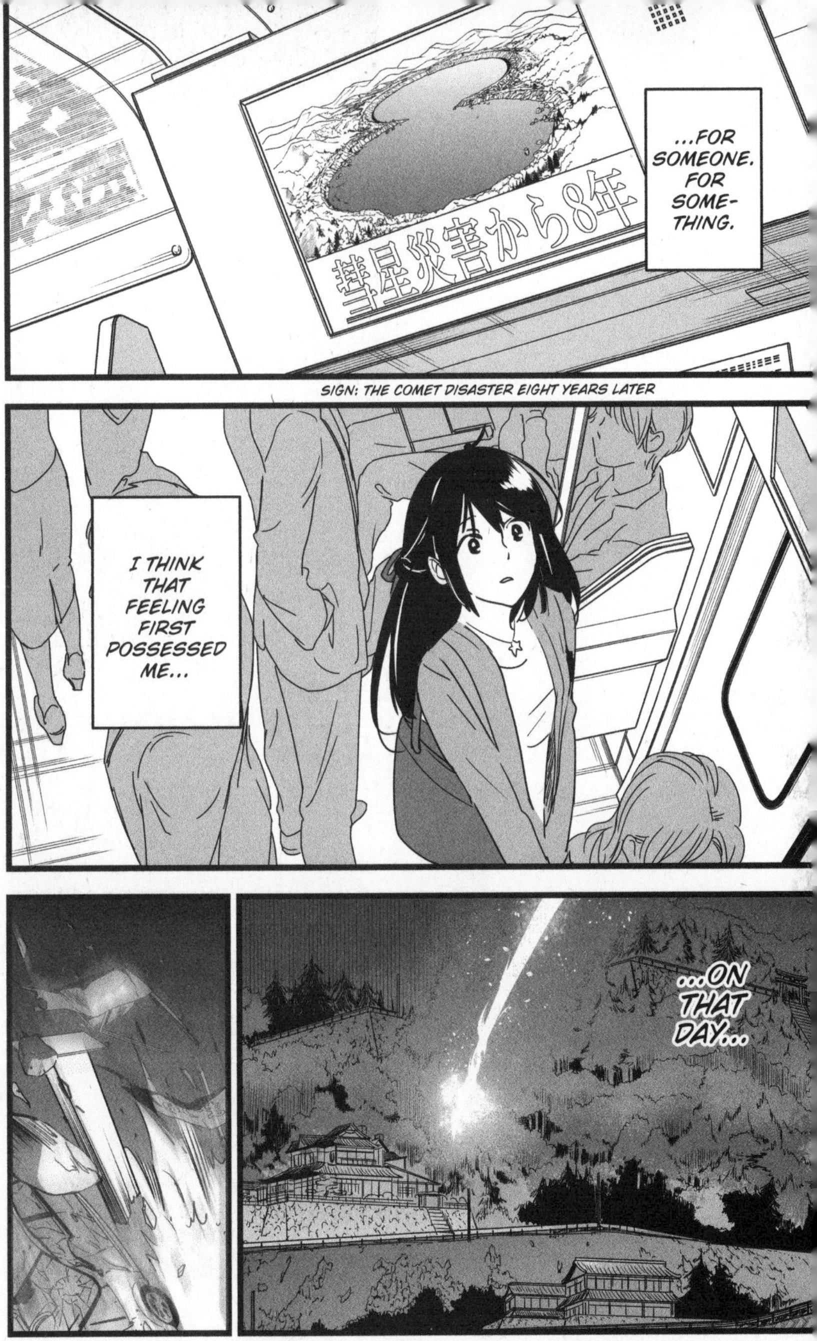
彗星災害から8年
...FOR SOMEONE. FOR SOMETHING.
SIGN: THE COMET DISASTER EIGHT YEARS LATER
I THINK THAT FEELING FIRST POSSESSED ME...
...ON THAT DAY...

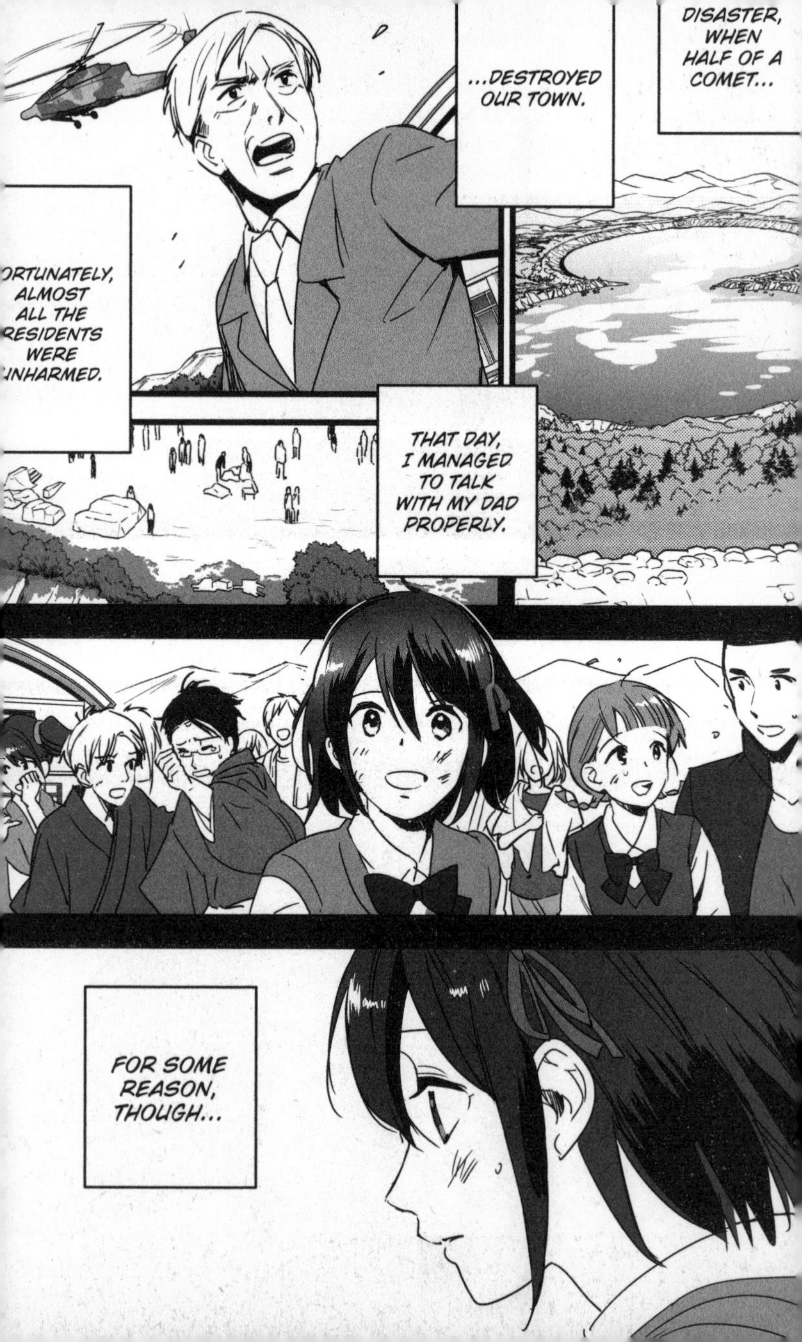
DISASTER, WHEN HALF OF A COMET...
...DESTROYED OUR TOWN.
ORTUNATELY, ALMOST ALL THE RESIDENTS WERE UNHARMED.
THAT DAY, I MANAGED TO TALK WITH MY DAD PROPERLY.
FOR SOME REASON, THOUGH...

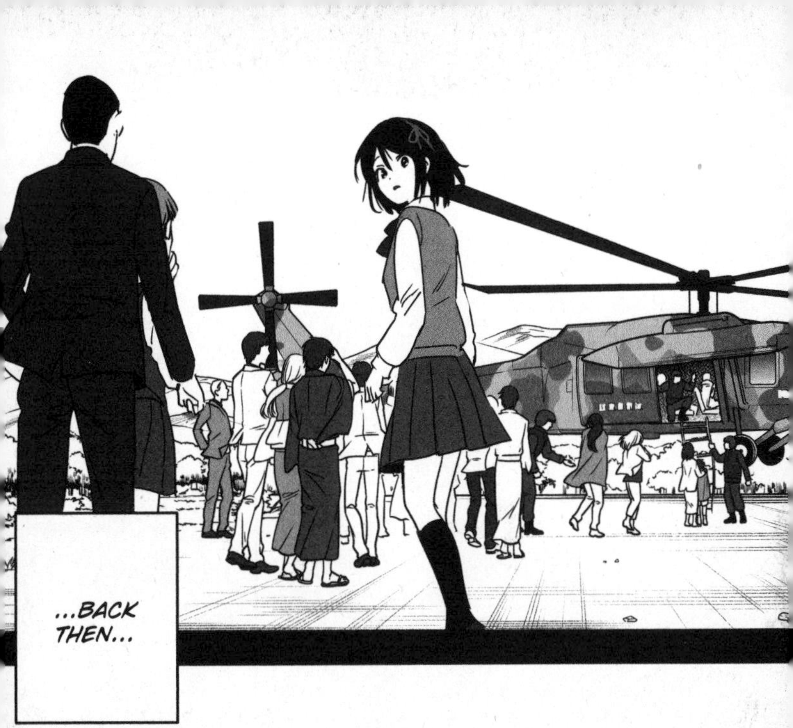
...BACK THEN...

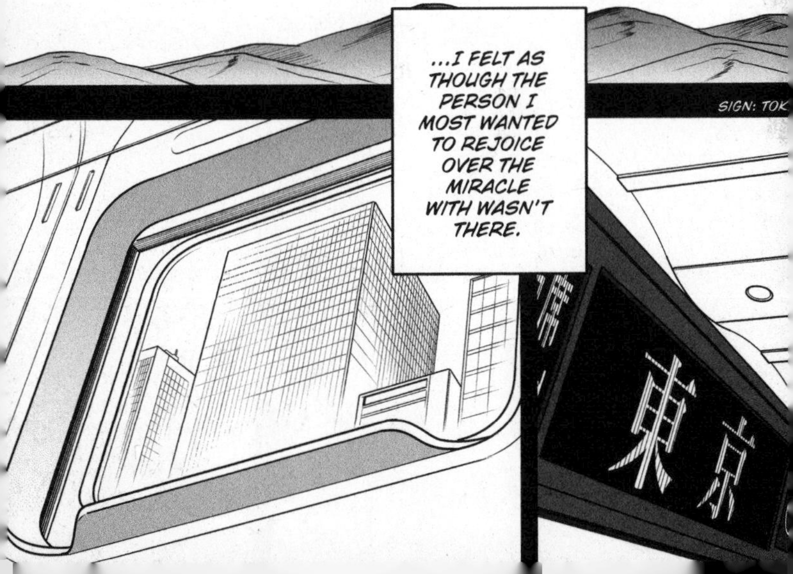
...I FELT AS THOUGH THE PERSON I MOST WANTED TO REJOICE OVER THE MIRACLE WITH WASN'T THERE.
SIGN: TOK
東京

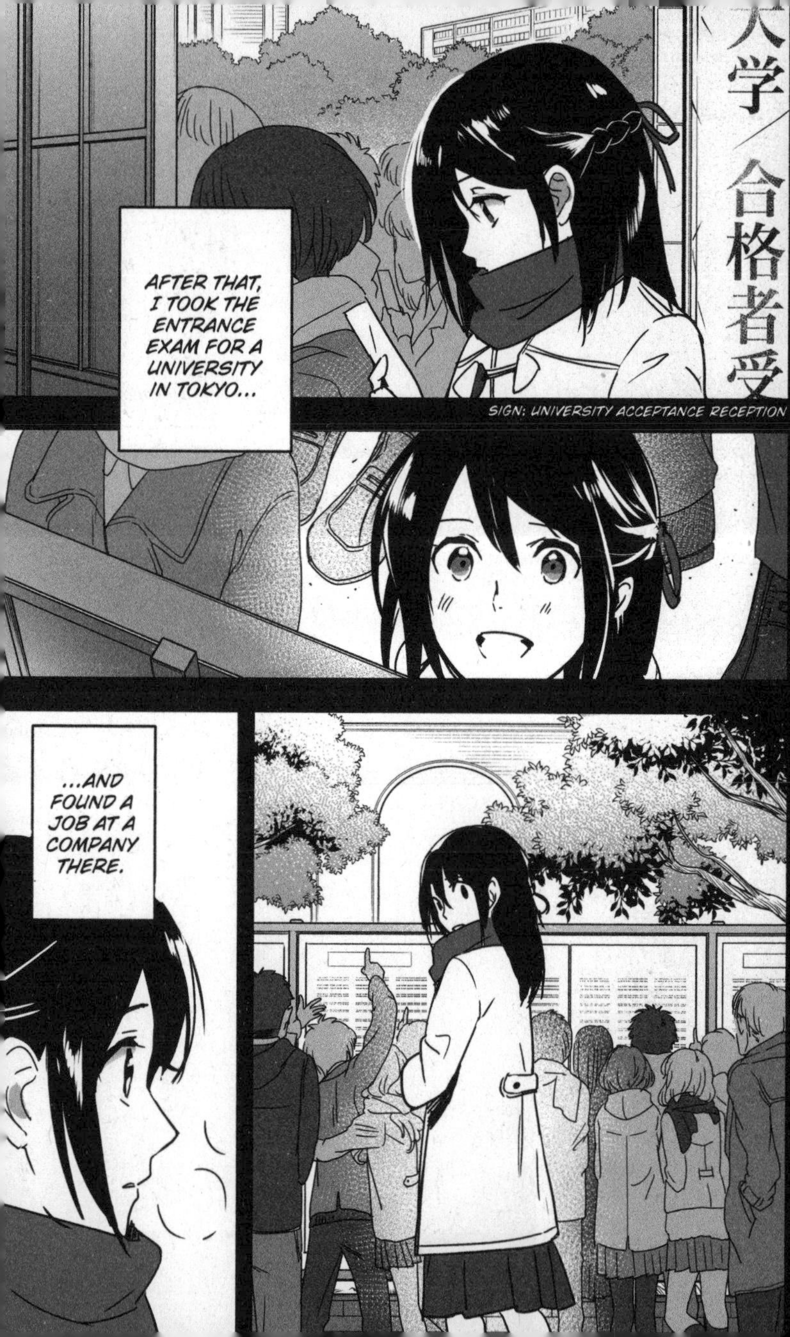
大学
合格者受
SIGN: UNIVERSITY ACCEPTANCE RECEPTION
AFTER THAT, I TOOK THE ENTRANCE EXAM FOR A UNIVERSITY IN TOKYO...
...AND FOUND A JOB AT A COMPANY THERE.

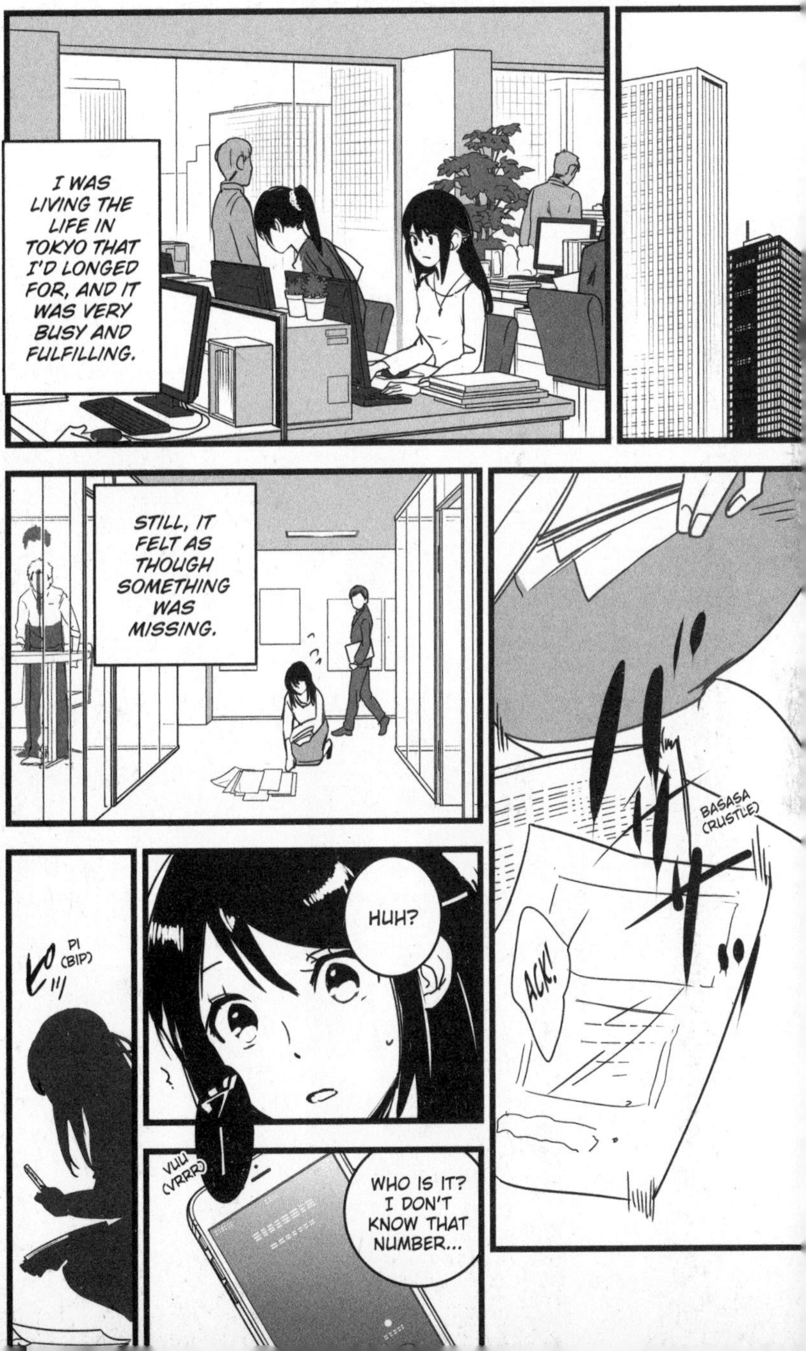
I WAS LIVING THE LIFE IN TOKYO THAT I'D LONGED FOR, AND IT WAS VERY BUSY AND FULFILLING.
ACK!
BASASA (RUSTLE)
STILL, IT FELT AS THOUGH SOMETHING WAS MISSING.
HUH?
VUU (VRRR)
WHO IS IT? I DON'T KNOW THAT NUMBER...
PI (BIP)

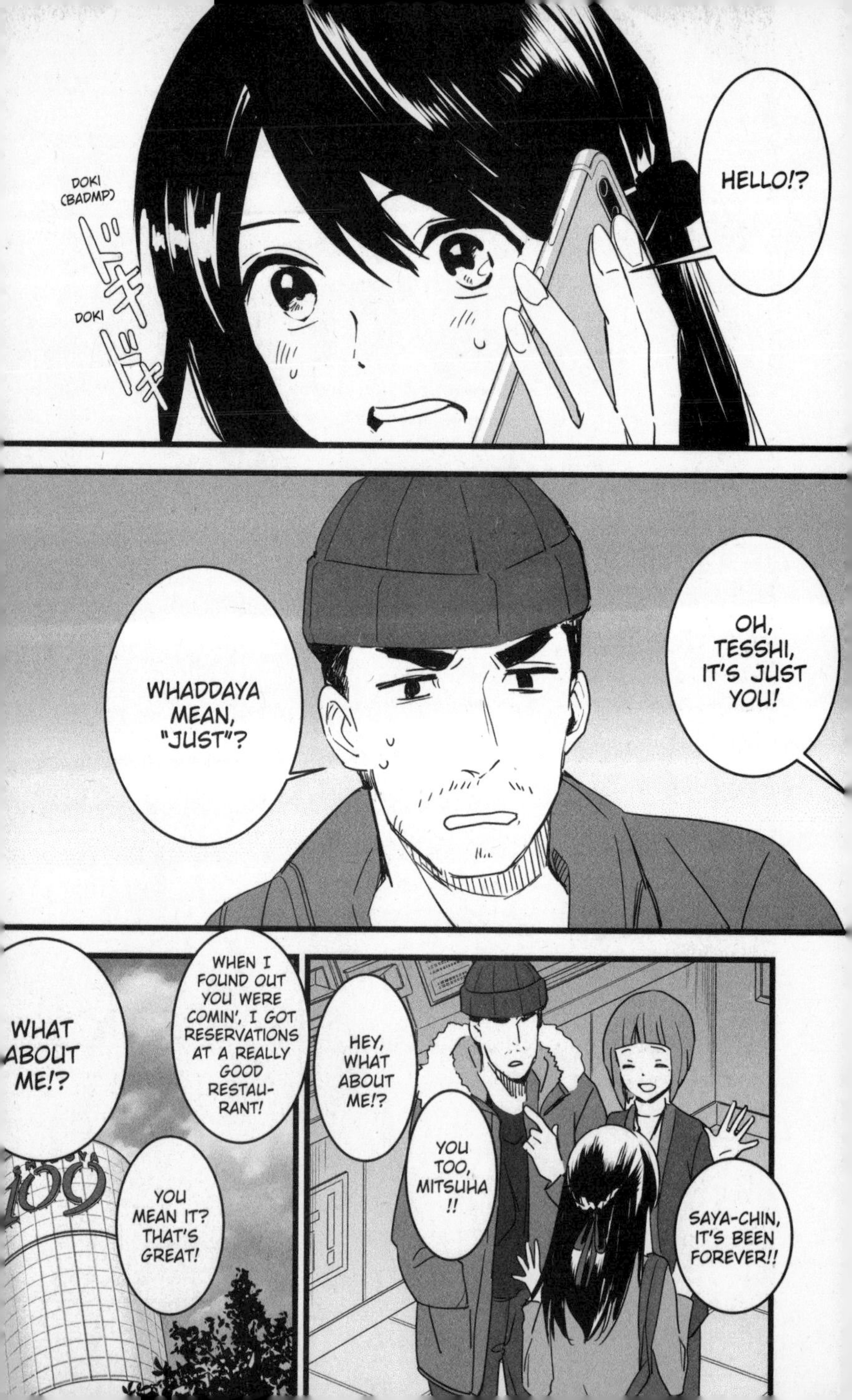
HELLO!?
DOKI (BADMP) DOKI
OH, TESSHI, IT'S JUST YOU!
WHADDAYA MEAN, "JUST"?
SAYA-CHIN, IT'S BEEN FOREVER!!
YOU TOO, MITSUHA!!
HEY, WHAT ABOUT ME!?
WHEN I FOUND OUT YOU WERE COMIN', I GOT RESERVATIONS AT A REALLY GOOD RESTAU-RANT!
YOU MEAN IT? THAT'S GREAT!
WHAT ABOUT ME!?
109

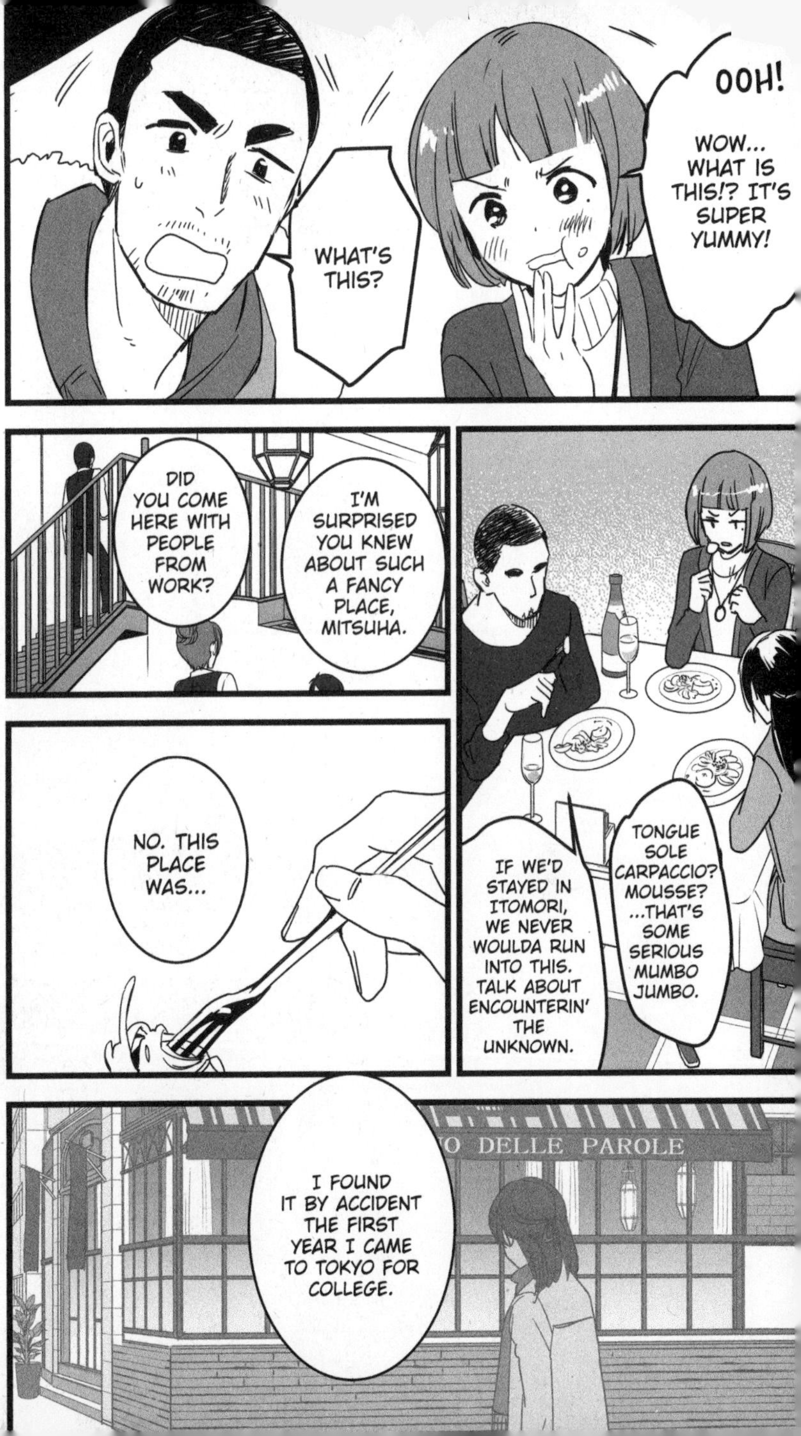
OOH!
WOW... WHAT IS THIS!? IT'S SUPER YUMMY!
WHAT'S THIS?
TONGUE SOLE CARPACCIO? MOUSSE? ...THAT'S SOME SERIOUS MUMBO JUMBO.
IF WE'D STAYED IN ITOMORI, WE NEVER WOULDA RUN INTO THIS. TALK ABOUT ENCOUNTERIN' THE UNKNOWN.
I'M SURPRISED YOU KNEW ABOUT SUCH A FANCY PLACE, MITSUHA.
DID YOU COME HERE WITH PEOPLE FROM WORK?
NO. THIS PLACE WAS...
O DELLE PAROLE
I FOUND IT BY ACCIDENT THE FIRST YEAR I CAME TO TOKYO FOR COLLEGE.

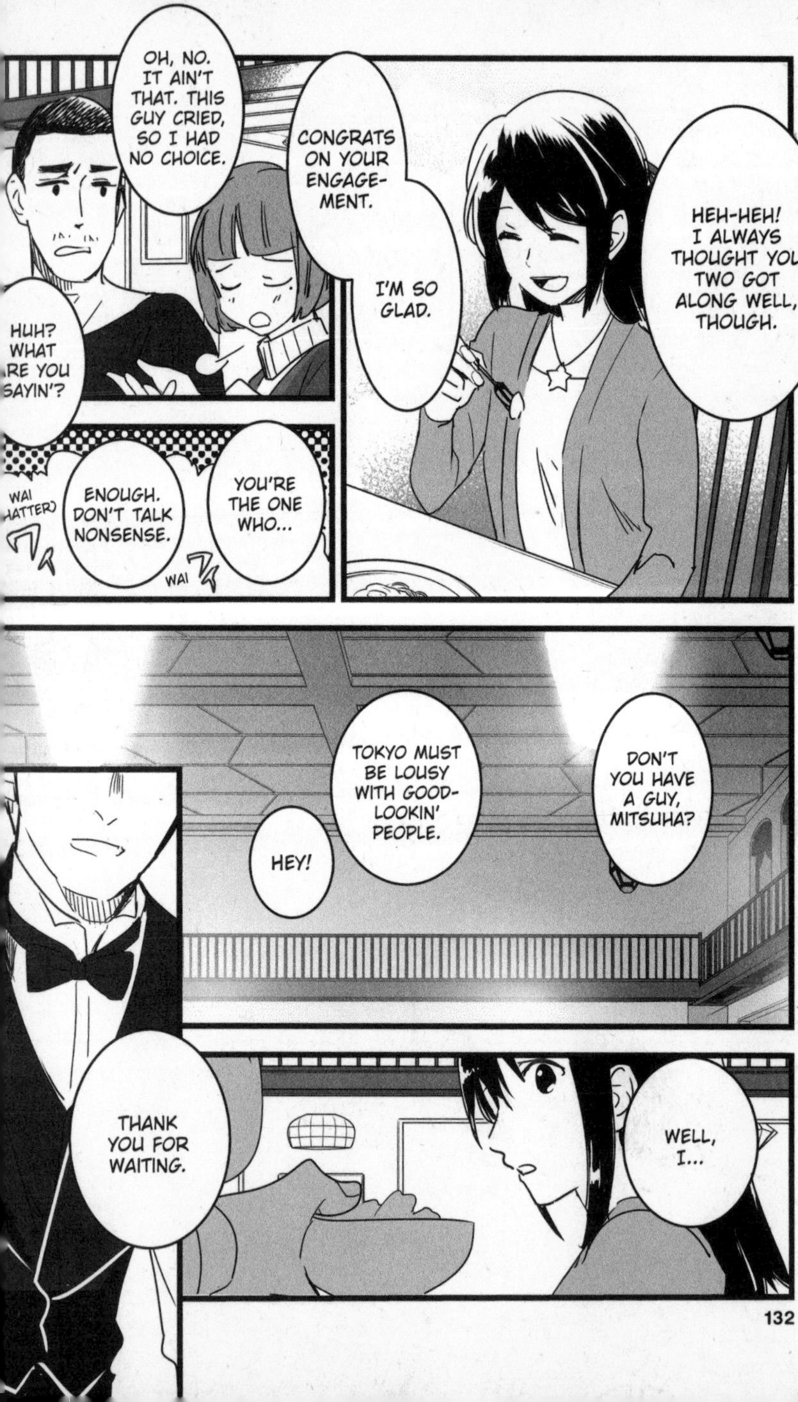
HEH-HEH! I ALWAYS THOUGHT YOU TWO GOT ALONG WELL, THOUGH.
CONGRATS ON YOUR ENGAGE-MENT.
I'M SO GLAD.
OH, NO. IT AIN'T THAT. THIS GUY CRIED, SO I HAD NO CHOICE.
HUH? WHAT RE YOU SAYIN'?
YOU'RE THE ONE WHO...
ENOUGH. DON'T TALK NONSENSE.
WAI
WAI HATTER)
DON'T YOU HAVE A GUY, MITSUHA?
TOKYO MUST BE LOUSY WITH GOOD-LOOKIN' PEOPLE.
HEY!
WELL, I...
THANK YOU FOR WAITING.

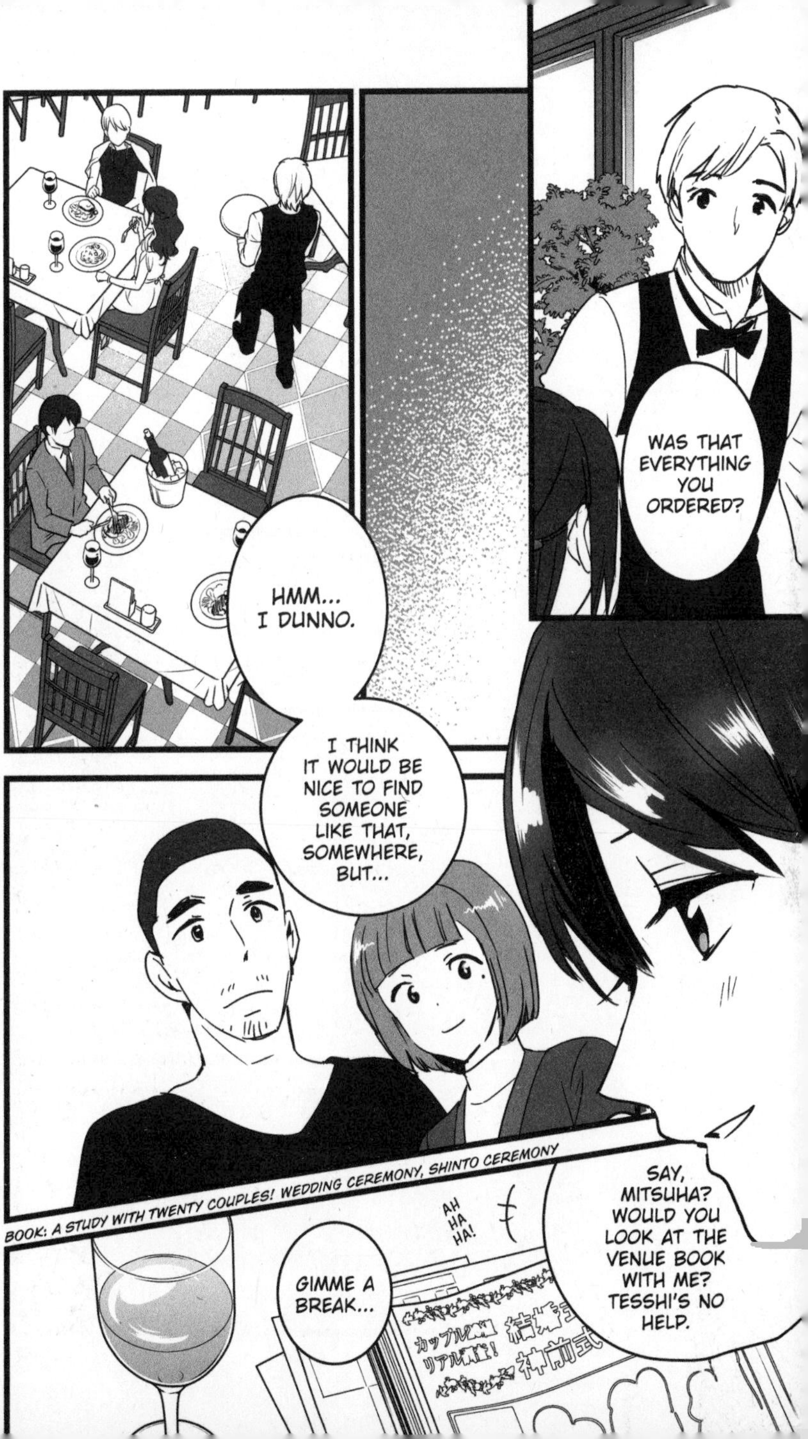
WAS THAT EVERYTHING YOU ORDERED?
HMM... I DUNNO.
I THINK IT WOULD BE NICE TO FIND SOMEONE LIKE THAT, SOMEWHERE, BUT...
SAY, MITSUHA? WOULD YOU LOOK AT THE VENUE BOOK WITH ME? TESSHI'S NO HELP.
AH HA HA!
GIMME A BREAK...
BOOK: A STUDY WITH TWENTY COUPLES! WEDDING CEREMONY, SHINTO CEREMONY

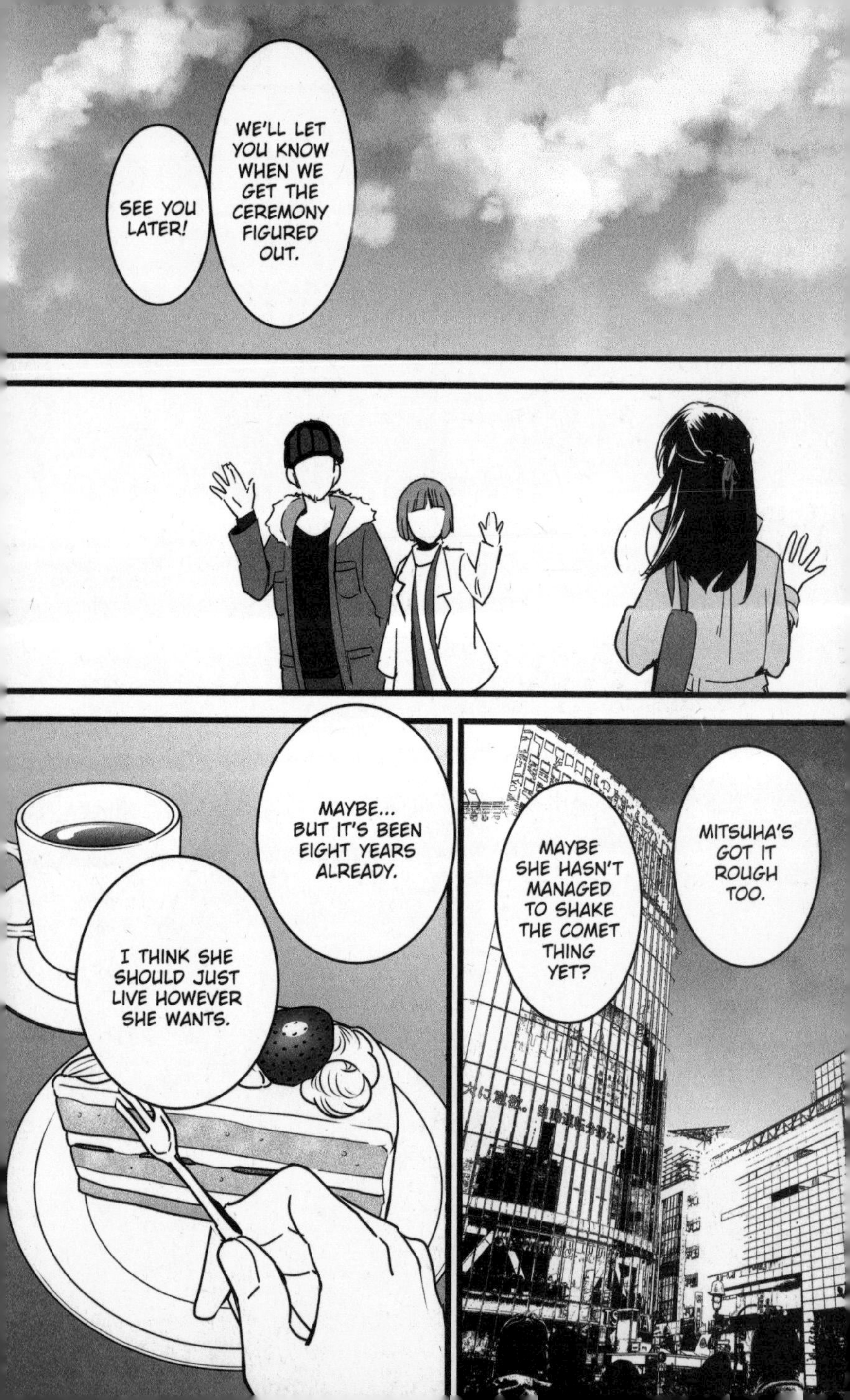
WE'LL LET YOU KNOW WHEN WE GET THE CEREMONY FIGURED OUT.
SEE YOU LATER!
MITSUHA'S GOT IT ROUGH TOO.
MAYBE SHE HASN'T MANAGED TO SHAKE THE COMET THING YET?
MAYBE... BUT IT'S BEEN EIGHT YEARS ALREADY.
I THINK SHE SHOULD JUST LIVE HOWEVER SHE WANTS.

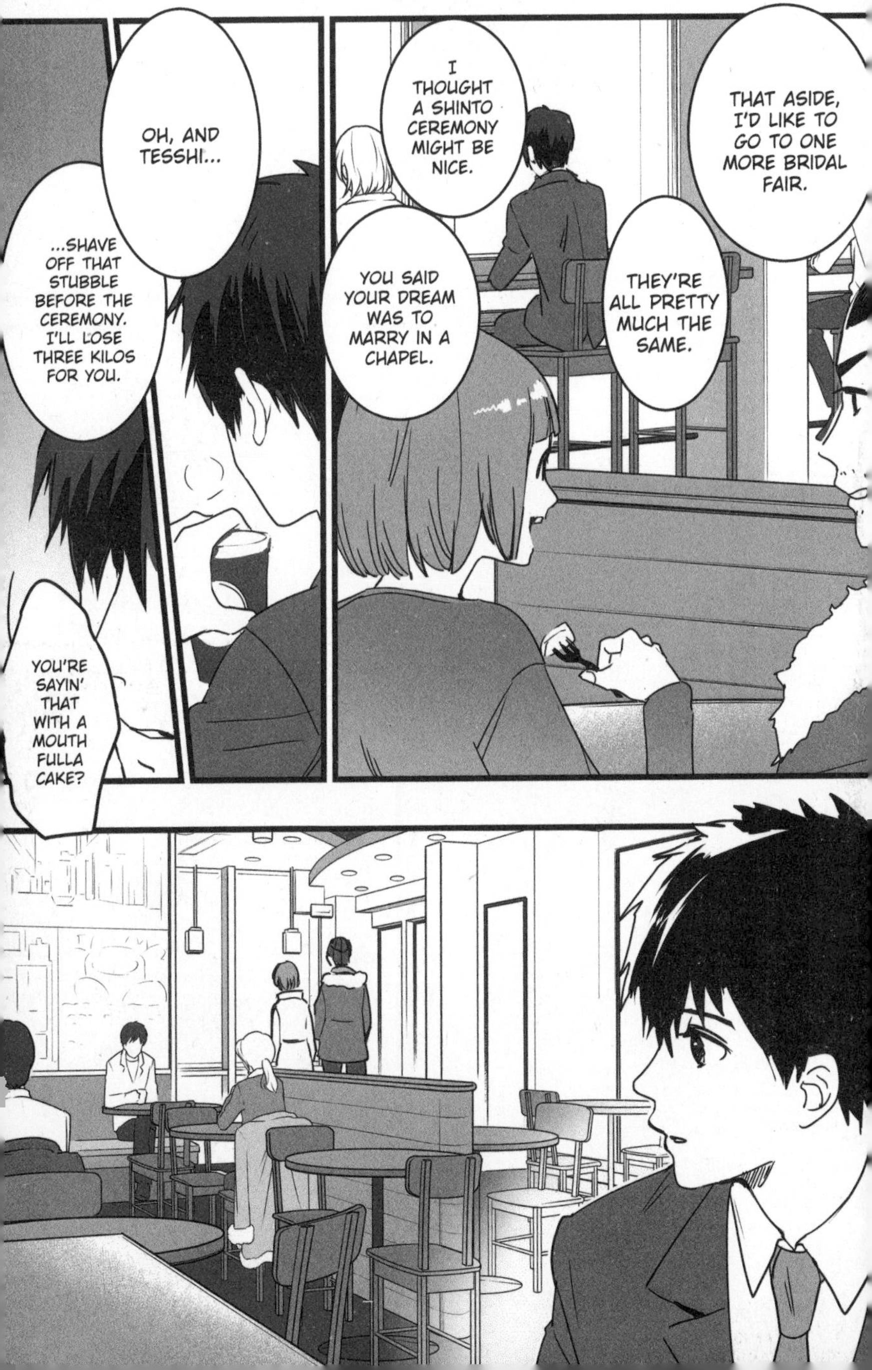
THAT ASIDE, I'D LIKE TO GO TO ONE MORE BRIDAL FAIR.
THEY'RE ALL PRETTY MUCH THE SAME.
I THOUGHT A SHINTO CEREMONY MIGHT BE NICE.
YOU SAID YOUR DREAM WAS TO MARRY IN A CHAPEL.
OH, AND TESSHI...
...SHAVE OFF THAT STUBBLE BEFORE THE CEREMONY. I'LL LOSE THREE KILOS FOR YOU.
YOU'RE SAYIN' THAT WITH A MOUTH FULLA CAKE?

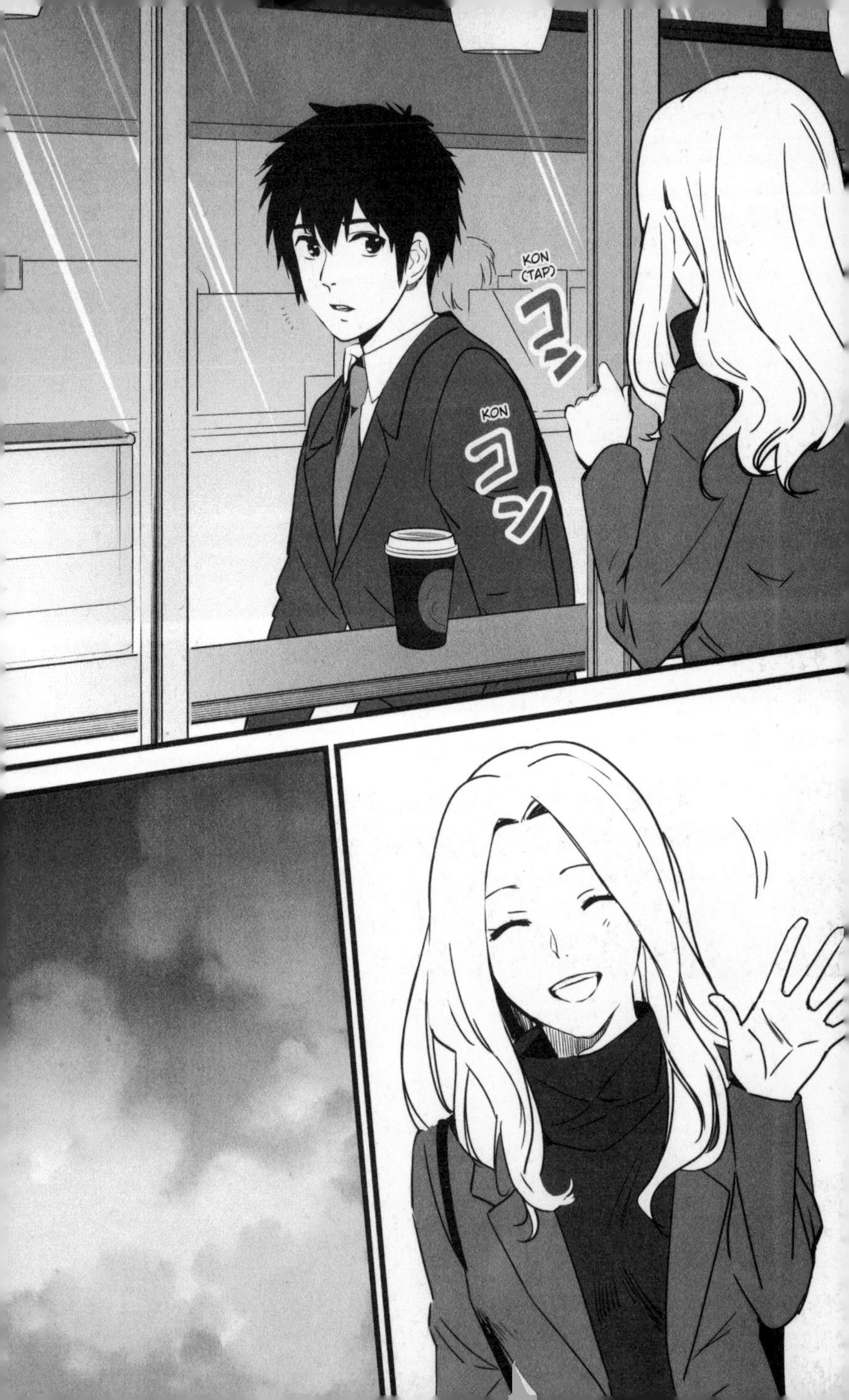
KON
(TAP)
コン
KON
コン

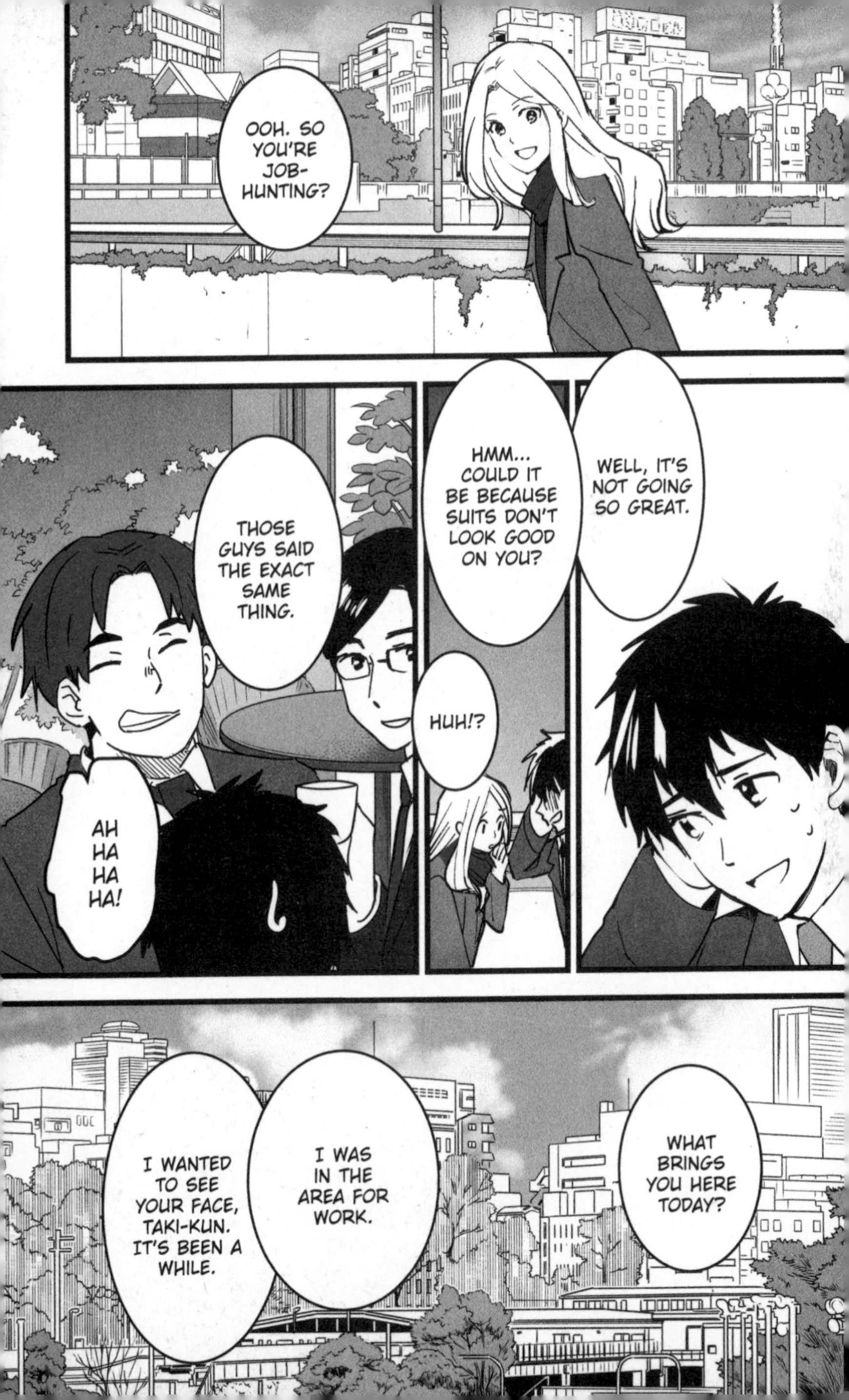
OOH. SO YOU'RE JOB-HUNTING?
WELL, IT'S NOT GOING SO GREAT.
HMM... COULD IT BE BECAUSE SUITS DON'T LOOK GOOD ON YOU?
HUH!?
THOSE GUYS SAID THE EXACT SAME THING.
AH HA HA HA!
WHAT BRINGS YOU HERE TODAY?
I WAS IN THE AREA FOR WORK.
I WANTED TO SEE YOUR FACE, TAKI-KUN. IT'S BEEN A WHILE.

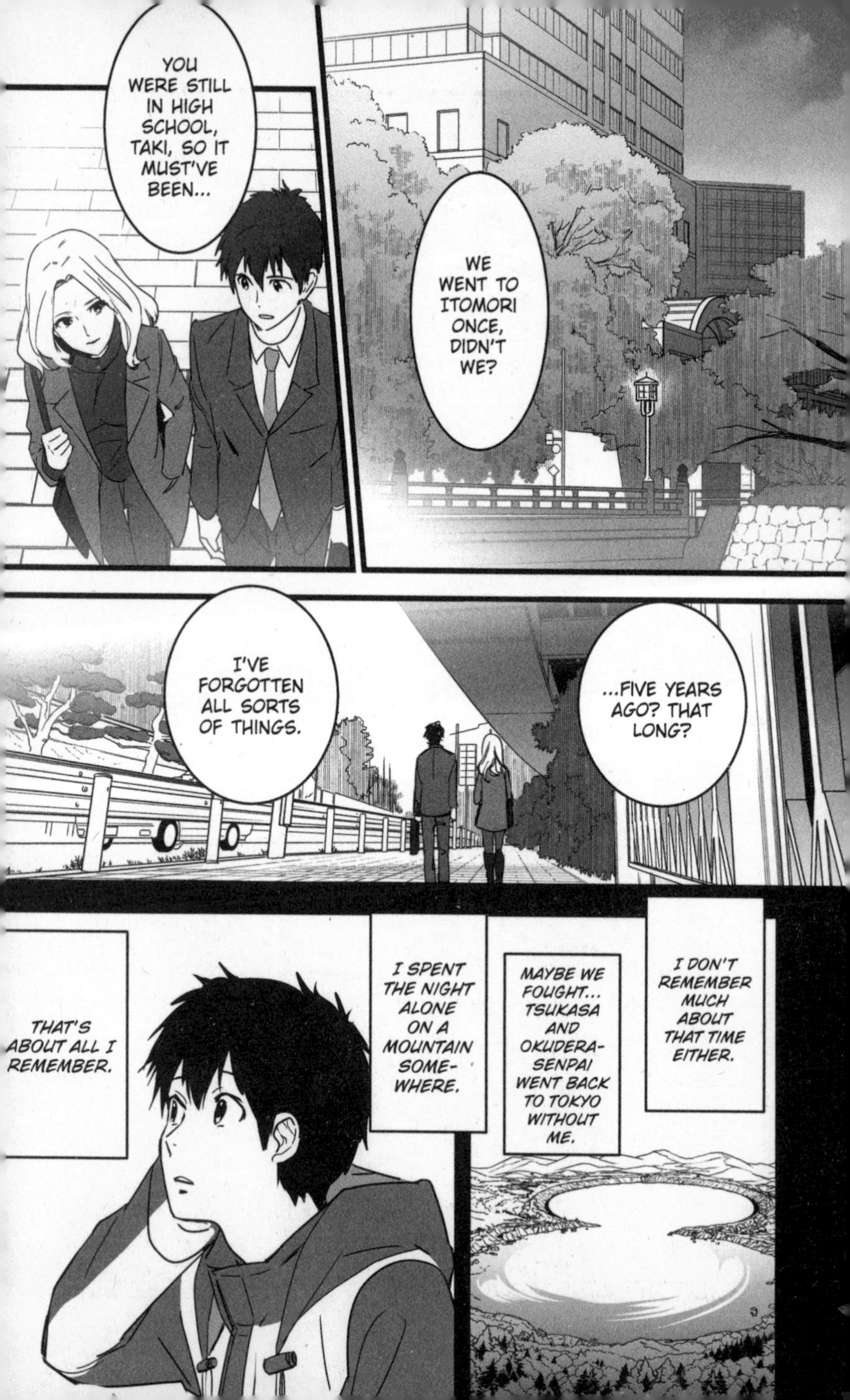
WE WENT TO ITOMORI ONCE, DIDN'T WE?
YOU WERE STILL IN HIGH SCHOOL, TAKI, SO IT MUST'VE BEEN...
...FIVE YEARS AGO? THAT LONG?
I'VE FORGOTTEN ALL SORTS OF THINGS.
I DON'T REMEMBER MUCH ABOUT THAT TIME EITHER.
MAYBE WE FOUGHT... TSUKASA AND OKUDERA-SENPAI WENT BACK TO TOKYO WITHOUT ME.
I SPENT THE NIGHT ALONE ON A MOUNTAIN SOME-WHERE.
THAT'S ABOUT ALL I REMEMBER.

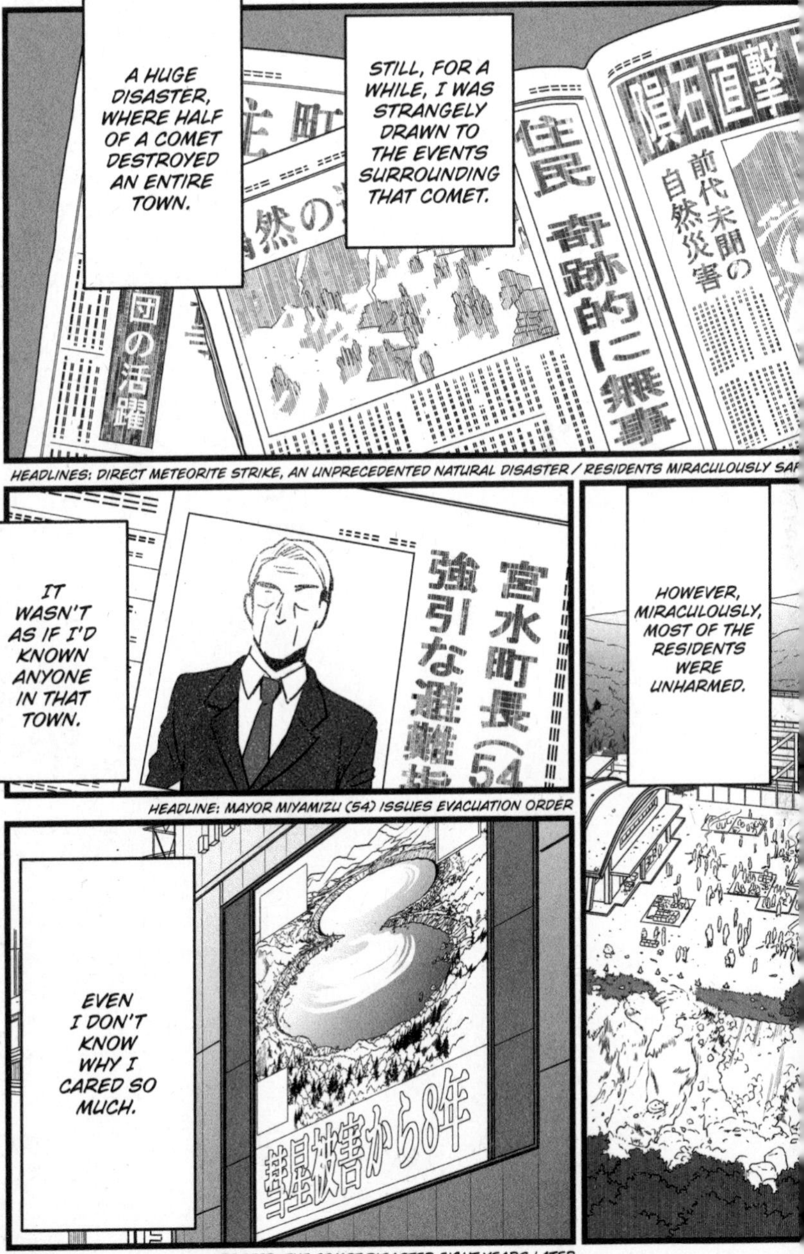
A HUGE DISASTER, WHERE HALF OF A COMET DESTROYED AN ENTIRE TOWN.
STILL, FOR A WHILE, I WAS STRANGELY DRAWN TO THE EVENTS SURROUNDING THAT COMET.
HEADLINES: DIRECT METEORITE STRIKE, AN UNPRECEDENTED NATURAL DISASTER / RESIDENTS MIRACULOUSLY SAF
HOWEVER, MIRACULOUSLY, MOST OF THE RESIDENTS WERE UNHARMED.
IT WASN'T AS IF I'D KNOWN ANYONE IN THAT TOWN.
HEADLINE: MAYOR MIYAMIZU (54) ISSUES EVACUATION ORDER
EVEN I DON'T KNOW WHY I CARED SO MUCH.
POSTER: THE COMET DISASTER EIGHT YEARS LATER

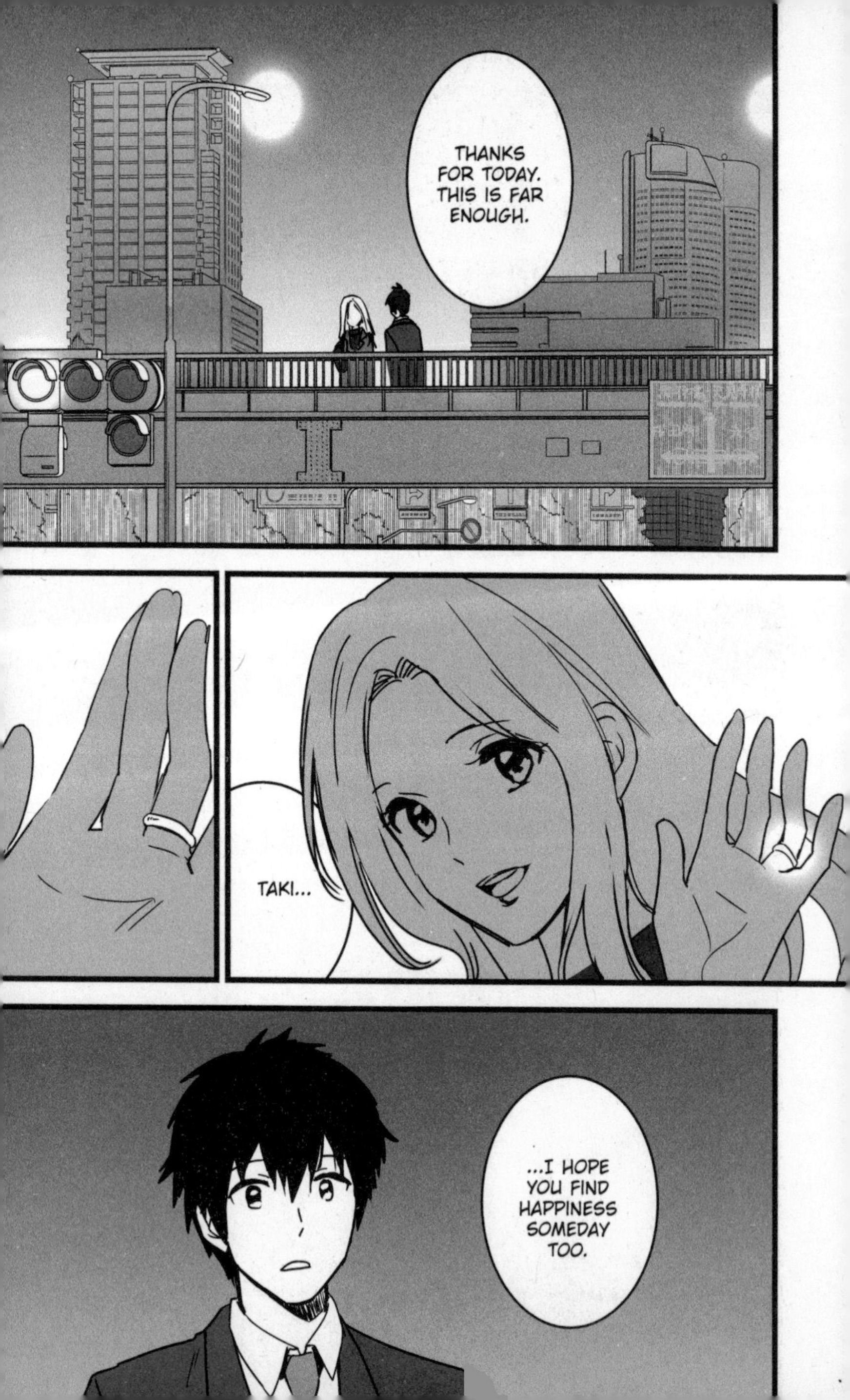
THANKS FOR TODAY. THIS IS FAR ENOUGH.
TAKI...
...I HOPE YOU FIND HAPPINESS SOMEDAY TOO.

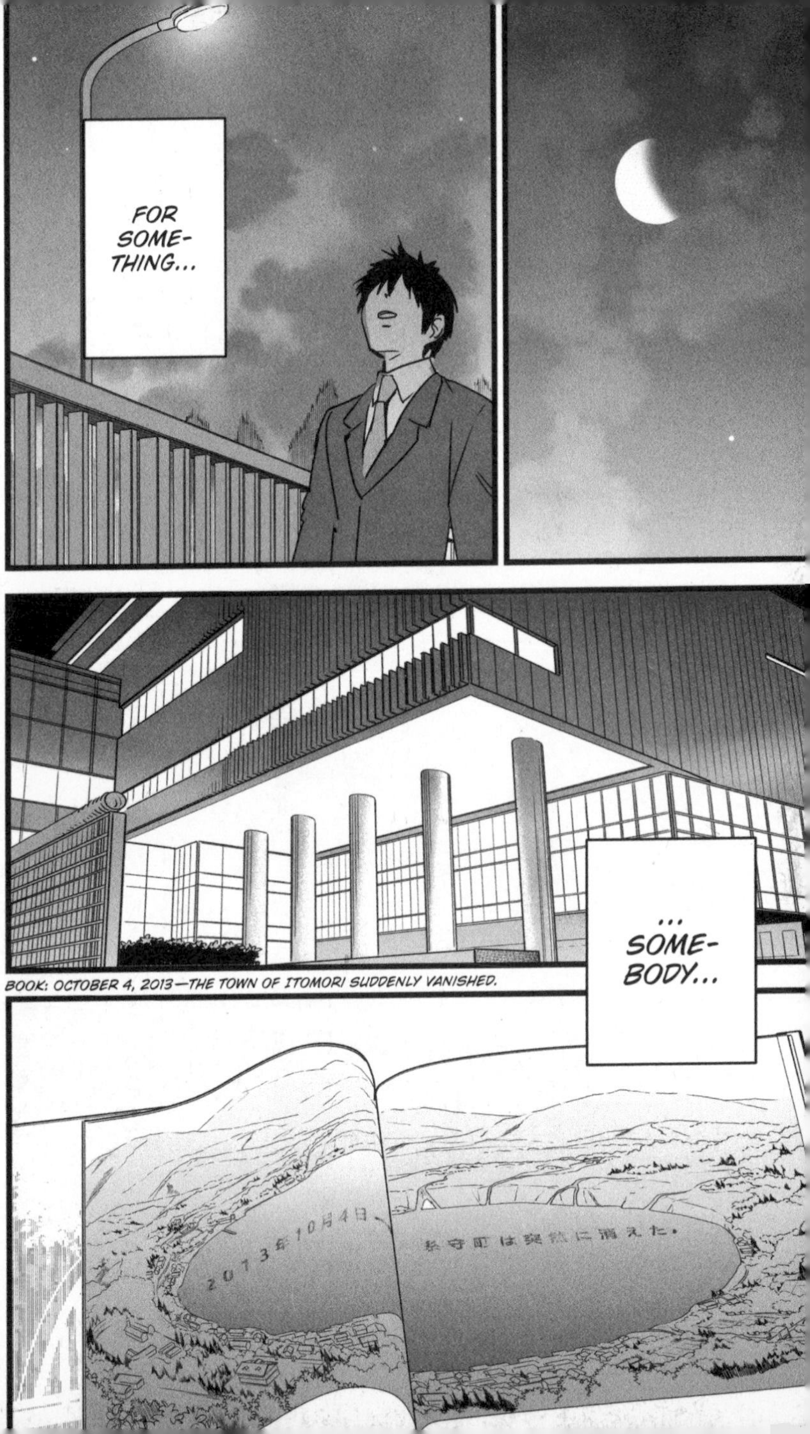
FOR SOME-THING...
...SOME-BODY...
BOOK: OCTOBER 4, 2013—THE TOWN OF ITOMORI SUDDENLY VANISHED.
2013年10月4日
糸守町は突然に消えた。

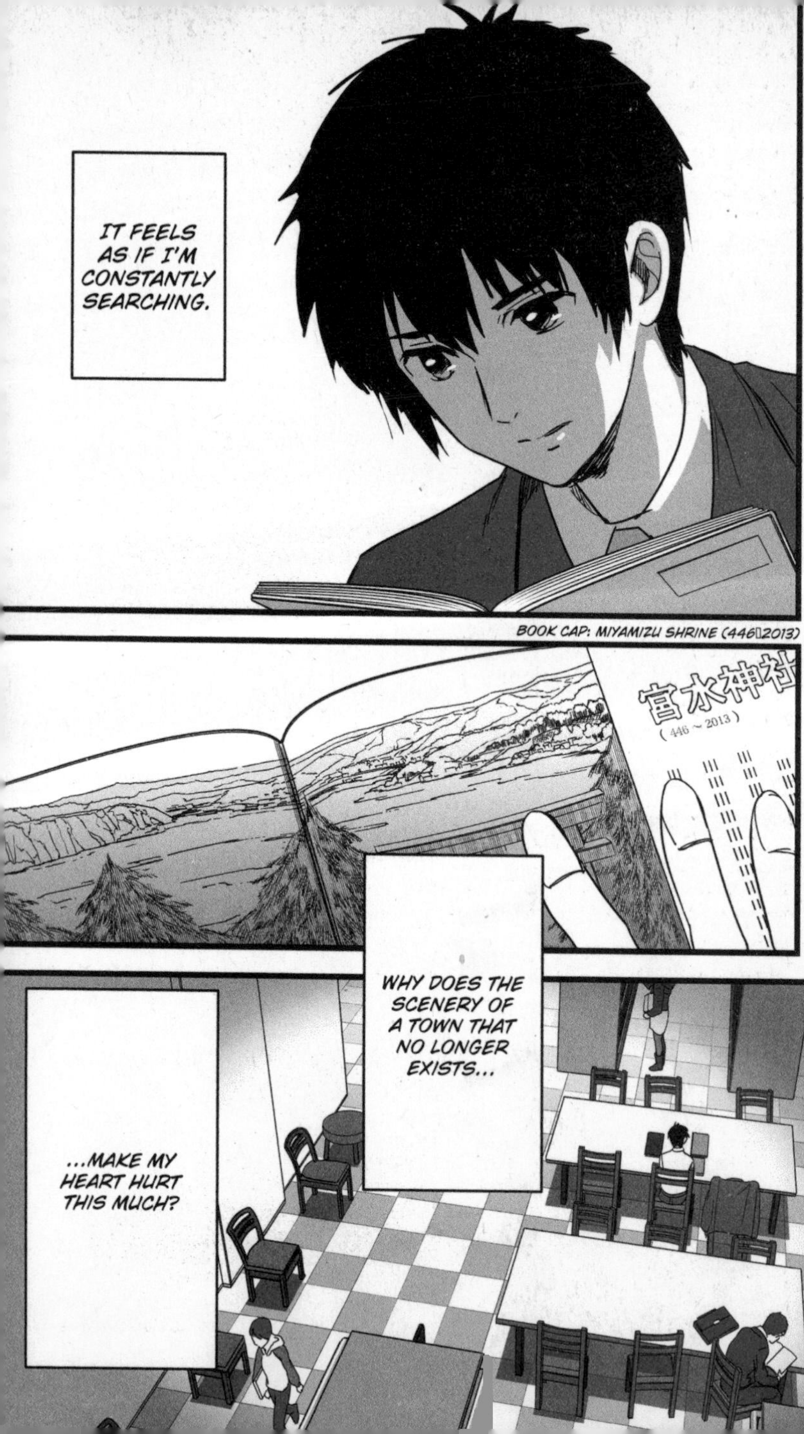
IT FEELS AS IF I'M CONSTANTLY SEARCHING.
BOOK CAP: MIYAMIZU SHRINE (446~2013)
宮水神社
(446 ~ 2013)
WHY DOES THE SCENERY OF A TOWN THAT NO LONGER EXISTS...
...MAKE MY HEART HURT THIS MUCH?

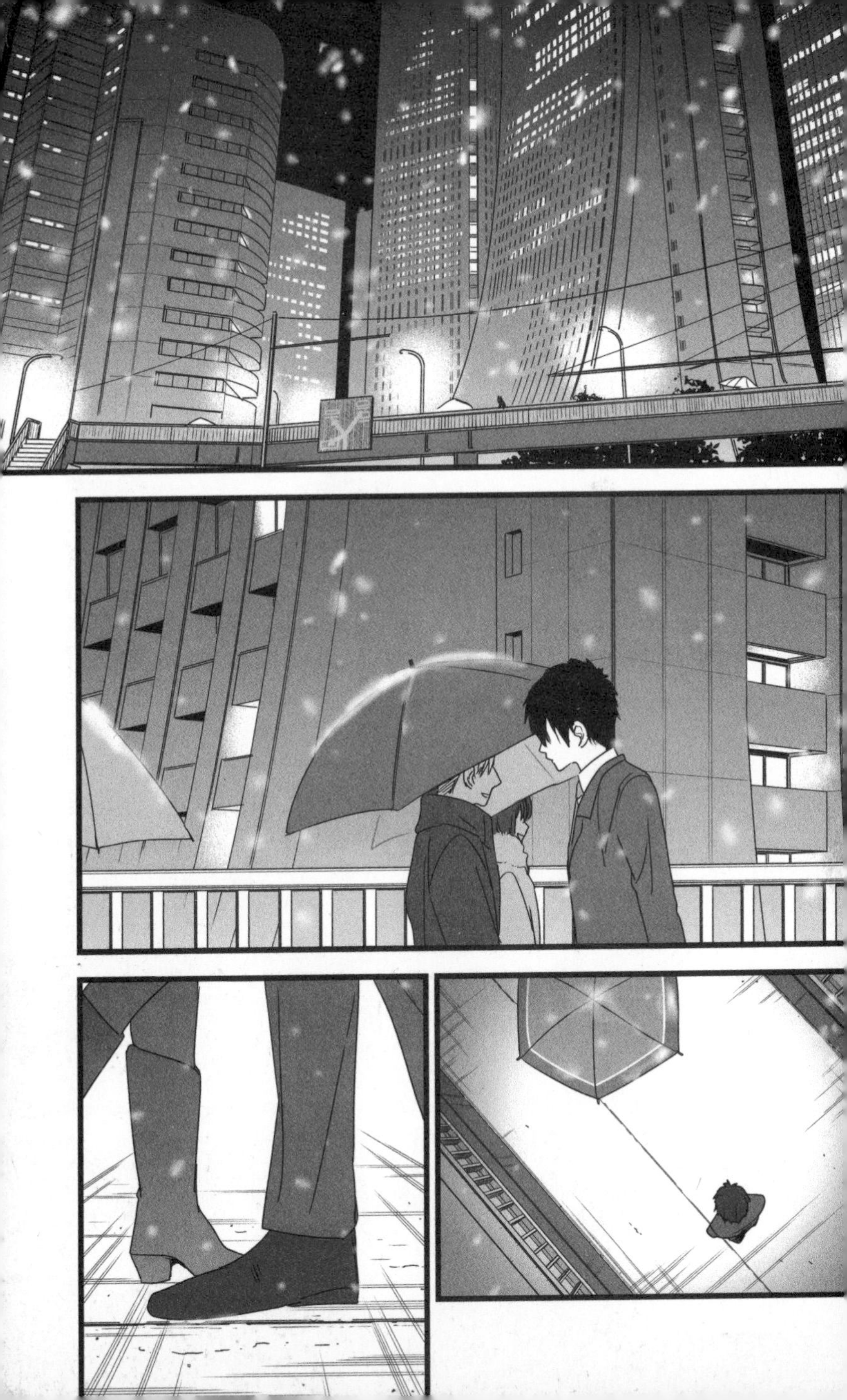

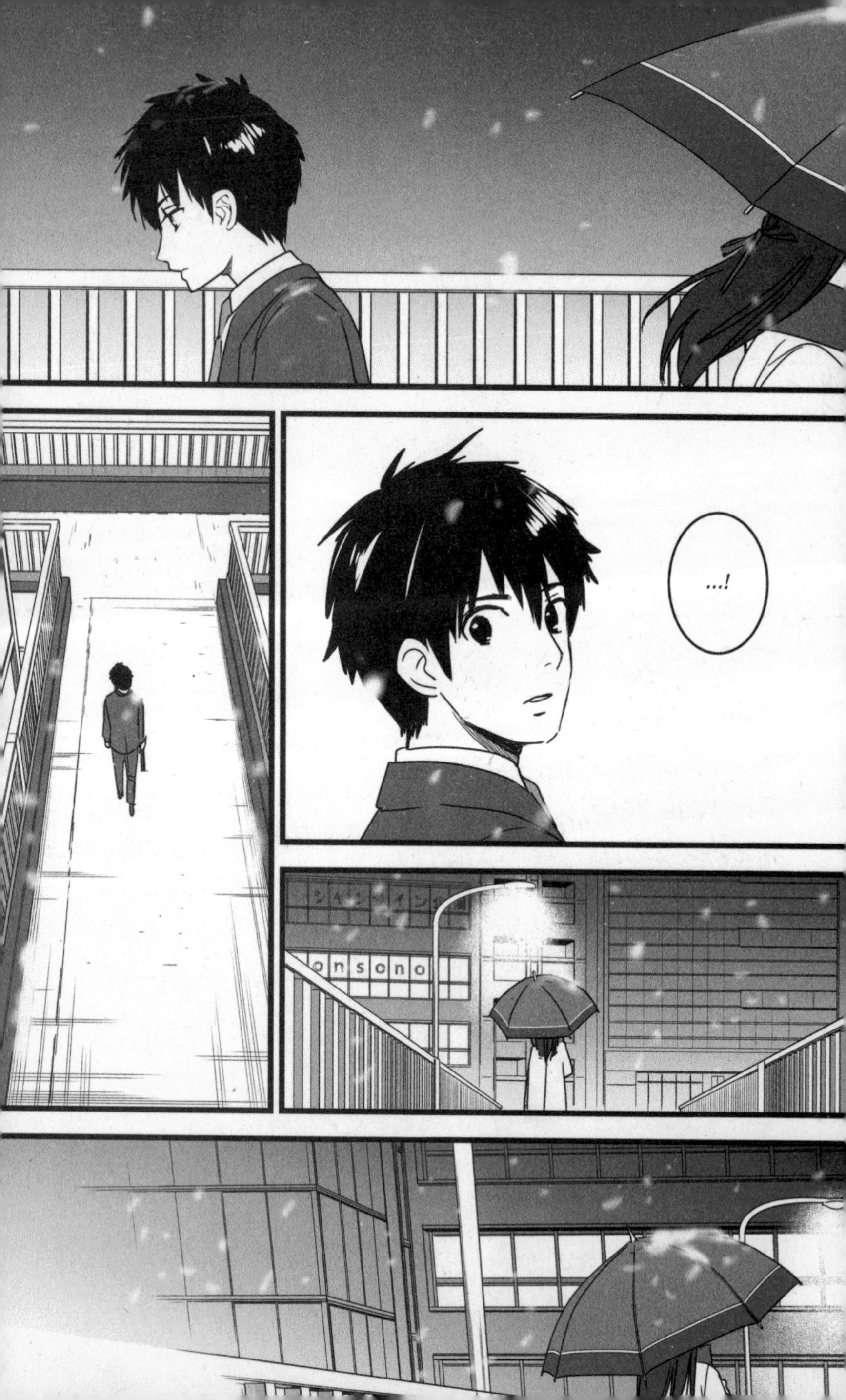
...!
onsono

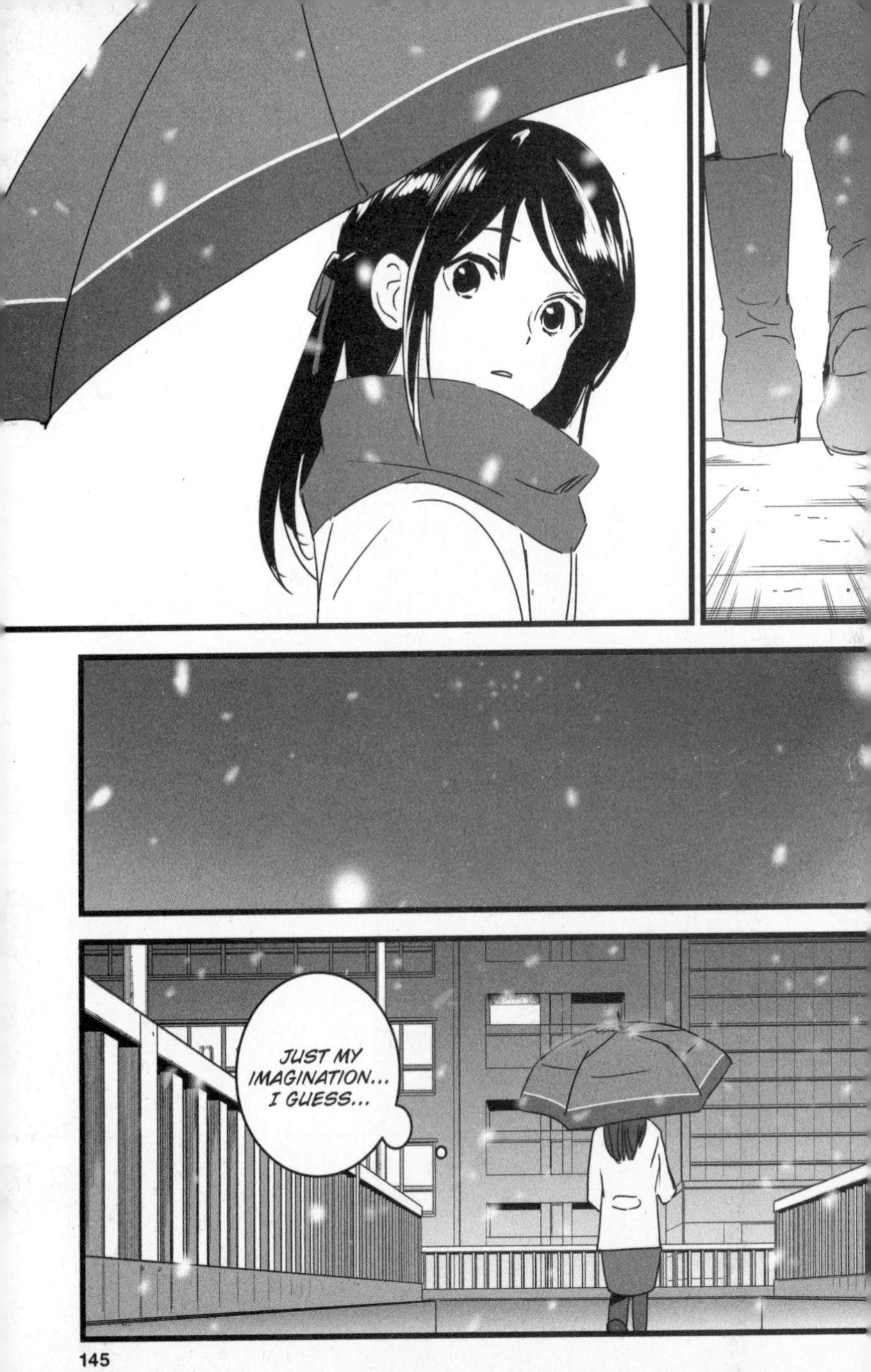
JUST MY IMAGINATION... I GUESS...

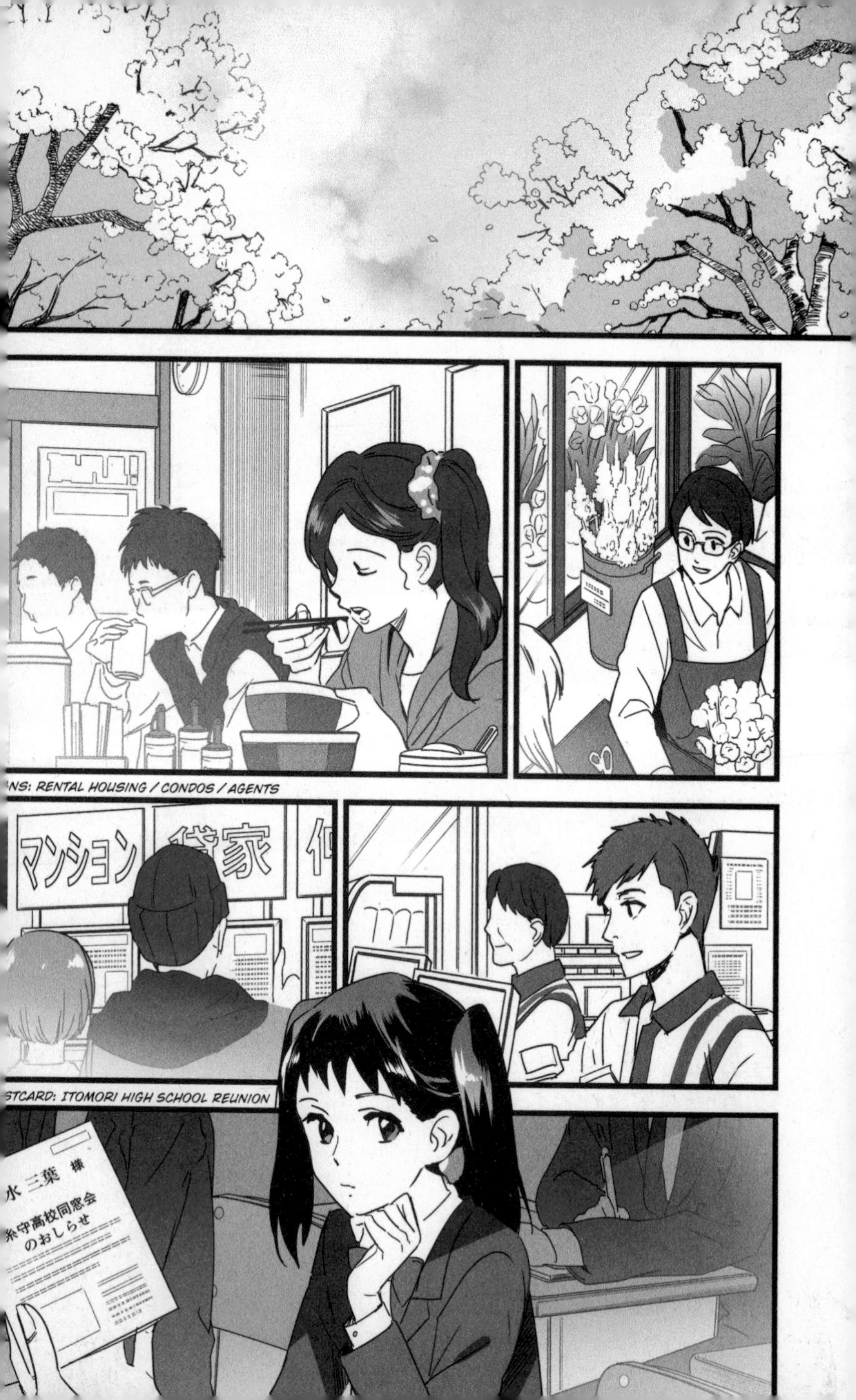
NS: RENTAL HOUSING / CONDOS / AGENTS
マンション
貸家
STCARD: ITOMORI HIGH SCHOOL REUNION
水 三葉 様
糸守高校同窓会
のおしらせ

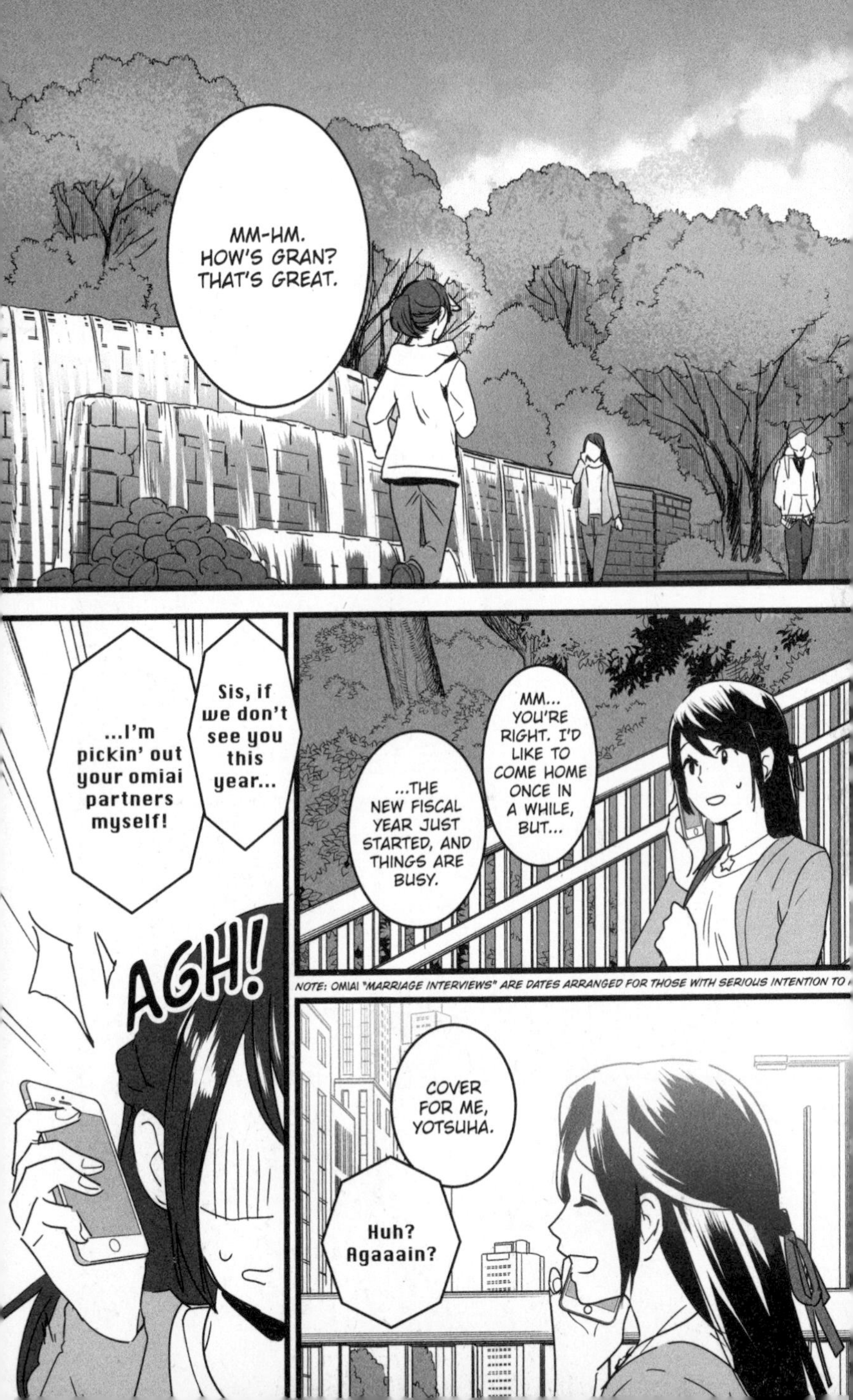
MM-HM. HOW'S GRAN? THAT'S GREAT.
MM... YOU'RE RIGHT. I'D LIKE TO COME HOME ONCE IN A WHILE, BUT...
...THE NEW FISCAL YEAR JUST STARTED, AND THINGS ARE BUSY.
Sis, if we don't see you this year...
...I'm pickin' out your omiai partners myself!
AGH!
COVER FOR ME, YOTSUHA.
Huh? Agaaain?

NOTE: OMIAI "MARRIAGE INTERVIEWS" ARE DATES ARRANGED FOR THOSE WITH SERIOUS INTENTION TO

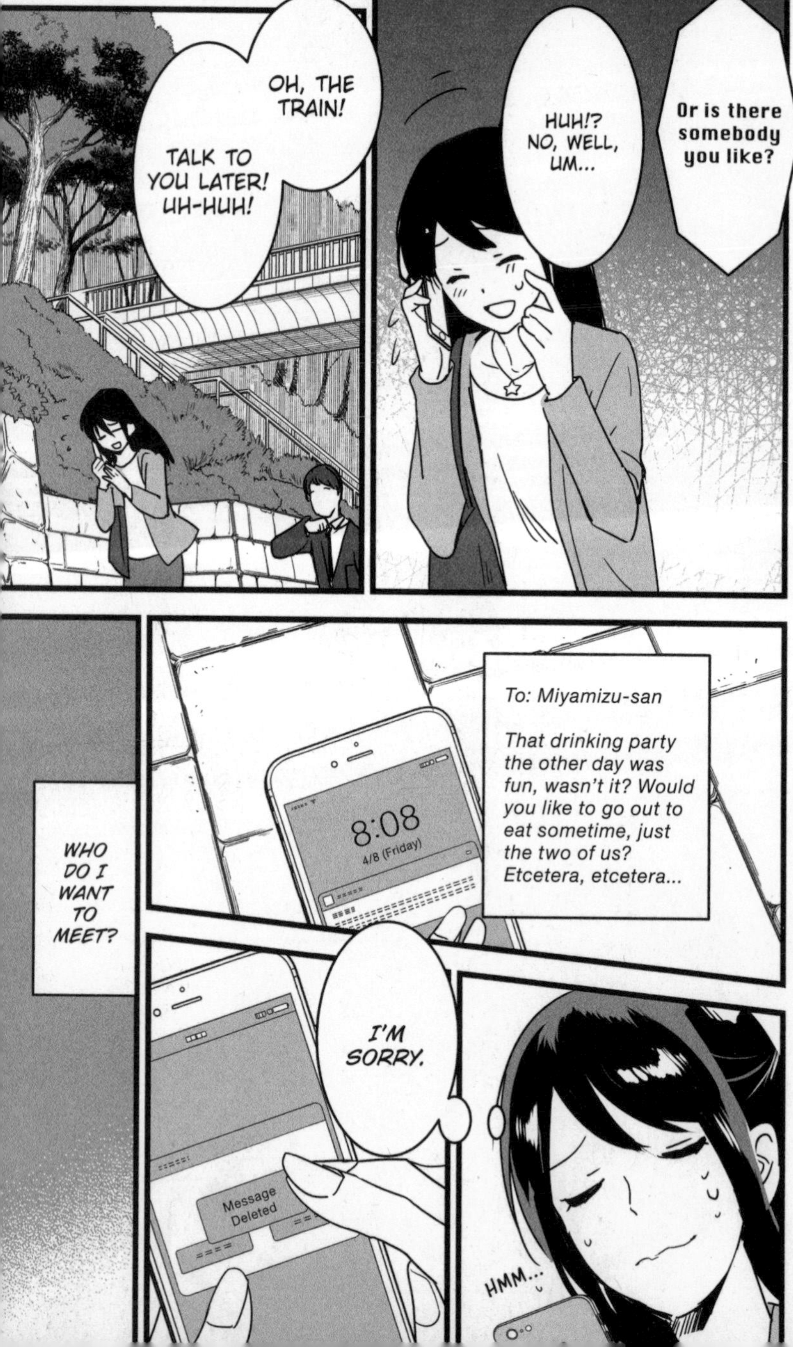
Or is there somebody you like?
HUH!? NO, WELL, UM...
OH, THE TRAIN!
TALK TO YOU LATER! UH-HUH!
To: Miyamizu-san

That drinking party the other day was fun, wasn't it? Would you like to go out to eat sometime, just the two of us? Etcetera, etcetera...
8:08
4/8 (Friday)
I'M SORRY.
HMM...
Message Deleted
WHO DO I WANT TO MEET?

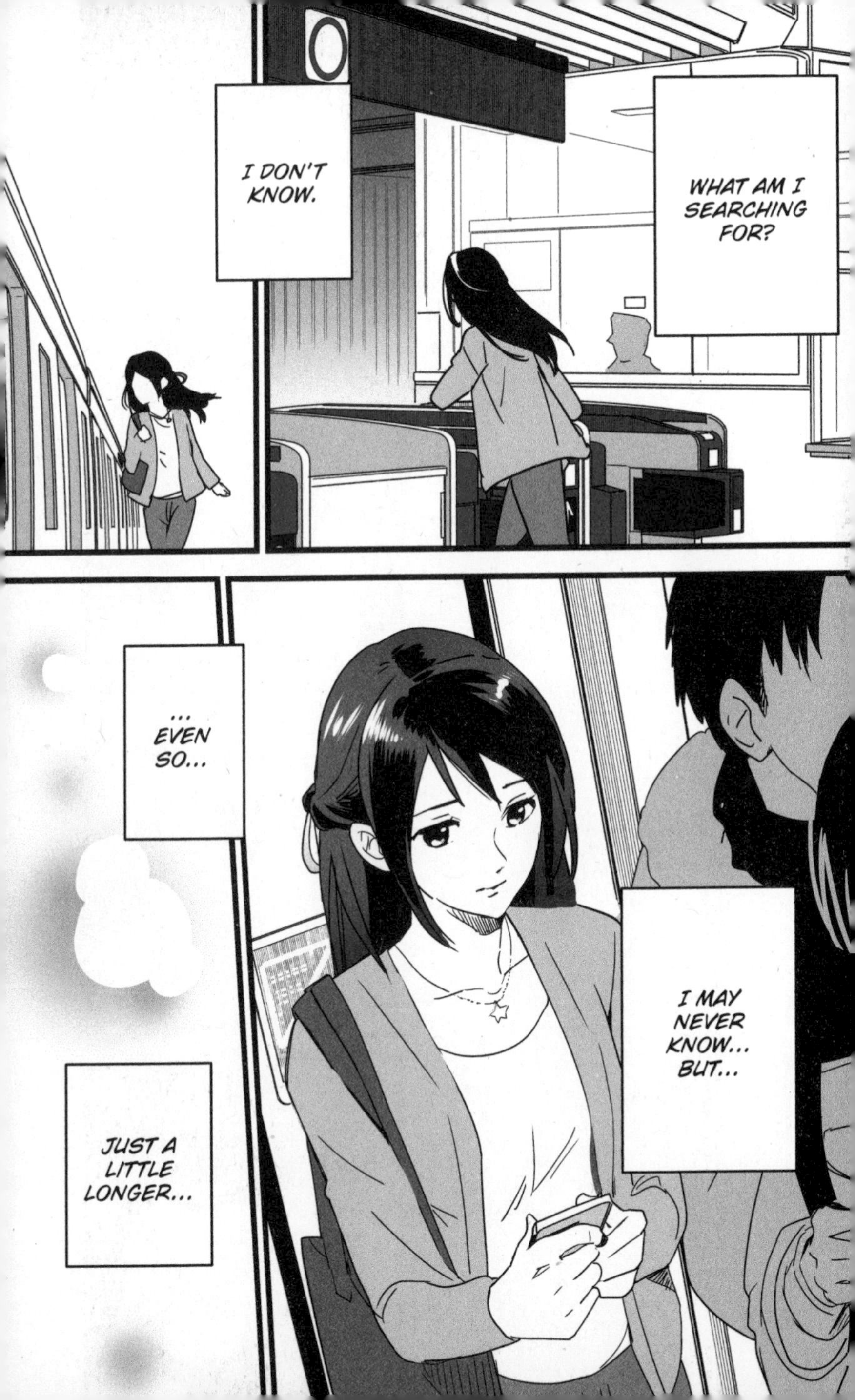
WHAT AM I SEARCHING FOR?
I DON'T KNOW.
I MAY NEVER KNOW... BUT...
...EVEN SO...
JUST A LITTLE LONGER...

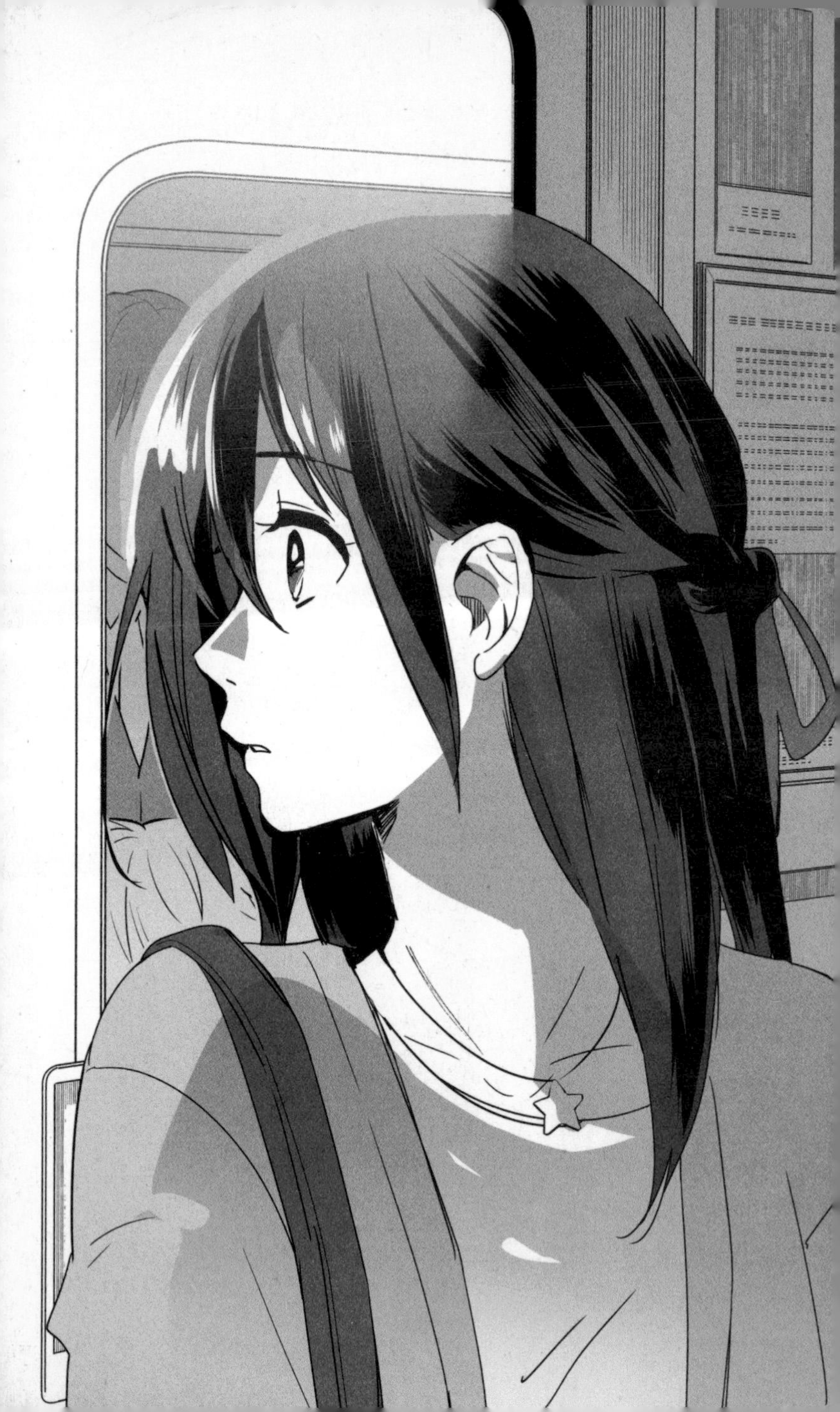

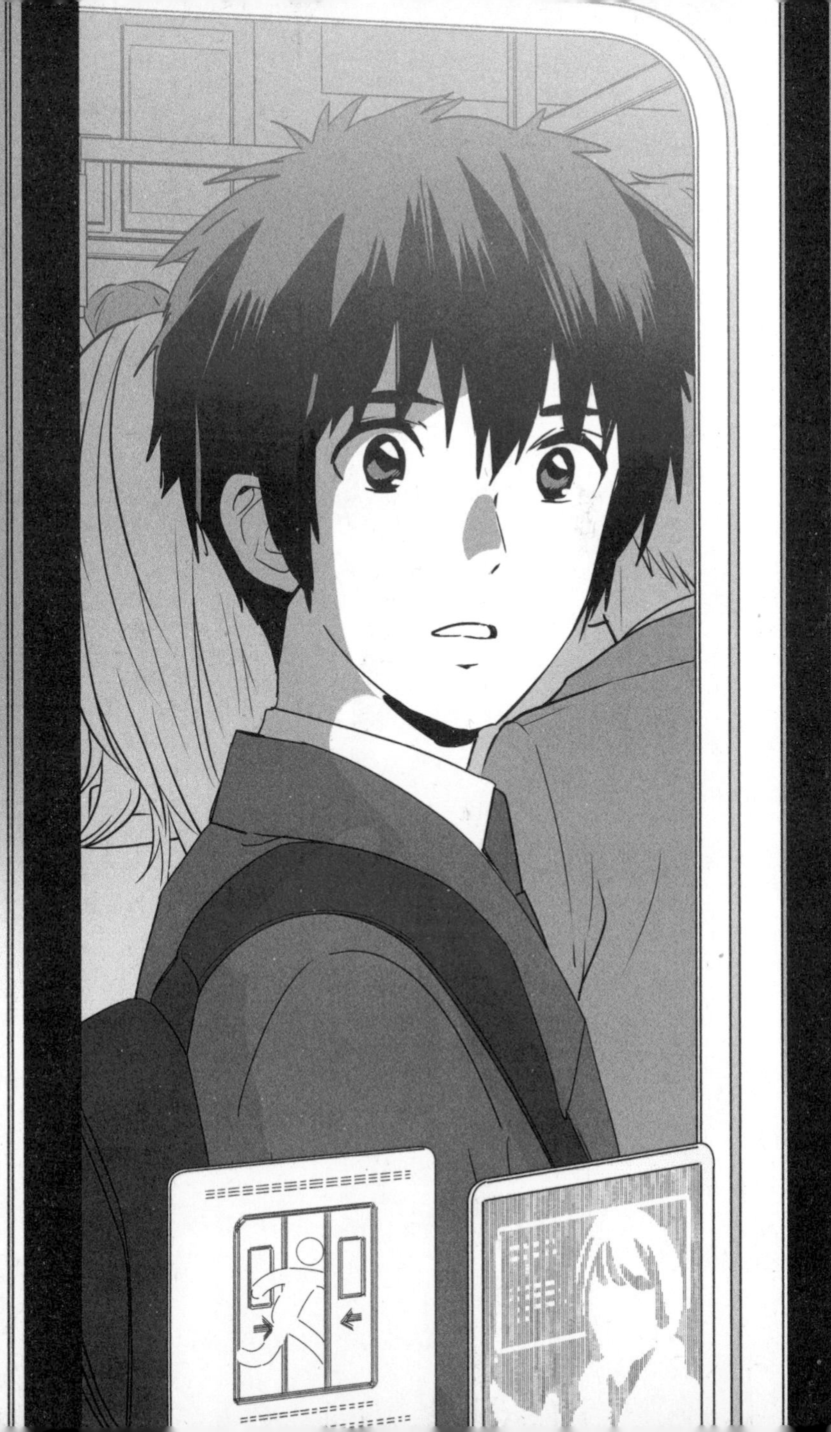

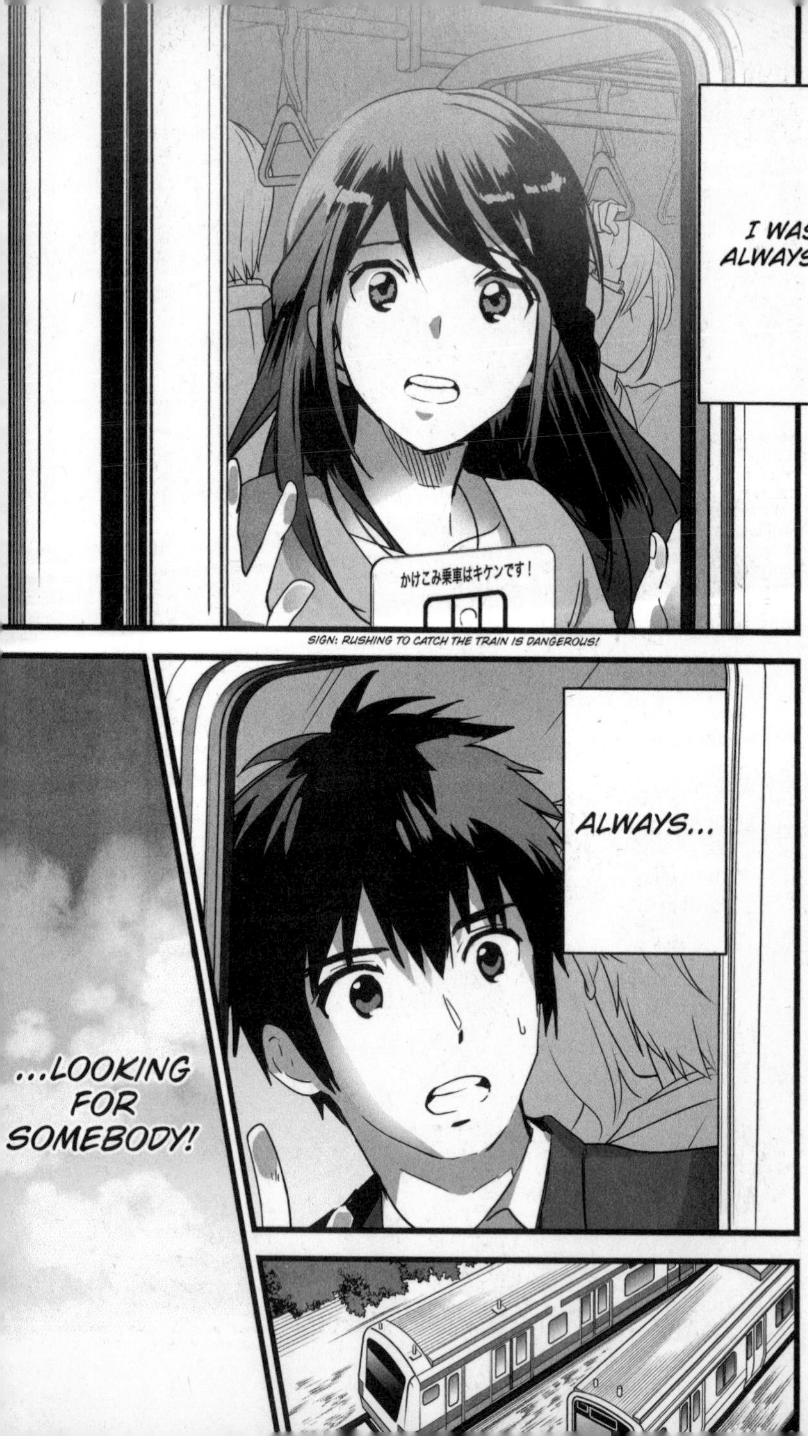
I WAS ALWAYS...
かけこみ乗車はキケンです！
SIGN: RUSHING TO CATCH THE TRAIN IS DANGEROUS!
ALWAYS...
...LOOKING FOR SOMEBODY!

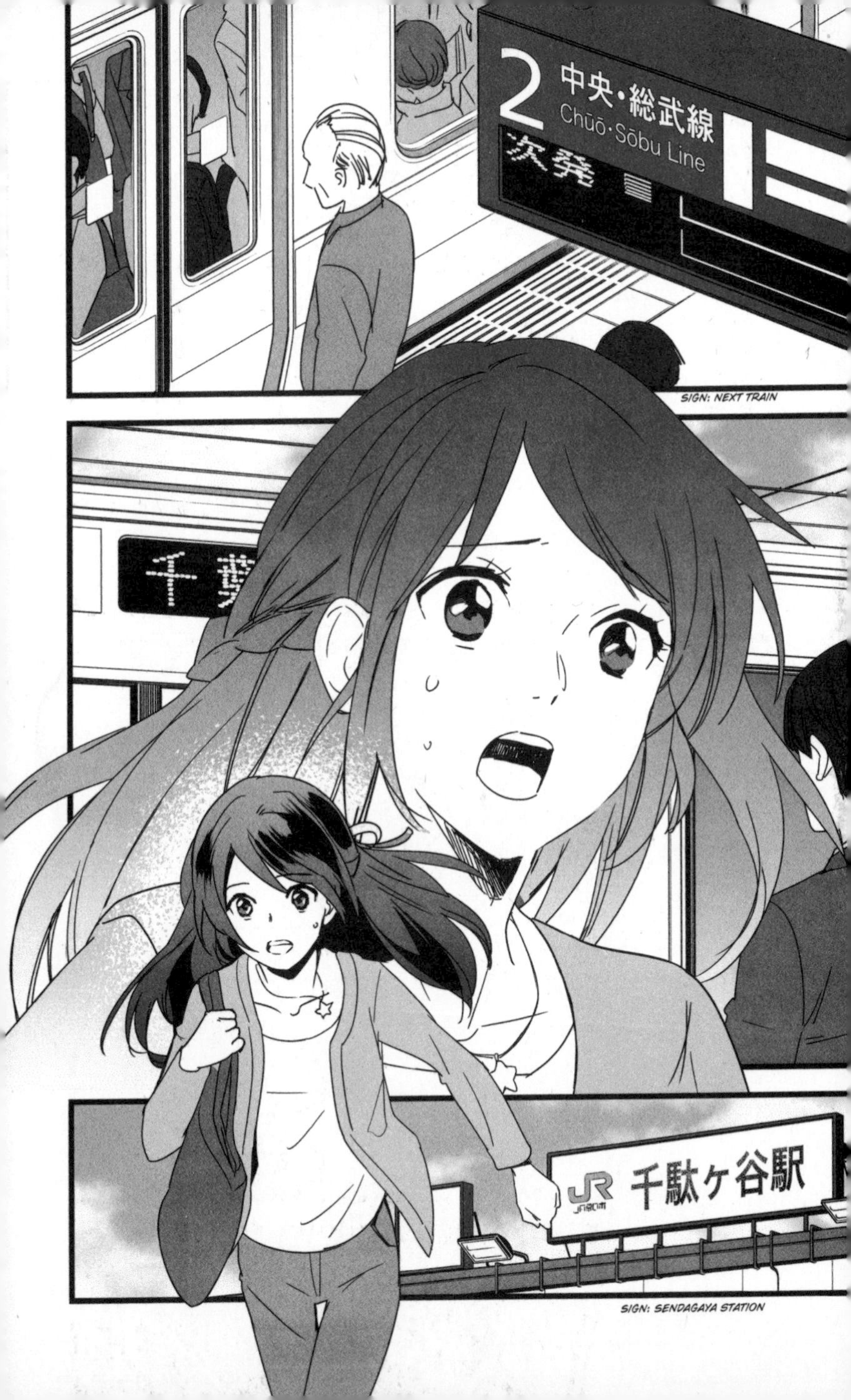
2
中央・総武線
Chūō・Sōbu Line
次発
SIGN: NEXT TRAIN
JR
千駄ヶ谷駅
SIGN: SENDAGAYA STATION

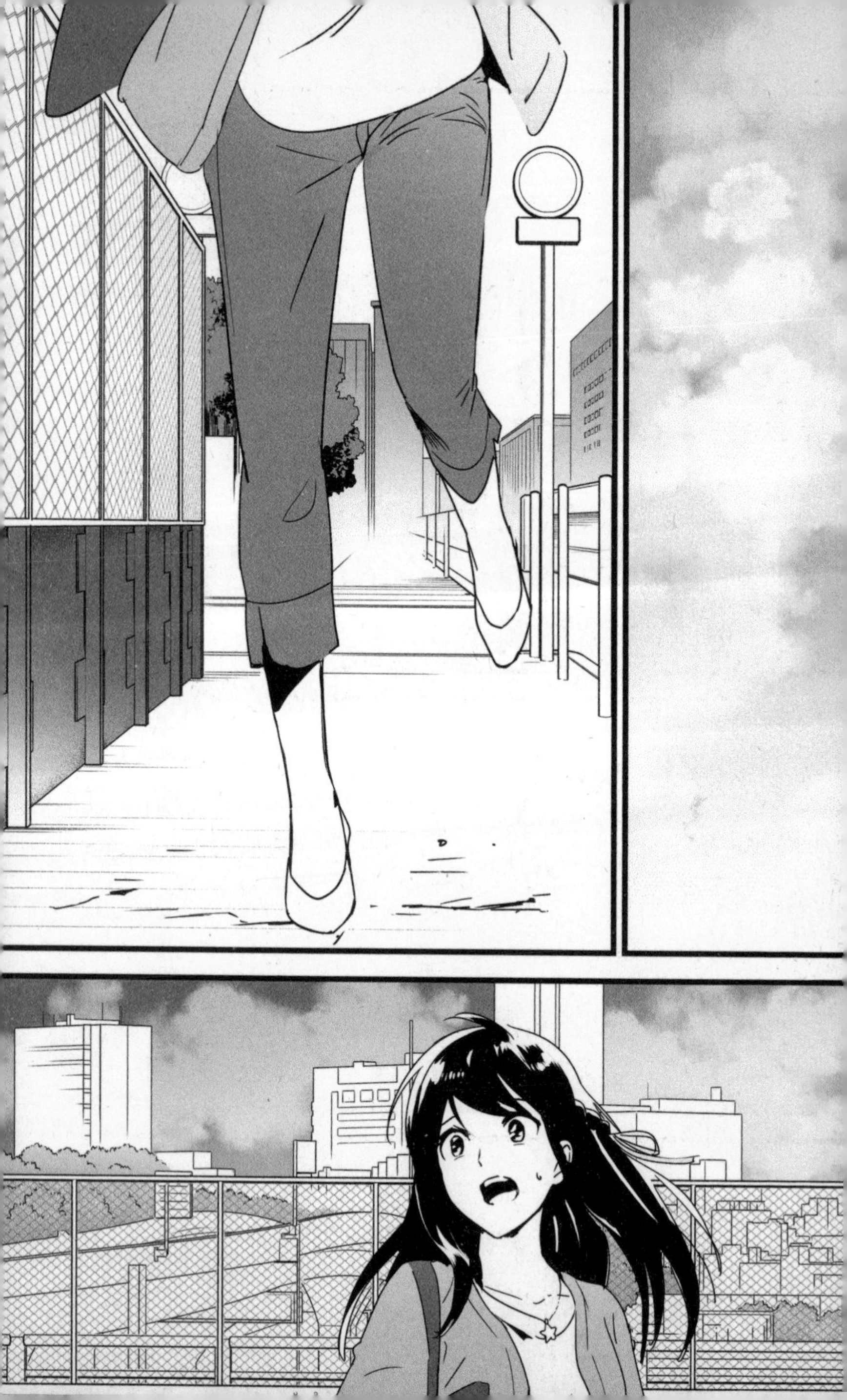

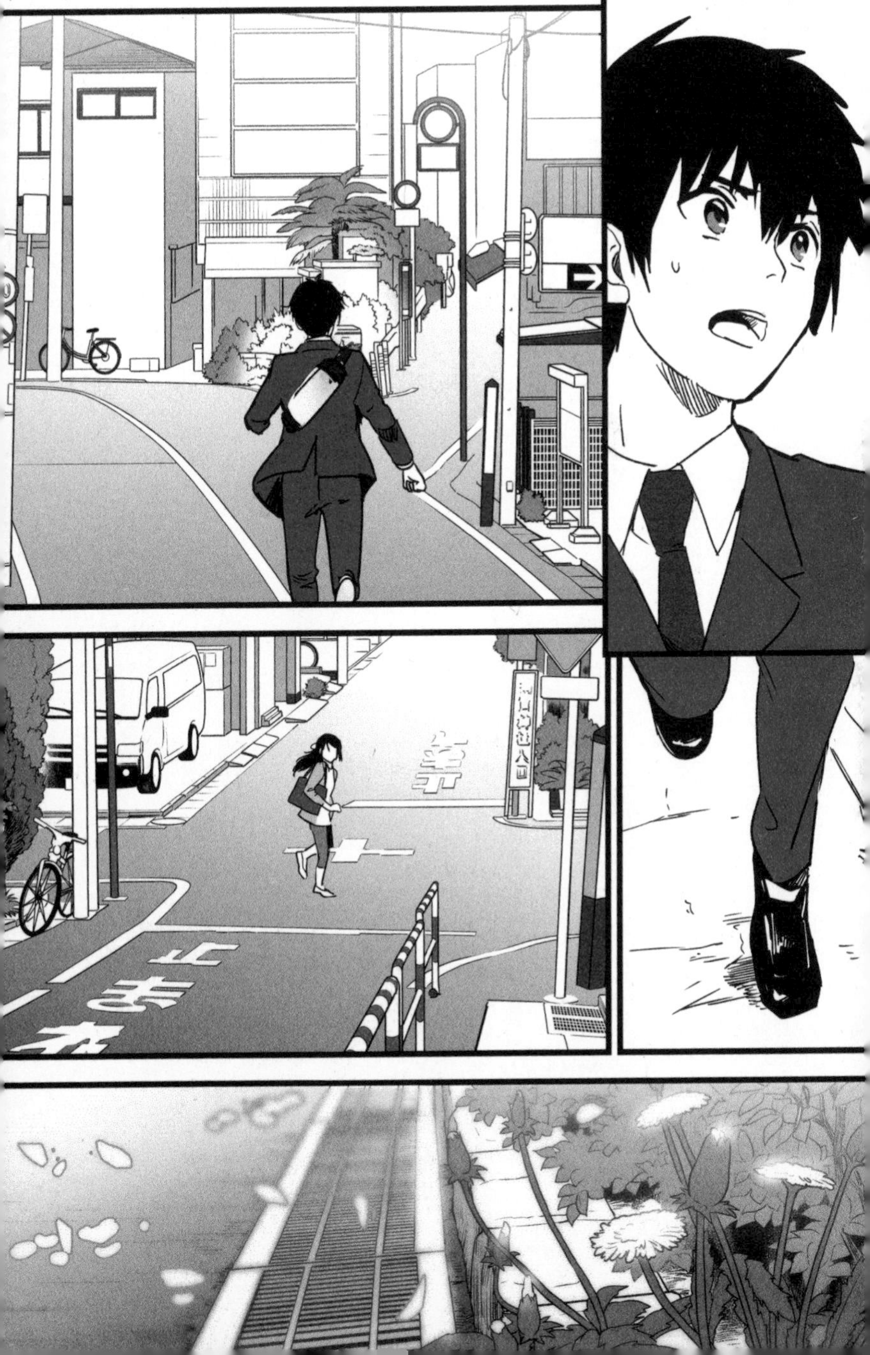

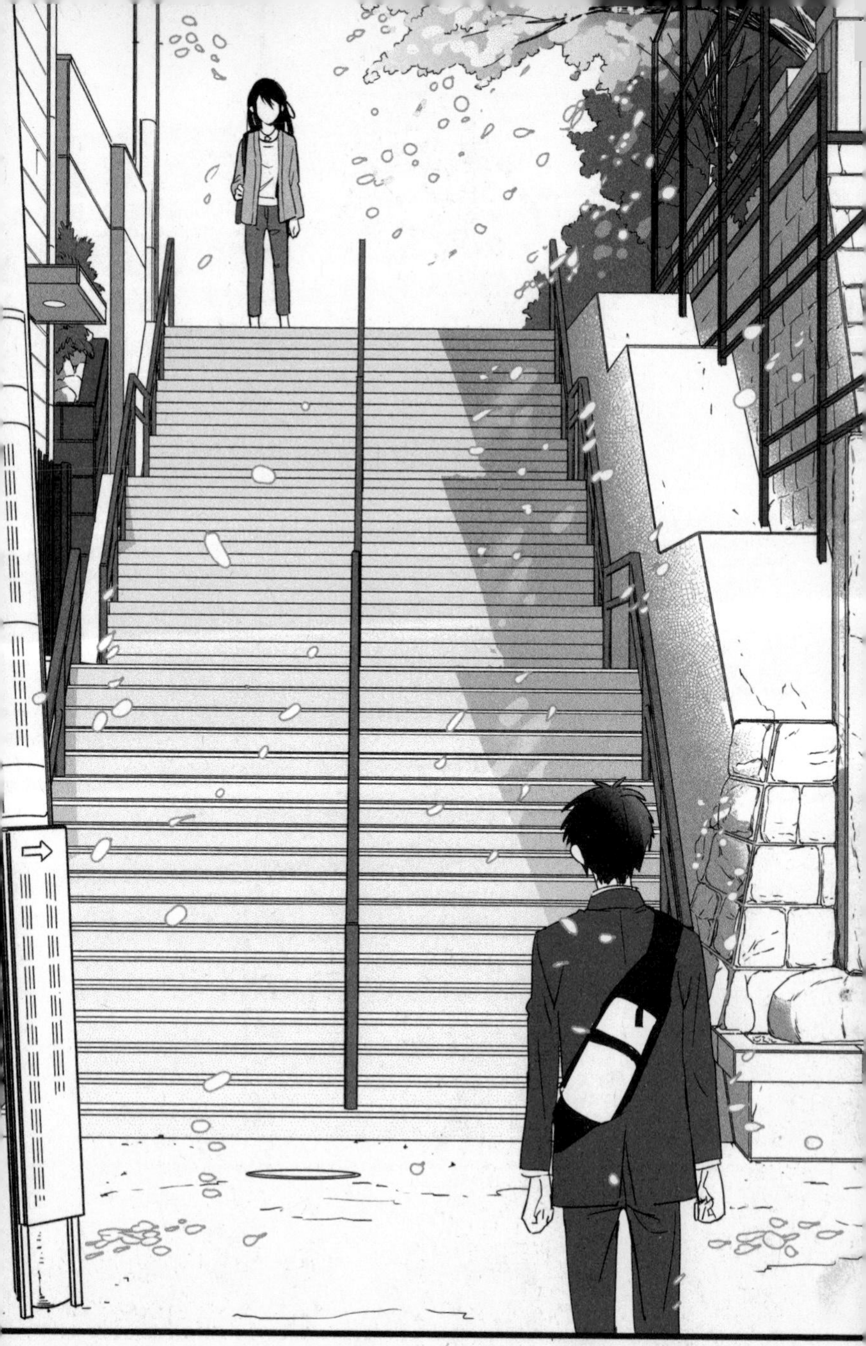

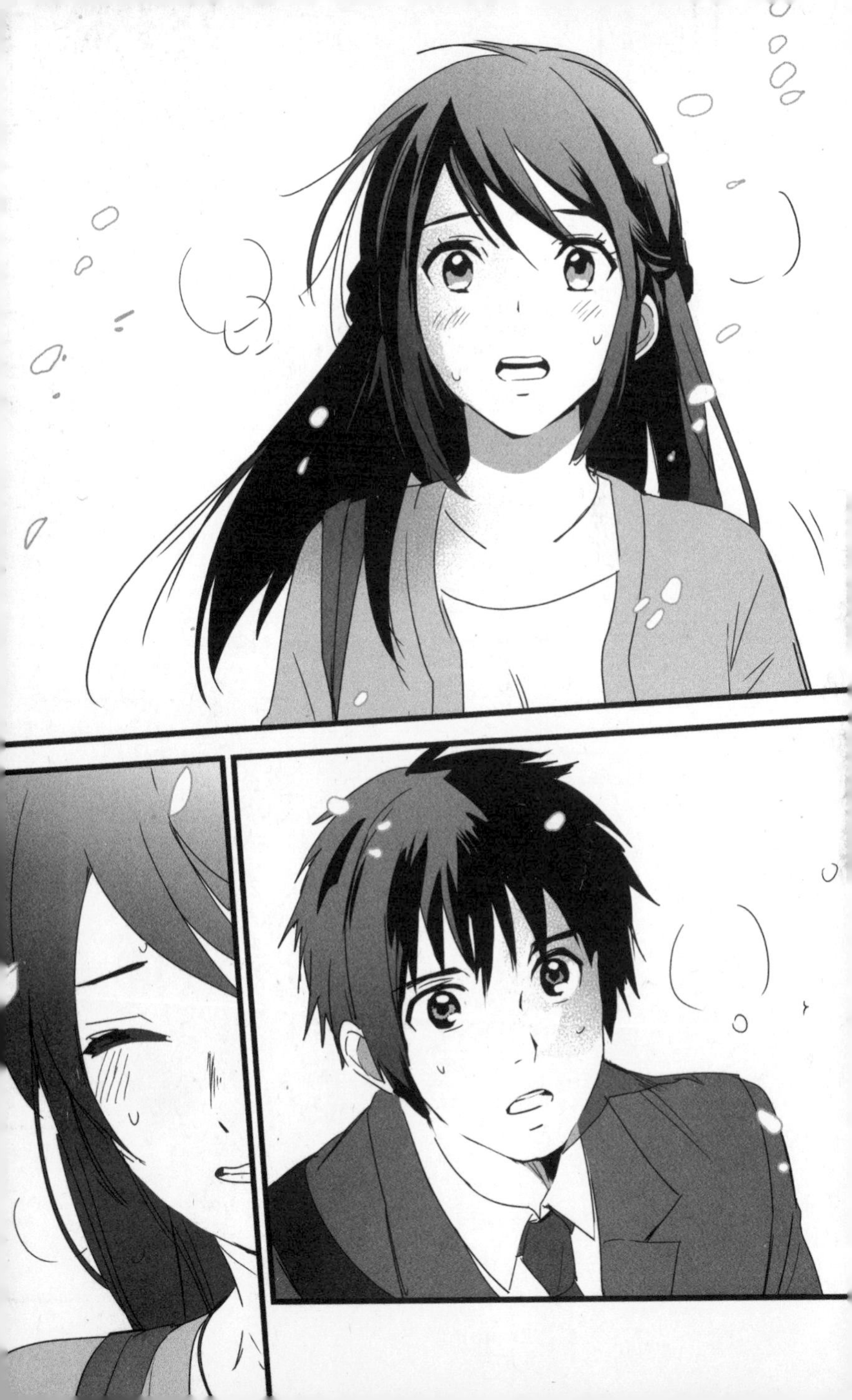

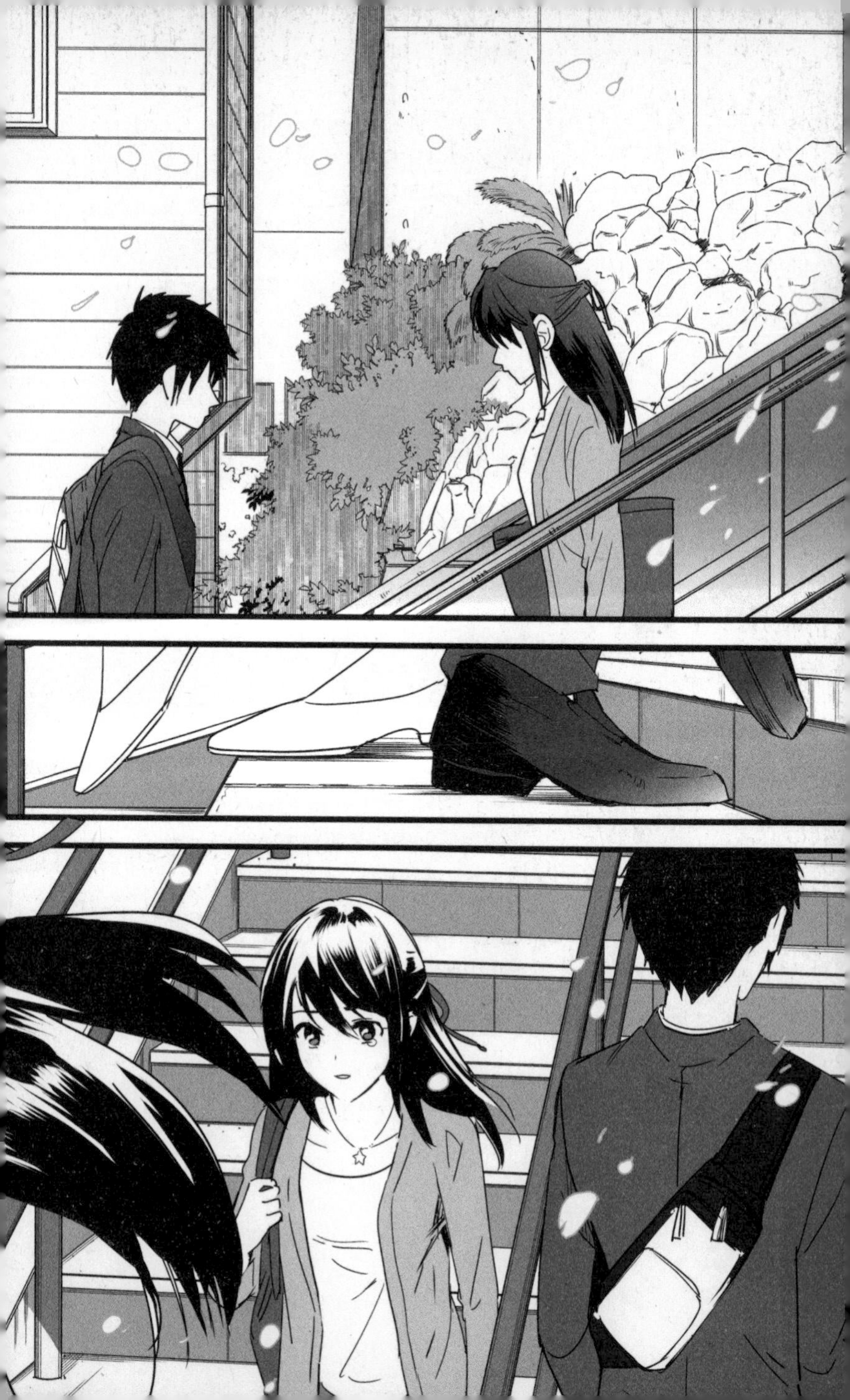

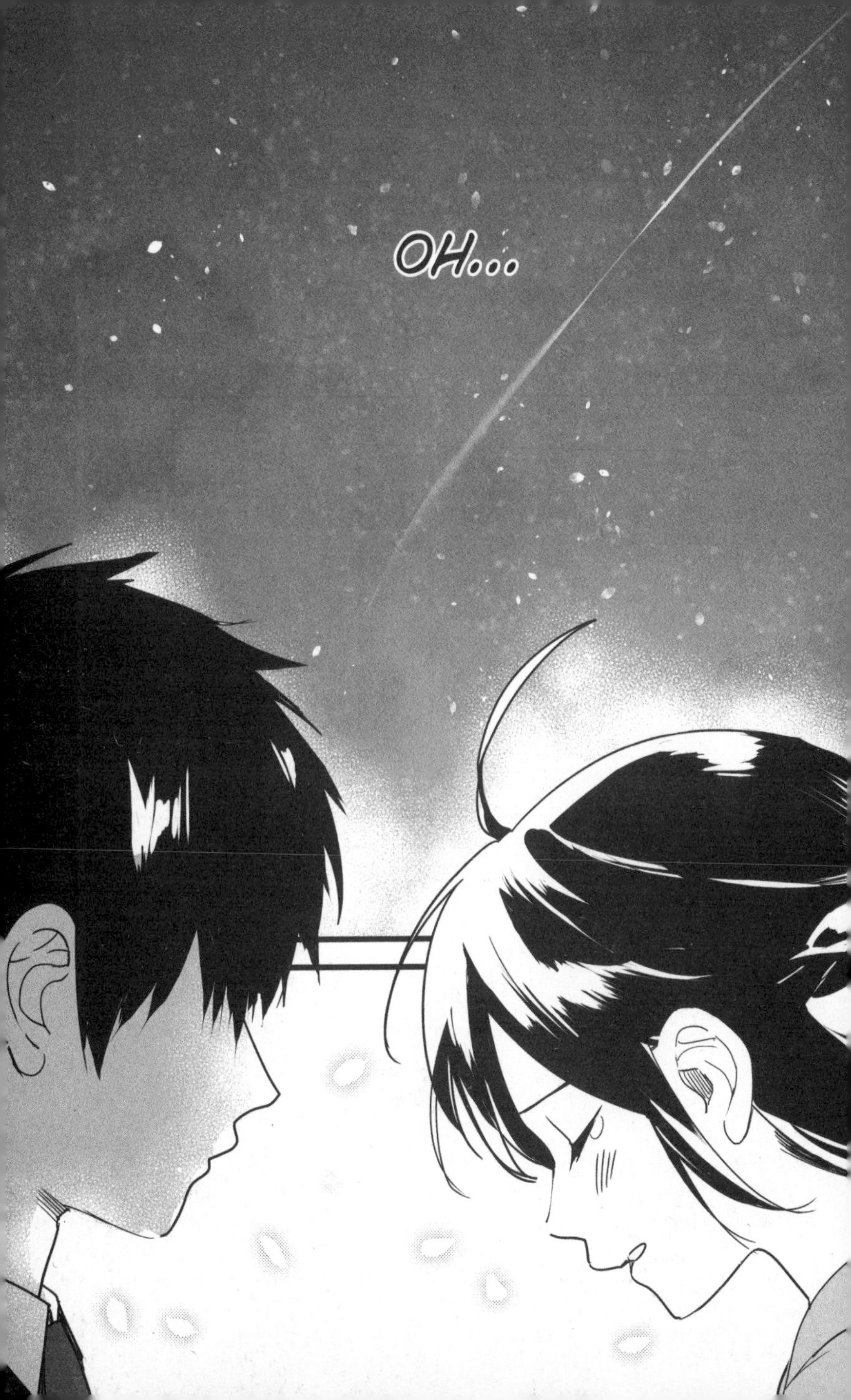
OH...

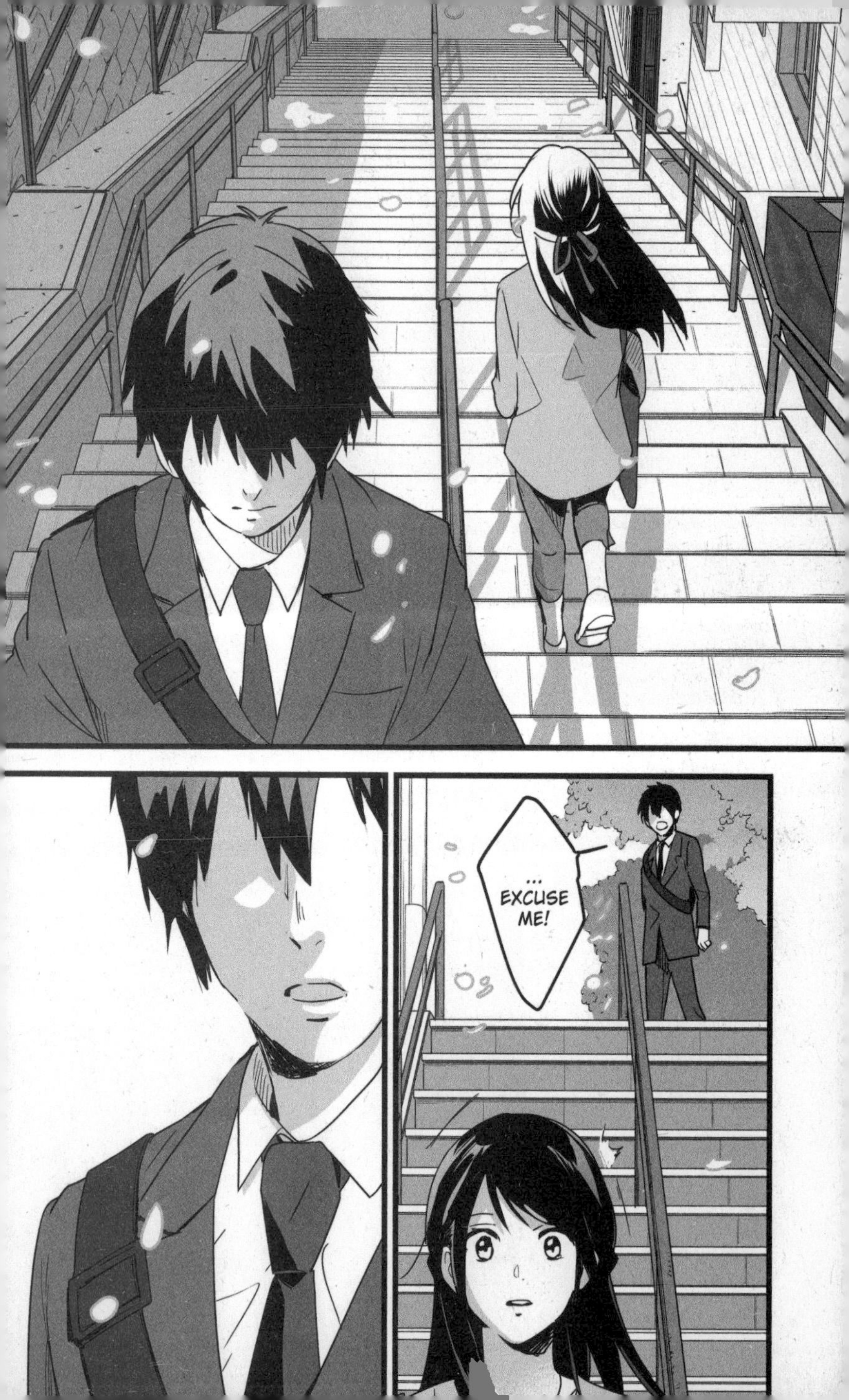
... EXCUSE ME!

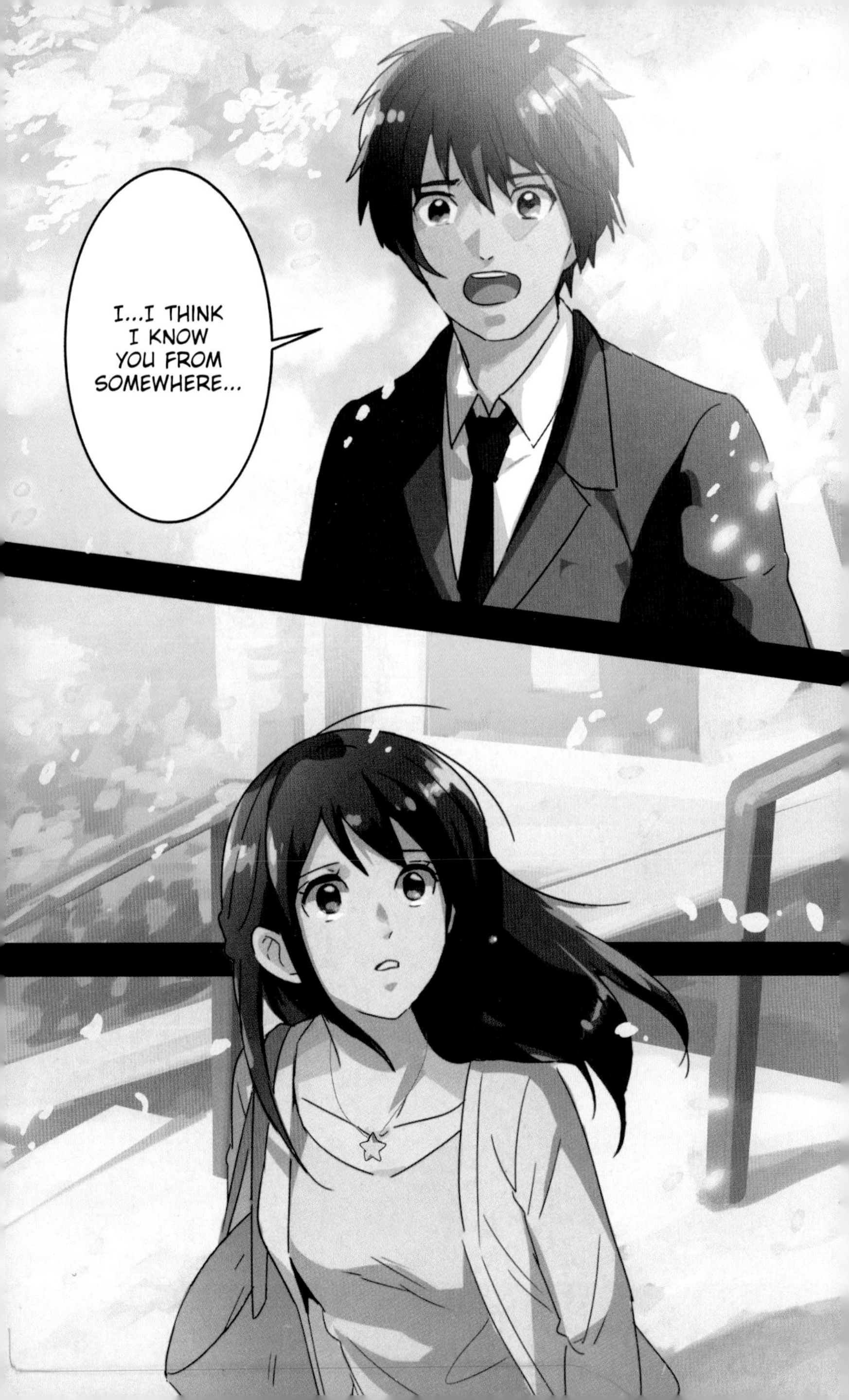
I...I THINK I KNOW YOU FROM SOMEWHERE...

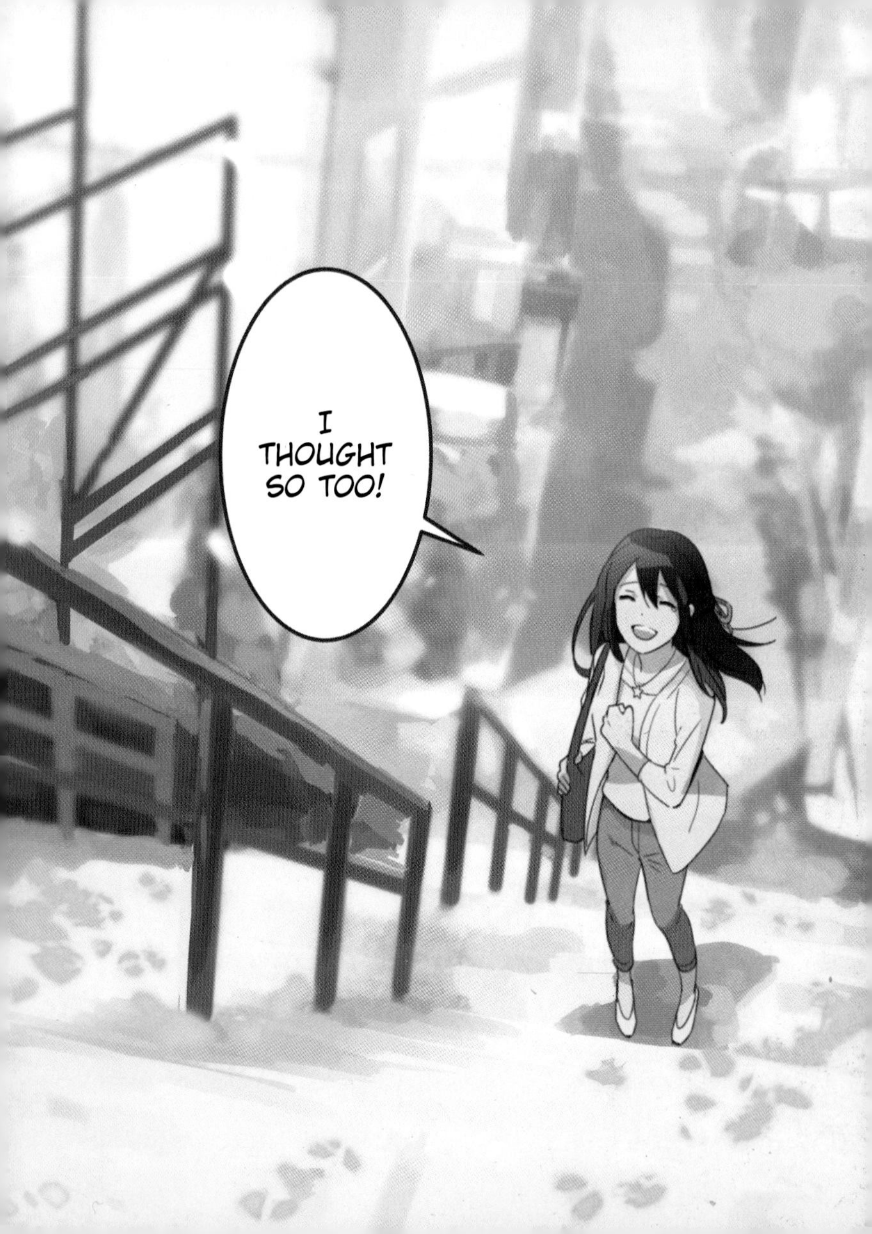
I THOUGHT SO TOO!

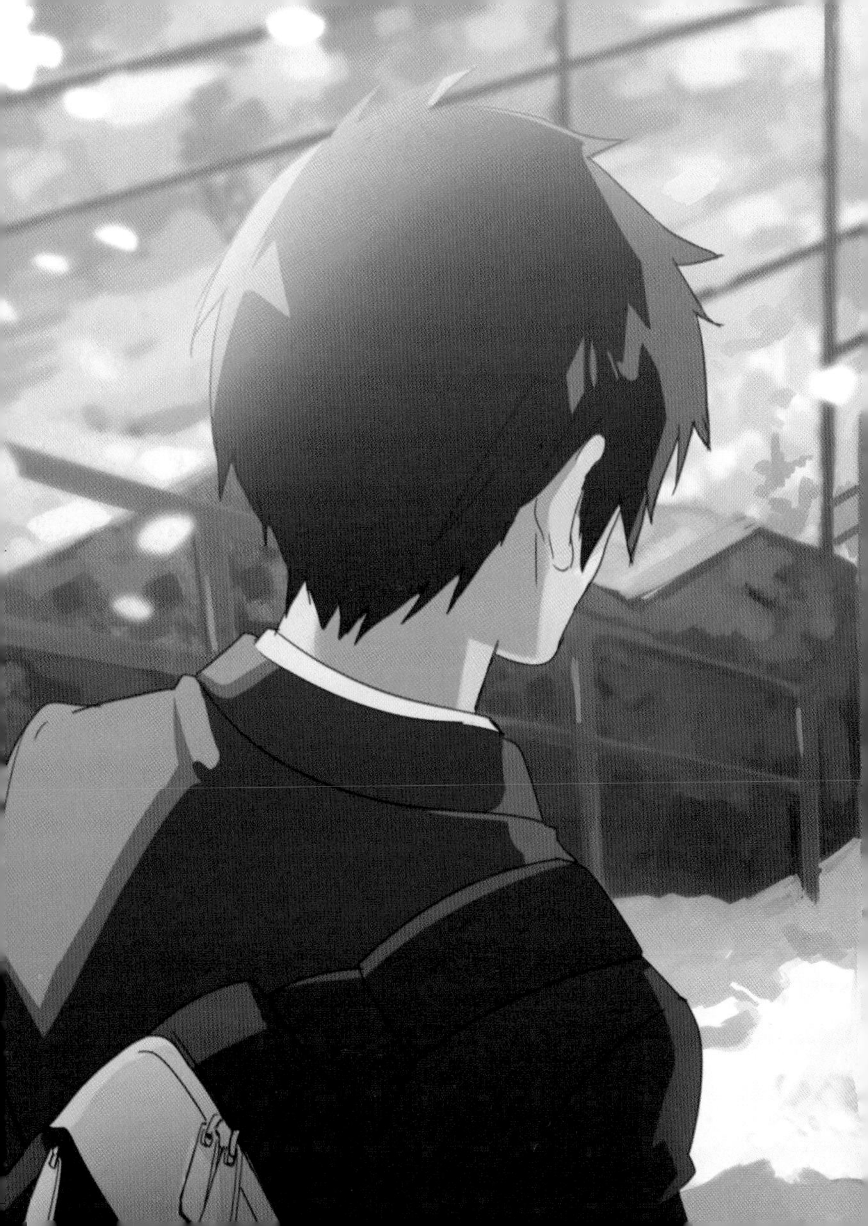

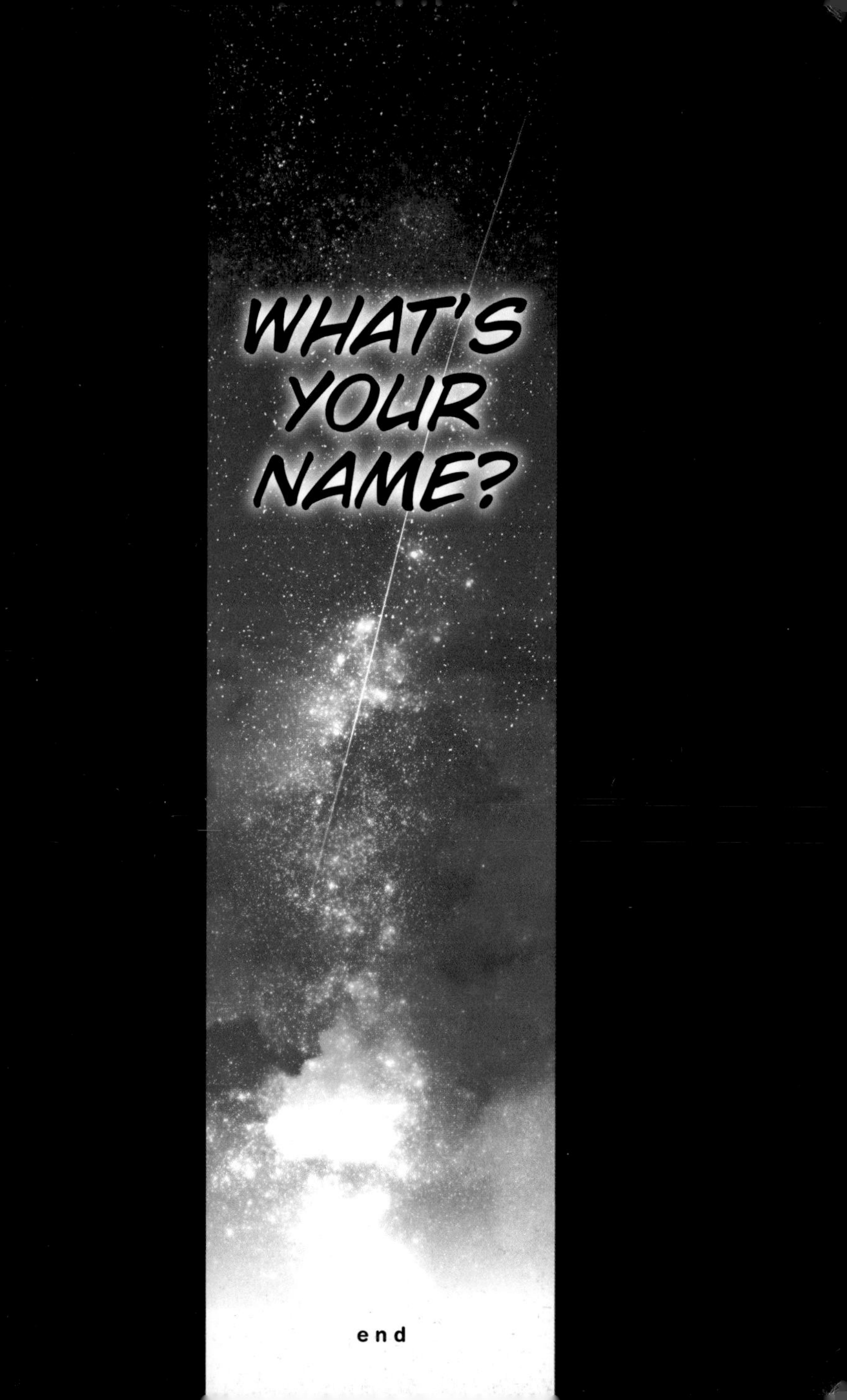
WHAT'S YOUR NAME?
end

# your name

the end


special thanks
akihiro-san
hisahara-kun

# your name

Translation: Taylor Engel
Lettering: Abigail Blackman

YOUR NAME. Vol. 3
©Ranmaru Kotone 2017
©2016 TOHO CO., LTD. / CoMix Wave Films Inc. / KADOKAWA CORPORATION / East Japan Marketing & Communications, Inc. / AMUSE INC. / voque ting co., ltd. / Lawson HMV Entertainment, Inc.
First published in Japan in 2017 by KADOKAWA CORPORATION, Tokyo.
English translation rights arranged with KADOKAWA CORPORATION, Tokyo through TUTTLE-MORI AGENCY, INC., Tokyo.

English translation © 2018 by Yen Press, LLC

Yen Press
1290 Avenue of the Americas
New York, NY 10104

Visit us at yenpress.com
facebook.com/yenpress
twitter.com/yenpress
yenpress.tumblr.com
instagram.com/yenpress

First Yen Press Edition: March 2018

Yen Press is an imprint of Yen Press, LLC.
The Yen Press name and logo are trademarks of Yen Press, LLC.

The publisher is not responsible for websites (or their content) that are not owned by the publisher.

Library of Congress Control Number: 2017934009

ISBNs: 978-0-316-52117-8 (paperback)
       978-0-316-52120-8 (ebook)

10 9 8 7 6 5 4 3 2 1

BVG

Printed in the United States of America